D1189898

THE ENGLISH
DEFENCE OF THE
COMMUNE

The English Defence of the Commune 1871

Edited and Introduced by

Royden Harrison

Merlin Press
London
1971

First published by the Merlin
Press Ltd., 11 Fitzroy Square
London W.1., and printed
by The Partisan Press Ltd.,
of Nottingham

73-19260

CONTENTS

Introduction

It is a grand fact about the Paris Commune that the passing of a hundred years has enhanced rather than diminished its claim upon our understanding, imagination and affection. Marx in his *Civil War in France,* insisted that the Commune was not to be regarded as the last act in the classic French revolutionary tradition, but rather as "the glorious harbinger of a new society". Twenty years later Engels advised the "German philistine" that if he wanted to know what was meant by the "dictatorship of the proletariat", he should look at the Paris Commune. For the successful revolutionaries of the twentieth century from Lenin to Mao, the Commune has been an experience to be revered as a brilliant anticipation of their own achievement: even when they muttered, as Lenin did, *"it was a government such as ours should not be".*[1] Nor did the Commune lose its importance as questions came to be asked about the nature and extent of the "success" of the great social revolutions of our own century. On the contrary, the point of reference began to change so that Paris in 1871 ceased to be considered as the aborted precursor of St. Petersburg in 1917 or of Peking in 1948 and was taken rather as the exemplar whose own standards might furnish a critique of the failures and deformities of its successors.[2]

The Commune was allowed only a few short weeks to establish its character. In certain respects that character remains ambiguous or controversial. Yet it did enough to establish its unmistakeable identity as the rule of the

7

Democracy; of the exploited rather than the exploiter; of the workman rather than the employer; of the tenant rather than the landlord; of the hard-pressed debtor rather than the well-heeled creditor. If it has to be thought of as the precursor of Russian Revolutions rather than in the line of French ones, then its affinity was with 1905 rather than 1917. It was a matter of instinctive and spontaneous response rather than of the deliberations of great personalities and the nice calculations of a centralised leadership. It was not the work of one predominant party, and almost all its parties found their existence fully compatible with the presence of factions. If the Commune came to establish the ascendancy of a new class it was resolved that this should never be confused with the rise of a new elite or the renewal of a bureaucracy which could exalt itself above society. It did not, in the manner of totalitarian regimes, compel participation by its citizens; their free participation was the condition of its life. It abolished standing armies, established churches, privileged officials, in favour of the hands, hearts and heads of the citizens themselves and it paid such professional leaders and officials as it needed, salaries which barely exceeded those of the average workman's wage. Full of enthusiasm for the direct administration by the working people of their own civil and industrial affairs, it had but a faint and indistinct appreciation of how those functions which had to be exercised by centralised authority at national level were to be conducted — but it had some appreciation. Full of a warm patriotism for the neighbourhood, for the community of Paris and for France, it nevertheless utterly repudiated chauvinism and national hatred. It tore down the Vendôme column as the symbol of national 'glory' and welcomed into its own ranks Germans, Hungarians, Russians, Poles and Englishmen. Full of enormous heroism it took to arms against impossible odds, but it displayed little lust for blood or vengeance. Its humanism, symbolised by the burning of the guillotine, was in the sharpest contrast with the ghoulish enthusiasm displayed by the Counter-Revolution: that

Counter-Revolution which in its hour of triumph, committed excesses nauseating even to its own sympathisers. It is small wonder that a new generation of revolutionary youth turns, once more, for inspiration to the Commune. For at one stroke the Commune established the dignity, capacity and heroism of the school teachers and artisans, workmen and washerwomen, students and governesses, who made up its ranks, while exposing the bad faith and brutality masked behind the bland assurance of the parliamentarians. Like all revolution it belonged to the youth, yet if it had a leader that leader was the old revolutionary and political prisoner — prisoner once again — August Blanqui. If it was a revolution of street fighting and barricades, that makes it seem less antique today, when the urban guerilla is being rediscovered, than it did a few years ago. Thus, it is not surprising that the reputation of the Commune, while experiencing certain vicissitudes, has grown over time and more particularly in the recent past. Scholars have sometimes said sensible things about the Commune; some of them have helped to restore the historical commune from those who would wantonly lay hold of it for their own partisan purposes, but such scholars have never understood it unless they have been able to recognise that when it was abolishing night work for journeymen bakers it was also affirming that it was about *la solidarité humaine.* To describe the Commune as sublime is but to state a fact about its nature. To ignore or deny that fact is to make Paris in the Spring of 1871 incomprehensible.

But how well was Paris in 1871 understood by the British working class? On the whole, historians of English Labour have been inattentive to this question.[3] On the other hand Frederick Engels dealt with the matter bluntly: "He thought the working class of England had behaved in a disgraceful manner: though the men of Paris had risked their lives, the working men of England had made no effort either to sympathise with them or to assist them".[4] If this was so it was not because the English working class had shown no internationalist sentiment nor capacity for action in relation to events abroad. On the contrary, the eighteen sixties were remarkable for the concern displayed by the British working class with foreign policy. They made the cause of Poland their own. They accorded to Garibaldi a reception which far surpassed in its magnitude and its enthusiasm anything which was ever given to the dignatories of established powers. Above all, during the American Civil War, ignoring the advice of many of their own leaders and most of their own journals, they came down decisively on the side of Abraham Lincoln and against all recognition and support for the Slave Power. If the organised workmen of the sixties, so largely made up of "the pompous trades and proud mechanics", had been as parochial and pedestrian as they have been represented as being then they would never have endorsed the *Inaugural Address* of the International in which Marx spared not one word for trade union struggles, but devoted himself entirely to political struggles and particularly to international politics. [5] Nor should it be imagined that this tradition was extinct by 1870. At the outset of the Franco-Prussian War the English workmen had denounced it as a conflict born of dynastic ambitions. After the defeat of Napoleon III and the proclamation of the Republic on 4th September 1870 they had demanded that Gladstone should recognise that Republic. Many of them went on to demand, unwisely in Marx's opinion, that Britain should be prepared for military intervention on behalf of France and in the interests of a peace without annexations or indemnities. Indeed, just as the identification with the Poles, the Italians and the Americans contributed to the development of the International and the Reform League in the mid-sixties so the identification with the new French Republic contributed to the dramatic growth of Republicanism in England at the beginning of the seventies. [6]

However, there can be no doubt that Engels was correct if he meant that the English workmen failed to impress upon Government and public opinion their attitude towards the Commune: if, indeed, they had any clear

10

attitude towards it. This was partly because of the very enthusiasm with which they had greeted the Republic of 4th September. They could fairly be reproached with having paid little heed to the warnings given in the *Second Address* of the International against placing trust in the men who succeeded Louis Napoleon. [7] George Odger and Charles Bradlaugh, the heroes of the new English Republicanism, were not well placed to understand or to defend the Commune when they had so recently been giving an unconditional support to the men who were to become the Commune's deadly enemies. But if the International itself could claim to have cautioned against an uncritical support for the Republic of September 4th, did it not also warn against any attempt at overthrowing that Government as a "desperate folly"? [8]

It will be necessary to return to the responsibilities of Marx, Engels and the International in relation to the English working class and the Commune. But before doing so it can be freely conceded that the labouring men of England were, as Marx alleged, deficient in the spirit of generalisation and in revolutionary ardour. Without these qualities they could not be expected to rise to the occasion. While the Communards were abolishing the pawn-shops, English trade union leaders were associating themselves with Rothschild in raising money so that the Parisian workmen could get their tools out of pawn. [9] While the Revolution in Paris decreed the remission of all rents for the quarters beginning in October 1870 through to April 1871, T. J. Dunning, the book-binders' leader and a respected school-teacher of English trade unionism, solemnly explained that economic categories were immutable and that the communards must be mad to even contemplate the abolition of rent. [10]

English working class women, mothers themselves, might curse the Queen and express the wish that all the 'royals' and their pauper pensioners were under the sod, but they had no intention of taking any direct action of their own to secure this result. The notion of shedding the blood of even the worst of their class enemies was remote and repugnant to them. The Irish might have taken a sterner view, but they were so distressed by the execution of the Archbishop of Paris that they made even the most peaceful demonstration on behalf of the Commune hazardous.

The silence of Marx, Engels and the International throughout the entire life of the Commune cannot be explained by any pessimistic estimate which they may have made of the likely response of the English working class to an appeal on the Commune's behalf. No such opportunist considerations deterred them from championing Paris after its fall. While the failure of the International to give a lead has some bearing on the failure of the British working class to make itself felt in relation to the Commune, it seems unlikely that the argument works the other way round. Engels explained that Marx was prevented by ill-health from completing his draft. [11] But had Marx been persuaded that it was necessary to rouse the English workers and had he been sure of the terms in which this should be done it seems unlikely that he would have allowed his own ill-health to stand in the way.

In fact, Marx's difficulty was that he had been opposed to the uprising and, even after it had begun, clung for a time to the hope that the Communards might reach a compromise with Versailles useful to the whole mass of the people. [12] Since Paris could not be led from London he was unable to recommend that combination of boldness and discretion which he favoured. Whatever he said was likely to be overtaken by events. While the Commune lived he was bound by his appreciation of its real nature: once it had fallen he was free to describe it, less in terms of what it was, than in terms of what it was trying to become. The early drafts towards the *Civil War in France* differ in some respects from the final version and are, perhaps closer to the historical commune. [13] Thus, once the Revolution had been suppressed by fire and sword, Marx (and still more explicitly, Engels) treated it as the first example of the

"Dictatorship of the Proletariat". But before the civil war had reached the full pitch of its intensity Marx wrote: "The Commune does not [do] away with the class struggles, through which the working classes strive to the abolition of all classes and, therefore, of all classes [class rule] because it does not represent a peculiar interest ... it affords the rational medium in which that class struggle can run through its different phases in the most rational and humane way. It could start violent reactions and as violent revolutions. It begins the *emancipation of labour* — its great goal — by doing away with the unproductive and mischievous work of the state parasites, by cutting away the springs which sacrifice an immense portion of the national produce to the feeding of the statemonster on the one side, by doing, on the other, the real work of administration, local and national, for workingmen's wages. It begins therefore with an immense saving, with economical reform as well as political transformation." [14]

Marx certainly intended to carry out the directive of the General Council and prepare an address on the Commune which would rally the workmen of all countries to its support. Moreover, he clearly had English working class opinion very much in mind. This is evident from such a passage as the following in the first unpublished draft: "The glorious British penny-a-liner has made the splendid discovery that this is not what *we* use to understand by self-government. Of course, it is not. It is not the self-administration of the towns by turtle-soup guzzling aldermen, jobbing vestries, and ferocious work-house guardians. It is not the self-administration of the counties by the holders of broad acres, long purses and empty heads. It is not the judicial abomination of 'the Great Unpaid'. It is not political self-government of the country through the means of an oligarchic club and the reading of the *Times* newspaper. It is the people acting for itself by itself".[15] It seems clear that it was neither ill-health nor fear of the hostility or indifference of the English working class which prevented Marx from acting on his instructions. Nor was it, one suspects, out of any hesitation to support men who had taken action which he had warned would be precipitate and unwise. The difficulty lay rather in arriving at an adequate characterisation of events in Paris: one which would contribute to the best possible outcome, affording an immediate guide to action while aiding the intellectual and organisational progress of the entire proletariat. Rapid changes in the political and military situation made it highly difficult, if not impossible, to respond in a way which was not likely to become counter-productive.

One of the minor curiosities of Marx's first unpublished draft is that it contained two paragraphs directed against the only organised grouping in England which was consistently defending the Commune week by week. Under the title "Workmen and Comte", Marx wrote: "If the workmen have outgrown the time of Socialist sectarianism" (the followers of Owen, St. Simon) "it ought not to be forgotten that they have never been in the leading strings of Comtism. This sect has never afforded the *International* but a branch of about half a dozen men, whose programm (sic) was rejected by the General Council." (The Proletaire Positivists of Paris were accepted into affiliation by the General Council on 8 February 1870 in Marx's absence. On 15th. March 1870 he complained that their Rules were too exclusive and contrary to the General Rules of the I.W.M.A.) "Comte is known to the Parisian workmen as the prophet in politics of Imperialism (of personal Dictatorship), of capitalist rule in political economy, of hierarchy in all spheres of human action, even in the sphere of science, and as the author of a new catechism with a new pope and new saints in place of the old ones." (This last reference is to one of Comte's final works, *Catechisme Positiviste,* which was the subject of much scorn. J. S. Mill ridiculed it. T. H. Huxley concluded that Positivism = Catholicism minus Christianity).

"If his followers in England play a more popular part than those in France it is not by preaching their sectarian doctrines, but by their personal valour, and by the acceptance (.....?.....) of the forms of working men (sic) class struggle created without them, as f.i. the trade-unions and strikes in England which by the by are denounced as heresy by their Paris co-religionists." [16] (This was not entirely accurate. Although the French Positivists were relatively less conspicuous in the Labour Movement than their English counterparts some of them took part in industrial disputes and held office in the Commune.)

Evidently dissatisfied with this treatment of the Positivists, Marx returned to the topic in a further passage on the "Comtist view". Here he condemned them for "complete ignorance" of the existing economic system and for their alleged failure to recognise that the working class aimed necessarily, historically and unavoidably at the negation of that system. He accused them, quite rightly, of being defenders of private property and seeking the "moralisation" rather than the expropriation of the capitalist. But he then went on to allege that "if they had lived in feudal times or in times of slavery they would have defended the feudal system and the slave system, as founded on the nature of things . . ."(This was to do a great deal less than justice to the notion of historical law and historical relativity with which Comte's system was profoundly imbued.) "Poor men! They do not even know that every *social form* of property has 'morals' of its own, and that the form of . . . ." – and here the fragment broke off. [17]

One can supply several good reasons which may have induced Marx to omit these passages and all explicit reference to the Positivists from the final version of his *Civil War in France*. First and most obviously there was that "personal valour" to which Marx himself referred. For example, how could he dissociate himself from E. S. Beesly, the English Positivist who had identified himself most closely with the Labour Movement? In 1867 Beesly had been threatened with dismissal from his Professorship at University College, London, for defending trade unionism during the hysteria which swept the middle class press at the time of the Sheffield outrages. In the Reform Club the attempt was made to have him 'blackballed' for contending that a trade union murder was neither better nor worse than any other kind of murder. Besides, Beesly had presided at the Inaugural meeting of the International and had furnished the best history of its activities which had yet appeared: a history in which Marx' learning and his leading role were explicitly acknowledged. [18] In his pamphlet *A Word for France* [19] Beesly, as Marx acknowledged, anticipated almost word for word much of the *Second Address* of the International on the Franco-Prussian War. During the Commune Beesly contributed weekly articles to the *Bee-Hive* [20] in which he defended working men's Paris against all comers and won himself the boundless hatred of 'respectable society' as a consequence. Marx had no choice but to express his admiration for Beesly's contributions to the *Bee-Hive* while adding that he was almost sorry to see his name appear in a paper which was sold "to Sam Morley and Co." [21] — Morley being the great textile manufacturer, philanthropist and purchaser, on behalf of Mr. Gladstone, of Labour Leaders. Characteristically Beesly disarmed the objection by taking up Marx's suggestion that he should contribute to the *Eastern Post*.

With an honesty bordering on truculence Marx advised Beesly: "as a Party man I have a thoroughly hostile attitude towards Comte's philosphy, while as a scientific man I have a very poor opinion of it." [22] To this Beesly replied: "I know very well that you are radically opposed to us Positivists, nor do I suppose it at all likely that you will ever alter your views. The one point we and you have in common is our indignation against the individualist theories of the propertied classes and their anti-social conduct. We both believe that the working class suffer terrible wrongs at the hands of the middle class, and that the social question is more important than the political .... No doubt whenever it becomes a practical question whether private property is to be abolished, you will find us opposed to you firmly. But it is likely that long before then we and you shall have been crushed side by side by our common foe." [23]

Marx tried to persuade Beesly that he was an exception: that he alone of the English Positivists had a sense for historical crises, but Beesly was not to allow that he could be separated, in any essential regard, from his friends. "You are quite wrong", he told Marx, "in supposing that my attitude differs in any respect from that of my co-religionists. Harrison at bottom agrees with me, though in writing he is inclined to be too diplomatic. in my opinion, and to spare the susceptibilities of the middle class." [24]

Here again Marx was in a difficulty. The Positivist, Dr. J. H. Bridges, went out of his way to publicly endorse the most "outrageous" contentions in the *Civil War in France*.[25] The Positivist, Frederic Harrison wrote contributions to the *Fortnightly* [26] which were not likely to be regarded as "diplomatic" by anyone who had not had the advantage of reading what Harrison had to say in private.

As I have always insisted, *civil war* in France has long been inevitable. There stands there the people of Paris and other large cities, for the purest, most honest, direct, and intelligent part of France, its real intellectual head and its true vital heart, who will have a Republic, and a real Republic, a government that is for the sake of the whole and not of the rich. Opposite stand the professional and trading class — mere adventurers who want to keep society as it is, and who alternately make use of armies, police, priests and peasants as their instruments. There stood the workmen resolved that society should not go on as it has done, armed and ready to fight. On the other side the rich resolved to keep society as it is, and ready to use any weapon, especially lying, fraud, legal and parliamentary chicanery and the rest of their dodges to keep society as it is . . . . Society as it is now constituted is not worth keeping together. The right to grind out of the workmen, his wife and child the uttermost farthing; to leave him naked, half-starved, ignorant, filthy, while you choke yourself with luxuries and cover the earth with your whims i.e. political economy, is a right he will not admit. Your right to property that is selfishly to consume, or wantonly to waste what the combined toil of many has made, is no right at all. *La propriété (comme vous la possédez) c'est la vol.* That is quite true. *Your* goods, *your* shops, *your* coffers! are being robbed! Yours? What made them yours? Society put you in charge of them, but from the ill-use you made of them Society takes them away from you.

Nothing that the rich can suffer, no death or torment, is worse than they deserve — lying, cheating, selfish, callous, calumnious brutes. There is only one word — *ces bougres du bourgeois* . . . .
Dimly and under many cries these workmen say — we want Society organised so that all its plums shall not fall on (sic) the rich, and all its weight on us — and that means the Republic — a government which is not the prize of a class — but the protection of the weak, and the helper of the suffering . . . .
Legitimacy of the National Representatives: I deny it all. I refuse to be bound by suffrages. The whole thing is a protest against the lying sham called universal suffrage. The whole theory of the suffrage is only one of the tricks of the *bougres*. It is not the national will, it is not even the majority. The best men have a *right* to serve the nation in a crisis. It is as Carlyle said — take away the bauble of the ballot box. The 2,000,000 workmen in Paris and other great towns are the 'best men'. There are not 2,000,000 *bougres,* not 500,000 but having hocused a lot of peasants they call themselves the majority. Majority or not we won't have them. Legitimate government be damned!
In an epoch of revolutions every government is but the issue of a fresh *coup d'état* . . . . But election or not I deny that suffrage is the source of right altogether. I fall back on force. And here we are. What do the *bougres* fall back on? Why force . . . .
I beg your pardon for the use of the word *'bougre'*. It comes from Marat and Père Duchesne. Nothing else can express the feeling of loathing and contempt we feel for the order. It is made up of idle bourgeois, money-makers, lawyers, priests and so forth and the official military, legal and literary creatures they employ." 27

It was pointless for Marx to separate himself from men who felt and wrote like this about the Paris Commune. It was made all the more superfluous because the English Positivists made no attempt to control the International or to confound Communism with Positivism. ("Nevertheless, confound them both" remarked *Punch.* 28) Had Marx included his paragraphs on the Positivists he would merely have raised the question as to how men whose theories were so wrong could perform actions which were so conspicuously right.

Beesly, Harrison and Bridges were by far the most prominent English defenders of the Paris Commune. It might, of course, be suggested that as followers of August Comte they were not really Englishmen at all, but Frenchmen in disguise. Such an opinion would be clever rather than correct. Since 1789 the English Democracy and English Socialism — particularly the Democracy — has had a powerful francophile component within its tradition. If some imagined that it was a gentleman that Jack would be if he spoke French, there were others who supposed that he would be a democrat and a revolutionary. (The curious breed of eccentric aristocratic radicals doubtless hoped for both results). Whenever the francophile tradition on the Left became a general reproach against English ways, it appeared to be extravagant and mannered, juvenile and absurd; affected and negligible. Whenever it was made to bite selectively on the problems of English culture and society it threatened to be disturbing and heroic. Thus, Edward Thompson has shown us that the English Jacobins at their best were *English* Jacobins. [29] Similarly Positivism in England was important to the degree to which it managed to become "intimately incorporated with the state of society."

Beesly, Harrison and Bridges met at Wadham College, Oxford, in 1848. They fell under the spell of their tutor, Richard Congreve, who was already deeply influenced by August Comte. Learning at Oxford still went through the exhausted rounds of a classical literary and aristocratic culture. Comte with his classification of the sciences; a classification completed by his own inauguration of the new science of sociology; came as the elaboration of the scientific spirit found in L'Ecole Polytechnique. At the same time he could not be accused of the philistinism characteristic of English provincial bourgeois culture of which Benthamism was the highest expression. Comte was historically minded: incorrigibly so. Through his discovery of the law of the three stages he seemingly established in organic unity an epistemology, a philosophy of history and a programme of social reconstruction. [30]

The English Positivists were able to put the new philosophy to useful work in the universities, in intellectual circles and in the Labour Movement because they adapted it to English conditions and needs. For Beesly, Harrison and Bridges Positivism was always to be a school rather than a church. Like the utilitarians before them they worked as a philosophical-political ginger group and did not allow themselves to be greatly inhibited by Comte's sectarian crotchets and shibboleths which would have prevented them taking such an active part in journalism and public life. When they insisted that they were "religious teachers" the English Positivists meant that they had found a way in which they could support the moral earnestness of their evangelical forbears by grounding it in the scientific attitude. If science, particularly geology and biology, appeared to undermine theological dogmas and thereby knock away the authority for the affirmations of religious and moral experience, Comte's Religion of Humanity purported to end the divorce between the world of fact and the world of value and to put our duties upon a demonstrable and scientific basis. If sensitive men were pained by the low notion of personal rewards and punishments which they discovered in established christian teaching, Positivism offered them an ideal of service to Humanity which was worthier as well as more intelligible. Finally, if unbelief was encouraged by the observation of how organised religion tended to identify itself with the rich and the powerful against the weak and the oppressed, Positivism came forward as a Labour movement bringing stern lessons for the rich and a promise of security and dignity for the workman and his family.

Comte had been the pupil of St. Simon, but whereas St. Simon thought of the working class only as the poorest and most numerous class, Comte saw it as an active force and even — subject to important qualification — as a revolutionary one. When Society reached its 'normal state', the workmen in conjunction with women and with the philosophers (positivist priests), were to constitute the Spiritual Power. While temporal power was to be concentrated in the hands of bankers and great captains of industry who would administer small territorial units in a planned manner, these capitalists were to be moralised by the Spiritual Power so as to ensure that they "lived for others". Comte recognised that to attain this normal state was bound to be a more or less arduous process. He anticipated sharp class struggles and considered that there might be a need for a transitional dectatorship in which power would be in the hands of a great proletarian governor. Comte's followers elaborated and interpreted these doctrines in different ways at different times. Thus, during the Revolution of 1848 the Parisian Positivists had argued that the workmen of Paris: "not having received a metaphysical education, have fewest prejudices; belonging to the most numerous class, their views have the greatest generality; having the interests which are least implicated in local affairs, they display the greatest disinterestedness; finally, being the hardest pressed by the need for social reconstruction, they are the most revolutionary section. On all these counts it is just that political power in France should belong to Paris; on all these counts also, power comes to the proletariat." 31

Marx's difficulty in relating the English Positivists' practice to their theory arose, in part, from his failure to recognise how deliberately latitudinarian they were and, in part, from his own polemical enthusiasm against Comte. Thus, he saw the French philosopher as the pedantic founder of a system based upon a shallow empiricism, while ignoring his attempt to inaugurate a new science of sociology grounded in an appreciation of laws of historical development. He saw Comte as the sentimental reconciler of opposites (Labour and Capital: Science and Religion: Order and Progress), without attending to the conditions upon which such reconciliations were to be effected. He was impressed by the fatuous promise of moralising the capitalist and accordingly wasted no time on the proposals as to how precisely the capitalist was to be taught rectitude. He saw the presumptuous Parisian who thought that "France ought to rule the world" and obscured the internationalist who looked to the "Republic of the West".

Respectable English society had, from the other side, an

equally one-sided and inadequate view of Positivism and Positivists. Sir Thomas Larcome, fearful for the security of Dublin Castle, had a file of newspaper cuttings of Positivist activities which he kept along with those relating to the International; adding a note to the effect that Positivists were much the same as Communists — irresponsible and seditious people. In a leading article entitled Our Own Reds, the *Pall Mall Gazette* declared that: "The Comtist agitators. . . make known to us a spirit as reckless, as cool-blooded, as well-leavened with political hate, as unscrupulous in the machinations of turbulence as ever possessed the revolutionaries of any age or nation — all of which we shall see fully displayed if malign chance gives them that ascendancy over working men which they strive so hard for." The very journals which gave hospitality to Beesly and his friends found space for furious attacks upon them. Thus, in the *Fortnightly* Colonel Chesney was allowed to make his readers flesh creep by assuming that the "malign chance" had come up and that the English Positivists and their working class friends had seized power. Fortunately Revolutions devour themselves and so, in Colonel Chesney's fantasy, the ruling triumvirate of Harrison, Beesly and Odger was soon forced to fight for its life against a new combination led by Congreve and Bridges. Similarly in the *Bee-Hive* Beesly was subjected to a whole host of personal attacks from middle-class contributors. It was suggested that he wanted a Revolution in England so that he could be made President of the Republic. His writings were described as "pestilential heresies" and after the Fall of the Commune he and his friends were directed, albeit with no result, to try "forty days of humility and silence."[32]

Frederic Harrison had imagined that among the ruling families there would be no objection to a little playful radicalism. He soon discovered that the defence of the Commune was not something to be lightly indulged in. When the Positivist, Henry Crompton, made some excuse for the Commune's execution of the Archbishop of Paris,

Arthur Russell could no longer dismiss him as a half
cracked academic but shrank back from him and "thought
how mischievous his folly might become, if he obtained
power". He denounced Beesly as "a tremendous fool".
Harrison and Bridges were for him "courtiers" who told
wild lies and wrote "criminal" articles in order to please
the ignorant workmen who employed them. [33]

Doubtless, Harrison was right in believing that there was
a good deal of silent sympathy among literary and scientific men for the Paris Revolution. Viscount Amberley himself, while remarking that he "rather agreed with Arthur
(Russell) in regretting that the English workmen should be
led by their sympathy for the Commune to palliate its
crimes", yet acknowledged that "there was a good and
sound case for the communal revolution, whether or not
the moment chosen was a right one, or the agents
worthy." [34] Captain Maxse in his "The Causes of Social
Revolt" (1872), expressed much the same feelings. More-
over there was a significant minority of journalists who
resisted the cry of respectable English Society for the humiliation of the "poltroons of Belleville" and who were sickened, as probably most Englishmen were sickened, by the
call in the *Army and Navy Gazette* for the vivisection,
without benefit of anaesthetic, of the roughs of Paris. [35]
John Ruskin himself, for a moment, was inspired to declare himself a Communist, "reddest of the red" but he
lost his sympathy for the communards once he was persuaded that they were laying waste to Paris in the interests
of their own defence, or in the frenzy of their defeat. [36]

As for the English workers, the factors responsible for
their relative inaction have already been considered. On
balance, there seems little reason to complain about the
assessment which "the Journeyman Engineer" made of the
state of working class opinion. [37] Of the English members
of the General Council of the I.W.M.A. only Lucraft and
Odger dissociated themselves from the *Civil War in France*.
Indeed, the Engineers, who had stood aloof from the International now availed themselves of its services. [38] While

the Positivists were almost alone among their mentors in trying to rouse workmen on behalf of the Parisians, there were others who helped to prevent them from becoming infected with the hysteria which marked the response of other classes. Their witness for the Commune, however halting and confused, was important and in the pages which follow the reader will find an attempt to recover voices long inaudible beneath the din which surrounded them. Yet it cannot escape notice that the most dist-inguished working class spokesman for the Commune, Thomas Smith, the Secretary of the Nottingham Branch of the International and the most original English thinker in the I.W.M.A., was deeply influenced by the traditions of positivist thought in France. Not that he was a Comtist anymore than he was a Marxist, but the pamphlet of this self-taught working man [39] (for such he appears to have been) has to be understood in terms of the methodology and the preoccupations of French thinkers who followed in the tradition inaugurated by Turgot and Condorcet. One may conjecture that he learned much from the French silk weavers who came to his native town and who helped to form the Nottingham (French) branch of the Inter-national. John Stuart Mill joined Beesly and Marx in ex-pressing his general admiration for Smith's achievement, but he added a rider to the effect that "the law of the Revolution" was a very un-English, and very French, way of thinking about social change, or rather of failing to think about it clearly. [40]

Thus, one is brought back to the admission, if admission it must be, that the English defenders of the Commune were pre-eminently franco-phils of one sort or another. But no apology is required for the predominance of their contribution to this volume. Their writings deserve to be remembered for their literary excellence: for the courage which it took to write them; and for the essential object-ivity and openness which distinguished them. Despite all their doctrinaire preoccupations, Beesly and Harrison and their friends saw the many-sidedness and complexity of the Commune without obscuring, as Harriet Taylor and others threatened to do, that its essential reality lay in the class struggle. While the Commune lived, they defended it. Once it had fallen they joined with Marx and a most motley cross section of English society in aiding the communard refugees. [41] "I have got a house", Frederic Harrison remarked to John Morley, "into which I am ashamed to bring one of these starving devils whom I call 'citizen' and address with 'fraternity' and whose shoes in the Kingdom of Heaven I am not worthy to black." [42]

Royden Harrison
Centre for the Study of Social History
Warwick University

NOTES

1. Lenin. V.I. *Two Tactics of Social-Democracy in the Democratic Revolution* (1905) in Sel Works Vol. III, p.95, (1936). Lenin charges the Commune with being a Government that "could not then distinguish between the elements of a democratic revolution and those of a socialist revolution".

2. The literature is well marshalled and reviewed in a controversial article by G. Ionescu, Lenin, the Commune and the State: *Government and Opposition*, Vol. 5 N *Page 4*. No. 2, (1970) pp 131-165.

3. But see H. Collins and C. Abramsky, *Karl Marx and the British Labour Movement* (1965) p.185 et seq and R. Harrison, E. S. Beesly and Karl Marx, International Review of Social History Vol. 4, Pts. 1 & 2 (Amsterdam) 1959.

4. Minutes of the General Council, I.W.M.A. 8th August, 1871 reprinted in *Documents of the First International* Vol. 4 p.256 (Moscow and London n.d.).

5. R. Harrison, The British Labour Movement and the International in 1864 in R. Miliband and J. Saville (editors) *The Socialist Register.* 1964 pp.293-308.

6. R. Harrison, *Before the Socialists* (1965) p.210 et seq.

7. Second Address of the General Council of the I.W.M.A. on the Franco-Prussian War in *Documents* op cit p.340.

8. Marx K. Kugelman. Confidential circular enclosed with letter of 28,March, 1870 in *Letters to Kugelmann* (1936) p.107.

9. R. Harrison, Before the Socialists (1965), p.232.

10. op cit p.233.

11. Minutes General Council I.W.M.A. 2 May, 1871 and 9 and 16 May. *Documents* p.184, 189, 194.
12. Collins H. & Abramsky C., Karl Marx and the British Labour Movement (1965) p.194 et seq. where the problem of "Marx's Silence" is identified and discussed.
13. *Archiv Marksa i Engelsa,* Vol. III Moscow (1934)
14. ibid p.332.
15. ibid p.288.
16. ibid p.346.
17. ibid p.358.
18. Harrison, R. Professor Beesly and the Working Class·Movement in (Briggs, A. and Saville, J. — editors) *Essays in Labour History* (1960) pp.205-241.
19. Reprinted on p.46
20. Reprinted on p.64
21. Marx K. to Beesly. E.S. 12 June, 1871 cited in Harrison. R. *E. S. Beesly and Karl Marx,* Int. Rev. of Soc. Hist. (Amsterdam) IV (1959) pt ii p.213.
22. ibid.
23. Beesly to Marx 13 June, 1871 ibid p.215.
24. ibid.
25. Reprinted on p.121
26. Reprinted on p.168
27. Harrison F. to Morley. J. 22 March, 1871 cited in R. Harrison. *Before the Socialists* (1965) pp.234-5
28. 9 December, 1871.
29. E. P. Thompson, *Making of the English Working Class* (1963) e.g. pp.498-9
30. Acton. H. B.Comte's Positivism and the Science of Society, *Philosophy* xxvi, 1951 pp.291-310. and Charlton D. G. *Positivist Thought in France During the Second Empire* (Oxford) 1959.
31. Cited in *Before the Socialists,* p.276.
32. For all this see my E. S. Beesly and Karl Marx p.211 et seq.
33. Russell, B. and P. *The Amberley Papers,* Vol. ii (1937) p.412 et seq.
34. ibid p.473.
35. 27 May, 1871. The Liberal Daily News, 25 March, 1871, referring to the Communards as "cowardly ruffians" added: "It is no less certain that the most humane amongst us would not be too scrupulous about the repressive measures which might be necessary to secure that end." i.e. the repression of the Commune.
36. Ruskin, J. *Fors Clavigera:* Letters to the Workmen and Labourers of Gt. Britain, Letter July 1st, 1871, p.4.
37. Reprinted below p.133
38. Collins H. and Abramsky C. op. cit p.212 et seq.

39. Reprinted on p.241
40. Elliott. H. (editor) Letters of J. S. Mill Vol. II p.346-8.
41. "Every day brings me letters in which the British public is displayed in all its colours — its eccentricity, its good nature, its profound generosity, its Yankee quickness to do a job, its impertinence, its selfishness, its hypocrisy. Pinching housewives write on scented notepaper for a 'distressed' maid-of-all-work at £1 per year . . . Procuresses want 'an inexperienced girl of 17'. Oxford men want a Communist by the next train to live with them. Well-to-do people offer a home and their friendship. An M.P. sends £100, an 'old housekeeper' sends £5 . . ." F. Harrison to J. Morley 13 February, 1871.
42. ibid. 11 January, 1872.

I

Richard Congreve

CONGREVE, Richard (1818-1899) Author, founder of organised Positivism in England. Born in Warwickshire in September 1818, the son of Thomas and Julia Congreve. Educated at Rugby under Dr. Arnold and elected to a scholarship at Wadham College, Oxford. After obtaining a first-class he was elected Fellow and tutor of Wadham, but resigned his fellowship in the eighteen fifties to devote himself to Positivist teaching. Comte required that Positivist Priests should be qualified medical practitioners. Accordingly, Congreve became a student at King's College Hospital and in 1866 obtained the membership of the Royal College of Physicians. In the following year he established the London Positivist Society.

As his former pupil, E. S. Beesly observed, Congreve delighted to bring into prominence the most unpalatable conclusions. One of his first public acts was to call upon Britain to surrender Gibraltar to Spain. As the strictest of the English disciples of Comte he disliked writing for the press, preferring to publish his writings as placards, leaflets, pamphlets or in such volumes as *Essays: Political, Social and Religious (1874)* His determination that Positivism should develop from a school into a church contributed to the separation which occurred between him and his most distinguished followers at the end of the eighteen seventies. After this time he became more and more a "back parlour Pope".

The War was a placard measuring 18in. by 11in. It was probably posted up upon the walls of London in late

August 1870. *Paris* appeared in English as a hand-bill printed on both sides. it was translated into French and used as a placard in Paris (See Le Chevalier: *Murailles Politique* (Paris).

THE WAR

In the Name of Humanity

I have no access to, nor have I any confidence in the Newspaper Press, I therefore adopt the Placard, the Street Press.

ENGLISHMEN, especially Englishmen of the Working Classes:

France, as the aggressor in this horrible civil war, for civil war it is, incurred just blame. Her Government deserves most blame, but the French nation must take its share.

But the attitude of the two parties is changing, has, in fact, already changed. The military spirit fostered in Germany beyond all due bounds, has thrown the nation on the French army, and in its triumph the German nation is throwing aside all its original moderation, and avowing plans of annexation and interference with the just independence of France. Germany is now the aggressor, France on the defensive. Germany is even rejecting the claims of the other States of Europe to have a voice in her settlement.

Whilst Louis Napoleon is officially the ruler of France, our Government cannot easily interfere, for he was the aggressor; though even this obstacle may, under certain circumstances, have to be set aside. But he may cease to rule at any moment. Should not England in that case actively interfere in behalf of France, if an energetic diplomatic remonstrance is not listened to? Should she not require of Germany the withdrawal of the German nation from the French soil, on the receipt of a fair indemnity in money, and under the guarantee that if France assumed the offensive England would join Germany to resist her?

These terms accepted by France and refused by Germany, we should support them by arms. No selfish abstinence from action, but war in union with France,—the

31

English and French armies side by side, as in the days of Cromwell or in the Crimea,—to drive back the German inroad—such is the policy I appeal to you to adopt. Arms, money, a fleet, and an army—we have all these means in our power. We might call on Italy and Spain to Join us; nay, even upon Austria and Russia. It is a policy of great sacrifices, but great interests are at stake. Think what the iron rule of Prussia may mean for the industrial movement, the interests of labour in Europe. There is once more a banding of powers against the Republic, in which lies the hope of social progress.

II.

As a nation we are being urged to imitate the example of Prussia, to organise society on a permanent war footing. A strong expression of your refusal to be drawn into such imitation, of your entire and unqualified reprobation of the whole military spirit, is, believe me, urgently needed. Your upper classes are radically unsound on this point. They are not industrial, they are retrograde and military; and that with the less excuse, in that our island position removes even the appearance of necessity. The public opinion of Europe should make it clear to Germany that her military regime is an unsocial and criminal disregard of the interests of Humanity. You, above all others, should stimulate that opinion.

III

One word more. Both Governments have appealed to the same God; and the German victory, at least, will be celebrated by thanksgivings, with the sanction of official Christianity. France, if victorious without Napoleon, will possibly not so insult the religious feelings of mankind. The Religion of Humanity would, by its very name, have protested against this aggression of France, as it would protest against the continuance of the war by Germany in a spirit of aggression and annexation. In the name of that religion I call on you to say loudly that in such a war there can be no triumph,—that the only feeling should be one of shame and sorrow; nay, even that no war in the present day can confer glory; that the reason and the feeling of mankind combine to refuse honour to any military excellence, be it of the pure fighter or of the life-long student of military schemes.

Richard Congreve,
17, Mecklenburgh Square, W.C.

PARIS

THE Prussian King, an old soldier, a mere soldier, incapable of any higher notion than that of a soldier's glory, impenetrable to all the better tendencies of our time, or viewing them with a King's instinctive hatred, is marching upon Paris. His attendant spirits, Bismarck and Von Moltke, those fell representatives of a retrograde policy of war, of ideas which are as inhuman as they should be extinct, are there to guide the Apostle of Absolutism, the crowned opponent of Republicanism, the more successful Brunswick of 1792. The German army, officered by the princes, nobles, and squires of Germany—men who are bred to think arms the only gentleman's profession—is tramping on to enjoy its insolent triumph; to humble the Republic, if possible to put it down; to dismember France; and to fill the Prussian treasury with money to be husbanded, according to the tradition of Prussia, for the next war.

The heroic city stands at bay. She has resisted for years the foul Bonaparte and his accursed regime. She has cleared herself so far as she could of this war. This the Prussian leaders know; and it is this very resistance that is the real crime of Paris in their eyes. It is the Republican party which has on all fitting occasions spoken out its hatred of Napoleon, and it is that party which is the real object of their attack. Paris resists the Hohenzollern as she has done the Bonaparte. She throws herself into the gap for France and for Europe, which needs as little a Prussian military monarchy to domineer over it as a Napoleonic. She thinks, and thinks rightly, that to repel this now causeless aggression is a duty at all risks; and finding her inspiration in her noblest self, she is, by the latest accounts, determined to fight it to the last. She may succeed, or she may fall, but her resolve is noble and wise—all that is noble and wise in Europe should sympathize with her.

The death-duel may even now have begun, and the city may have heard the first boom of the Prussian artillery. And we—what are we doing? What is England doing? Her Queen is in the Highlands, away from the care and trouble; reading, possibly, with sympathy the last devout despatch of her royal compeer of Prussia, and indulging in satisfaction over the glorious prospects of her daughter's husband. Her Ministry is silent, and apparently careless. Her Premier visiting exhibitions, or Clumber. Her Foreign Secretary enjoying Walmer. Her First Lord of the Admiralty in Belgium;—the rest, here, there, and everywhere. Her nobles and gentry are bent on their annual *game* destruction—is it not the season of that mighty interest? Her commercial classes counsel peace, her press preaches submission. No hand is raised;—no voice, even in sympathy.

Men of London, we may awake one morning and find that the death struggle is over, and that through the smoking ruins of Paris, bombarded and taken by storm, the ministers of German vengeance and German greed are raising their hoarse psalm—it will be, of course, a psalm!—of triumph to the God of Battles.

And the infamy of this result will slowly settle down into the minds of Englishmen; and slowly too, perhaps, will visit the Ministry under which it was suffered.

But what can England do? Why, her Government might acknowledge the French Republic, and speak, in the face of Europe, her disapprobation of the Prussian attack. France would be grateful even for that. There have been statesmen of England who would have done more, who would have been able to pierce the sophisms of Prussian policy, and to see that the issue is now clear between the peace and orderly progress of Europe and the triumph of a great military monarchy; and, true to her traditions of resistance to such an evil, they would have called the nation to another great effort. We have no such statesmen.

Men of London, none better than you can realize Paris

girdled in with that iron instrument of destruction. You can speak. Do so, and clear yourselves. Meet and speak. Lend a voice to England. Say that you, the heart of England, have no part nor lot in your Government's supineness and impassivity; that as you sympathised with Germany in her original wrong, so you look with abhorrence on her present attitude of triumphant aggression, as fatal to her own best interests as it may be to those of European civilization.

Come what may, I, and those who think with me, have done what we can—will continue to do what we can.

Paris! Noble and Holy City! there are true English hearts who, in this thy supreme hour, watch thee with hope and admiration; would encourage thee in thy great daring; will, if thou fall, honour thee and avenge thee in the noblest way, by continuing thy mission. Thy lesson of courage and sacrifice shall not be lost.

Richard Congreve.
17, Mecklenburgh-square, Sept. 10, 1870.

II

E. S. Beesly

BEESLY, Edward Spencer (1831-1915) Professor, author, journalist, Positivist. Born January 1831 in Feckenham, Worcestershire. Father, the Rev. James Beesly. Mother, a daughter of Gerald Fitzgerald of Coolaknowle, was Irish. According to the *Times,* 9th July, 1915 "he was descended from Theofano, the wife of Emperor Romanus II". Entered Wadham College, Oxford 1849. Here met Frederic Harrison and John Henry Bridges. Beesly came to Positivism more slowly than Bridges or Harrison. Nevertheless, he was a foundation member of the London Positivist Society which was established in 1867.

From 1854 to 1859 Beesly taught history at Marlborough College. 1860 appointed Professor of History in University College, London, having become Principal of University College Hall in 1859. During the building workers' fight against the system of payment by the hour 1861-62 Beesly emerged, along with the Christian Socialists and his fellow Positivists, as a determined advocate of the claims of Labour. He immediately used his newly won influence among workmen to involve them in political action. For some years Frederic Harrison had been urging him to work with Bright and to help effect a new social and political alignment. On March 26th, 1863 John Bright presided at a great meeting in St. James Hall, London. This was a trade unionists' meeting for Lincoln and against the Slave Power: against British intervention on behalf of the Confederacy and in favour of Reform at home. Beesly not only spoke at this meeting: he played a most important part in organising it.

A month later, he presided at a Trades Society Demonstration on behalf of the Poles. At the end of the year he translated George Odger's address to the Working Men of France. Thus, Beesly was the obvious choice as chairman at the Inaugural Meeting of the International Working Men's Association held at St. Martin's Hall London on 28th September, 1864. Although he presided, Beesly declined an invitation to join the I.W.M.A. He did establish increasingly friendly relations with Karl Marx and the German Socialist provided him with the materials which he used for a detailed account of the origins, aims and structure of the International which appeared in the *Fortnightly Review* for November 1870. By this time Beesly expressed privately his regret at not having associated himself more closely with the work of the I.W.M.A. He considered that its principal usefulness lay in its opposition to militarism and war: an opposition which he took to be quite a different matter than the "hollow sentimentalities" of the Peace Society.

Just as Beesly encouraged the growth of an internationalist spirit among workers without joining the International, so he encouraged trade unionists to go in for political action without allowing himself, at first, to be identified with the Reform League. In 1865 he considered its programme to be too modest and too shallow to arouse the workers' enthusiasm. With the appearance of the Cave of Adullam he warmed to the struggle. He became a Vice-President of the League: urged workers to follow Bright without losing sight of the hostility between their interests and those of middle class radicals: and recommended the formation of a Reform Constabulary or workers' Defence Corps. (*Bee-Hive* 25th November, 1866): He spoke at numerous Reform meetings including the important one held in the Agricultural Hall on 11th February, 1867 at which he seconded a resolution introduced by Ernest Jones. He always advocated Reform in terms of the desirable consequences which he expected to follow from it rather than with regard to "metaphysical" arguments respecting its rightness in the abstract.

Beesly tried to avoid becoming involved in the quarrels which beset the trade union movement in the sixties. However, his sympathies lay with official leaders. As a member of the Committee for the Benefit of Miners (1864) he supported Alexander Macdonald against the attacks of the *British Miner.* In 1865 he defended Applegarth and the Junta in the London Trades Council against George Potter and the *Bee-Hive.* (See his letters in the *Bee-Hive* of 11th February, 21st March, 2nd August, 23rd and 30th September, 1865). He gave a most sympathetic account of the 'New Model' in his "The Amalgamated Society of Carpenters and Joiners", *Fortnightly Review,* March 1867 and was made an honorary member of that Society on 6th January, 1868 (Monthly Report A.S.C. & J February 1868).

After the Sheffield outrages, 1865-66, Beesly privately advised the trade union leaders to discover the culprits. When it was established that William Broadhead was the ring-leader, the London unions met in the Exeter Hall on 2nd July, 1867 to dissociate themselves from his crimes. Beesly observed that a defensive attitude was a weak attitude: that a trade union murder was neither better nor worse than any other sort of murder: and pointed to outrages which had recently been perpetrated in the interests of capital. His speech was widely condemned in the press: it was proposed to blackball him from the Reform Club and to dismiss him from University College. Having survived these attacks, Beesly proceeded (August 1867) to draft a policy entitled, 'The General Election of 1869 : Programme for Trade Unions.' A six point platform intended to secure the independence of the workers in relation to the middle-class radicals. It was endorsed by the Bradford branch of the Reform League and Beesly defended its principles in letters to the *Bradford Review* (14th September, 9th November, 7th and 21st December, 1867). The Conference of Amalgamated Trades found it too ambitious. Beesly did secure its support for a Bill described as the Trade Societies Act, 1868 which he drew up in conjunction with his fellow Positivist and brother-in-law, Henry Crompton.

In the early sixties Beesly compromised himself in the eyes of some workmen by his apparent sympathy with the Second Empire. By the end of the decade he had lost all confidence in Napoleon III and was looking forward to the approaching Revolution. After the proclamation of the Provisional Government in 1870, Beesly and his fellow Positivists campaigned for recognition of the Republic by England. By the beginning of the 1871 they were demanding British military intervention in the interests of the territorial integrity of France. Between 25th March and 17th June, 1871 Beesly contributed a dozen articles to the *Bee-Hive* in defence of the Paris Commune. He was active on behalf of the Communard refugees.

Beesly saw the Criminal Law Amendment Act of 1871 as the result of the defeat of the Commune and of the readiness of certain trade union secretaries to sell themselves to the Liberals during the General Election of 1868. George Howell found these hypotheses disagreeable. He was still more exasperated in the following year when he and Alexander Macdonald were subjected by Beesly and Frederic Harrison to severe public criticism for their allegedly secretive, weak and dishonest management of trade union affairs in the lobby of the House of Commons. (For Beesly's criticisms see *Bee-Hive* 31st May, 14th June, 6th and 20th July, 3rd and 24th August, 1872). At the beginning of 1873 Beesly was pressing for the Gas Stokers Committee to organise the mass agitation which the Parliamentary Committee appeared unwilling to encourage. Increasingly his advice was followed and this culminated in the dinner in honour of five cabinet makers who had been imprisoned for peaceful picketing. It was in May 1875 that Beesly suggested that the London Trades Council should organise the dinner and he presided.

When Odger died in 1877 Beesly led the funeral procession and delivered the eulogy. The death or retirement of old friends among the Labour leaders combined with the open split among the Positivists themselves (1877-78) to diminish Beesly's influence in the trade union world. His close association with the Union leaders finally ended as the result of the Irish question 1881-82. In 1867 Beesly and his fellow Positivists had drafted a petition in favour of the Fenian prisoners which Bright had introduced into the Commons and which caused a great stir. Beesly consistently opposed colonialism and imperialism. In the early eighties, in the press and from the platform, he opposed Coercion in Ireland: defended the Land League: and championed Home Rule or even complete independence. This position ended Beesly's long association with Lib-Lab trade union leaders such as Henry Broadhurst, while it brought him into association with some of those who were to contribute to the socialist revival. He took part in the conference out of which the Democratic Federation emerged. H. M. Hyndman always referred to him with respect and affection. Beesly never pretended to be a socialist, but he preferred the militant or Marxist variety to reformists and Fabians.

Beesly's concern for Ireland twice led him to override Positivist scruples respecting candidatures for Parliament. In 1885 he stood as a Liberal, Home Rule man in Westminster where he was defeated by a Tory by 3, 991 votes to 1,737. In the following year he again lost to a Conservative this time in East Marylebone, by 3,101 to 1,616.

In 1893 Beesly resigned his Chair at University College and founded the *Positivist Review*. In 1901 he moved to St. Leonards and in the following year ceased to edit the *Review*.

In 1869 Beesly married Emily, the sister of Henry Crompton. They had four sons. He died at St. Leonards, 7th July, 1915 and was buried beside his wife in Paddington Cemetery, on 10th July, 1915. He was the first

University teacher who closely committed himself to the British Labour Movement.

"A Word for France" was written during the first week of September 1870. It is reprinted here because it is representative of the line which the English Positivists were taking on the eve of the Commune. (Congreve used the placard, "the street press" while J. H. Bridges followed Beesly's example in a pamphlet entitled "Why we should stand by France"). However, the great interest of *A Word for France* is the way in which it anticipated the Second Address of the International on the Franco-Prussion War. As Marx acknowledged there were passages which coincided "almost literally". In particular, this applied to the terms in which the two documents characterised the Prussian military system. They also corresponded to one another closely in the way in which they insisted upon the changed character of the War: in emphasising the bourgeois republicans' fatal dread of the French working class and in the manner in which they disposed of the German claim to "a sound strategic frontier."

Beesly was as impressed by the coincidence of opinion as Marx. On 14th September, 1870 he wrote to the German Socialist: "I now recognise as I never did before, the usefulness of the International, and I regret that I have not co-operated with it actively in the past, though I have always sympathised." Marx suggested that Beesly should write an account of the International for the *Fortnightly Review*. This was done on the basis of materials supplied by Marx himself and duly appeared in the issue for November 1870. It was by far the most complete and authorative account of the I.W.M.A. to have been written at that date. However, Beesly made rather light of theoretical questions and recommended the 'practical English element'. He regarded it as sufficient unto the day that the International was republican and anti-militarist. "Let not cynical politicians imagine", he wrote, "that the protest of the workmen of Europe against war is to be ranked with the hollow unreasoning sentimentalities of the press, the pulpit and the countinghouse. In England they mean to have their way about this thing and they will grind to powder all institutions, classes and interests that attempt to militarise them, whether as regulars, militia, reserves, volunteers or anything else."

On 20th September, 1870 Beesly had written to Marx about the improvement in public feeling on the Franco-Prussian War. He added "I do not anticipate that England will act even in the mildest way. But all this excitement is leavening the mass for us. "Unfortunately, the Positivists were not content with rousing workmen to press for Gladstone's recognition of the French Republic. From hinting at the need for armed intervention, they passed on to open demands for it and Congreve presided over an Anglo-French Intervention Committee. By January Marx was expressing concern that members of the International should follow the Positivist lead and call for war upon Prussia if she refused to make peace on reasonable terms. At the end of the month Engels initiated a full-scale debate in the General Council in which he argued that had the workers confined themselves to getting Gladstone to recognise the French Republic they might have succeeded. However, there were "others who were not satisfied with this. I mean the Comtists, Professor Beesly and his friends . . . the Comtists are not properly a working-class party. They advocate a compromise to make wages labour tolerable, to perpetuate it; they belong to a political sect who believe that France ought to rule the world. In their last declaration, which was signed by several members of the Council, they demand that France should be restored to the position it occupied before the war. Before the war, France was a military power. The Comtists asked for intervention, and as soon as that was done the working-class movement split up . . . . How could people who were not able to compel the Government to recognise the Republic, force the same Government to go to War for the Republic?"

Subsequently, the Positivists came to acknowledge the substantial correctness of Engels' judgement. After the War and the Commune, Congreve spoke to his French co-religionists about the great qualities of the English working class. "They were", he said, "practically unanimous in proclaiming the French Republic and always insisted that the Government should recognise it without delay. But when it came to the question of war, the division was very pronounced: they drew back before this prospect, and this division was fatal to the exercise of all serious influence upon the general politics of the country."

*   *   *

Professor Beesley on the Paris Revolution

The immediate object of these remarkable articles was to keep workmen 'sound' on the Commune and to immunise them against the hysteria being spread by the middle-class press. The *Standard* of 21 March described Paris as a Red Republic "dominated by thieves, rowdies and demagogues" of the city. The Liberal *Daily News* of 25 March characterised the Communards as "Cowardly Ruffians" and affirmed that "the most humane amongst us would not be too scrupulous about the repressive measures which might be necessary" to extinguish the Revolution. The *Daily Telegraph* dismissed the revolutionaries as "assassins" and "convicts" and this sort of language was employed by most of the papers for most of the life-time of the insurrection.

It seems unnecessary to give detailed editorial notes. The "Polish General" referred to in the article for 22nd. April was Jaroslaw Dombrowski: the "Prussian" who was described as "elected to the Commune" was, presumably, Leo Frankel. For the rest, the interested reader will find notes on the communards referred to in F. Jellinek, *The Paris Commune of 1871* (1937). Governor Eyre, who is twice mentioned, was the Governor of Jamaica who had, in 1865, resorted to martial law, frequent hangings, burnings and flogging to suppress a disturbance at Morant Bay. Beesly had been associated with J. S. Mill, Huxley, Darwin and others in demanding (unavailingly) that Eyre should be brought to justice. The reference in the final article to "the contemptuous refusal of unionist demands in the present session of Parliament" relates to the refusal of the Gladstone Government to secure the right to peaceful picketing and to protect workmen from prosecutions for conspiracy arising out of trade disputes.

Although the *Bee-Hive* printed Beesley's articles in a prominent position it opened its columns to furious attacks upon the Commune and its friends. A short history of the paper will be found in S. Coltham, George Potter, the Junta and the Bee-hive *International Review of Social History*. (Amsterdam) vol X (1965) Parts 1 & 2.)

A WORD FOR FRANCE

Addressed to the Workmen of London

My object in writing these few pages is to place before such workmen as may read them some considerations upon the struggle now proceeding on the Continent, looked at from the workman's point of view. Floods of printed matter are poured forth on this subject every day by our journalists and literary men, and a workman has no information except what comes from their pens. They judge this, as all other questions, without reference to his interests and sympathies, of which they are both ignorant and careless. A private writer has little chance of reaching many of his countrymen. Still, every one may do something towards the formation of public opinion, and therefore I publish this little pamphlet with the hope that it may arrest the attention of some of our London workmen, who have known me long enough to be well assured that I have their interests really at heart.

Great as is my admiration for France, firmly as I believe that her pre-eminence is for the good of Europe, I have always condemned her jealousy of German unification. I have always held that if any people of German blood (or, for the matter of that, of any other blood) desired to enter the Prussian kingdom, France had no title to interfere. In 1864 I was one of the very few Englishmen who maintained the right of Prussia to rescue Holstein and the German parts of Schleswig from the domination of the Danes; and I wrote letters signed with my name in the *Daily News* and the *Beehive* in support of that opinion. When war was declared last July, I desired that France might receive a sharp lesson, bitterly as I grieved that such a lesson should be needed; for it was impossible to persuade oneself that the whole guilt lay with the vile man who governed France. It was clear that a portion of the nation had wel-

46

comed the war. What portion it was I will explain presently. It is enough here to admit that the French people allowed itself to be represented by the war party, and therefore deserved to pay the penalty. I feared greatly lest the Germans should have been taken unprepared, and lest the work of 1866 should be undone. I feared it, because it was clear that Germany was bent on union, and that any interruption of the process would only prolong a mischievous struggle. I feared it still more for France herself, believing that a victorious campaign would reawaken in her people the taste for conquest and military glory which was rapidly dying out. I welcomed the first successes of the German arms, as putting an end for ever to French dreams of territorial extension on the side of Germany. I even desired that the French army should suffer a decisive overthrow, believing that to be the shortest path to the re-establishment of a just peace, and the deposition and condign punishment of Napoleon. I could not think it possible that any responsible German statesman, even if as swollen with stupid pride as the old sovereign of Prussia, or as unscrupulous as Bismarck, would seriously propose to rob France of the smallest portion of her soil.

But it seems I was mistaken every way. It is clear that the thirst for territorial plunder, the propensity to bully and tyrannize over a fallen enemy, is quite as strong among these gentle Germans as ever it was among the French. No sooner have they obtained military advantages, than they proclaim their intention of annexing two French provinces and limiting the numbers of the French army, while they would retain their own military organization now known to be far the most formidable in Europe. Now what is this but an imitation of the outrageous treatment of Prussia by Napoleon I. sixty years ago? It is a crime, not merely against France, but against Europe, for it ensures the renewal of the war at no distant date. If Prussia, when a small nation of 7,000,000 souls, and without allies, but inspired by a patriotic hatred of foreign domination, contrived, under the very eyes of such a sharpsighted statesman as Napoleon I., to prepare in secrecy a fine army of well-drilled soldiers, is it to be supposed that a great country like France, however she may be humbled for the moment, will not soon be ready and eager to renew the struggle, even single-handed? But she will not stand alone. Russia, Austria, and Italy are already uneasy at the threatened preponderance of Germany, and from one or all of them France would sooner or later obtain assistance. Thus the overbearing ambition of Prussia would prolong indefinitely the misery of Europe.

Putting aside for the moment the question whether a million and a half of Frenchmen are to be transferred from one nation to another, like so many sheep, it is clear that there is not the smallest excuse for this atrocious demand. Germans pretend that they require the Vosges Mountains as a frontier for their protection against France. But, in the first place, does any man in his senses believe that after this astounding display of the united feeling and military strength of Germany, France will ever again cherish the dream of conquering or dividing her? And, secondly, is it not a fact that the possession of her present line of frontier, backed by the strong positions of Cologne, Coblenz, Mayence, and Rastadt, has been found admirably adapted to repel the first rush of invasion? It was arranged in 1815, with a view to that very contingency. For fifty-five years it has proved sufficient for its purpose, and though the declaration of war the other day was a surprise, and the French army was first in the field, it never found its way three miles across the border. The claim of a new frontier therefore is not merely unreasonable, it is impudent, and is to be regarded as a manifestation of the new-born arrogance and territorial greed of the German people. Woe to Belgium and Holland, to Denmark and Switzerland, if this detestable spirit is not promptly and sternly repressed by united Europe.

We are all of us apt, during a great war, to award our sympathy, not so much with reference to the immediate occasion of the quarrel, as in accordance with a sentimental preference for one or other of the combatants. I do not say that this is to be regretted. On the contrary, sentiment is upon the whole the safest guide for the great mass of a nation. It kept our people right during the American war, and I trust it now. Let me suggest a few reasons why the humiliation of France by Germany should be repugnant to the sentiment of English workmen.

France is the only country in Europe which has been thoroughly revolutionized. There alone has the working class once and again risen in its might, and at a critical moment taken the destinies of its country into its hands. The heroism, the self-denial, the lofty aims of the French workman, in the revolutions of 1792 and 1848, are the glory of their class throughout Europe. They invested it with a new dignity, and if the London artizan finds himself not without importance in English politics, if he sees other classes fain to assume a respectful attitude towards his, if there is a growing belief that society will in the end be organised with a view to the greater happiness, not of its richer but of its poorer members, let him remember that this is mainly due to the example French workmen have given of what they claimed, what they could do, and what they could suffer. It is in France that the struggle between employer and employed has raged and will again rage most fiercely. There it is that the victories of labour will first be won. In France alone the soil belongs to the people. It was wrested from the nobility, gentry, and clergy by the first revolution, and its produce now enriches, not idle land-lords or grinding farmers, but the peasants who cultivate it. Should not the English workman feel that his interests are bound up with the welfare of the only nation in which his class has obtained preponderance?

Turn to Germany. I have nothing to say against the German workmen. They are, I believe, a worthy and excel-lent class. But, they are sadly behindhand. Well educated they may be—or rather well instructed, which is not quite the same thing; but their instruction has not emancipated them from superstitious, old-world ideas. They still bow their necks patiently under the yoke of a privileged class. Prussia has a stupid old king, who detests popular liberty and claims to govern by divine right, as the Stuarts did in England. Imagine divine right in the nineteenth century! There is a parliament, indeed; but when a few years ago it presumed to oppose him, he collected the taxes in spite of it, and imprisoned members who made speeches he did not approve of, exactly as our Charles I. did. When the law courts decided in their favour, he displaced the judges, just as our James II. did. There is a numerous nobility, puffed up with the pride of birth to a degree we cannot conceive in England, and always ready to support the King against the People. His minister, Bismarck, delights to call himself the King's "vassal", and has often ostentatiously proclaimed that he is responsible only to the king. All this the educated Prussians tamely put up with. When Charles I. endeavoured to use his English subjects to conquer the kindred country of Scotland, our ancestors seized the opportunity to shake off his yoke. But when the King of Prussia summoned his subjects to war against their kinsmen of South Germany, in 1866, he found a passive and even cheerful obedience. In the French army a large proportion of the officers rise from the ranks. This was one of the many points of equality established by the old revolution. Marshal Bazaine began life as a private soldier. In the Prussian army such a phenomenon is unknown. The officiers are taken exclusively from the upper classes. They are, it is true, obliged to serve one year as privates, but when that year is over, they step into the position reserved for their birth. Perhaps some one will reply, that the commissions are kept for gentlemen in the British army. Very true; more the shame for a people calling itself free. But, after all, ours is a volunteer army. If a man chooses to enlist with the knowledge that he can never rise, and will always have to be ordered about by a gentleman, it is his own look out. But in Prussia, every man is obliged to serve in the army for three years; and at the expiration of his active service, he is still enrolled in his regiment, so that though he goes back to industrial occupations he is no better than a soldier on furlough. Let an English labouring man ask himself how he would like to be hopelessly bound for life to the condition of a private soldier, with the neighbouring squire or his employer for his commanding officer; and then let him say what the Prussian working men must be like, who can tamely submit to such degradation. Four years ago this system existed only in Prussia, but since the war of 1866 it has been extended over North Germany, and men who were born citizens of the free town of Frankfort now see their sons drilling under Prussian nobles and squires. I say, that until Germany has had *her* revolution, until her people have brought their princes, aristocracy, and gentlemen as low as France brought hers in 1792, an English workman cannot look on German conquests as anything but a calamity to freedom and progress.

But let us regard this Prussian military system from another point of view. It is exciting much attention just now. Many English Liberals are fascinated by it. Make every citizen a soldier, they say, and England will be powerful abroad, while her liberties would be secure at home. What would be the effect of this system on our political liberty may be seen most clearly by asking ourselves how it would work in any individual case. When political feeling runs high, when there are gatherings in Trafalgar Square and processions to Hyde Park, a London workman is master of his own actions. He can attend public meetings, he can consult with his friends, he can arrange with them how to act in certain emergencies. If he thinks a demonstration unwise or premature, he can walk out and look at it with his hands in his pockets; if he thinks it useful he can join it; if he thinks it wants putting down he can get sworn in as a special constable. But if he was No. 999 in the reserve of a regiment, at the first symptom of commotion he would be summoned to report himself at head-quarters, he would have some Lord Elcho for his colonel, some master builder or master tailor for his captain, and his foreman for serjeant or corporal. Standing in the ranks in his barrack-yard he would have little means of learning what was going on, or of consulting with the friends he trusts, still less of himself contributing to form public opinion; and he would be liable at any moment to be ordered to do something which his conscience abhorred. To put it shortly—How can liberty be rendered surer by making every private citizen amenable to martial law? Such an arrangement might suit the noblemen and game-preservers, the great employers, and west-end shopkeepers, but if the working-men, the destined rank and file of this precious militia, who have got the franchise at last, and can make their weight felt at a general election, if they allow Lord Elcho, or any one else, to get such schemes any further than the columns of the *Times,* they will deserve to lose their liberties and to become as patient uncomplaining tools of despotism as Prussians.

But this is not all. Let us suppose the Lord Elchos sent to Jericho, their hares and pheasants exterminated, and their estates divided among the labourers who cultivate them; let us suppose Buckingham Palace turned into public offices, and Windsor Castle let in apartments—would it then be desirable that every citizen should be a soldier? Certainly not; not though every officer, from the lance-corporal to the commander-in-chief, were to be elected by ballot and universal suffrage. In what, broadly viewed, has modern progress consisted? In the demilitarising of society. There was a time when this dream of foolish lords and gaping liberal journalists was a reality. Some six centuries ago, and even later, every gentleman was a soldier. He would have thought it beneath his dignity to be anything else; and the lower classes, though wishing for nothing so much as peace, had to follow their lords to their constant wars, so that probably no poor man ever went through life without having used his bow or pike in battle. From this state of things we gradually emerged. Instead of every man being taken away from his business to fight, the service was devolved upon a special class paid for the purpose.

Thus not only was an economy effected by the well-known principle of a division of labour, but the large mass of the population ceased to be infected with the turbulent, violent, anti-industrial habits of military life. The dislike of soldiering, a trade never willingly adopted now-a-days, except by idle persons fit for nothing else, is one of the chief marks of the advance we have made in civilization. France is always supposed to be the most warlike country in Europe. Well, there is no country where the lower classes hate soldiering so much. The army has to be filled up by conscription—the "tax of blood"—as it is called. The conscript is drawn by lot, all the family savings and as much as can be borrowed besides, are eagerly given to buy a substitute for him. But the poorest have to go. It is certain that any government of France which should declare the conscription abolished, would be enthusiastically supported by the peasantry. But what do we see in Prussianized Germany? A return to the old barbarous manners which made every man a soldier. The whole population is classified for military service according to age, just as it was in ancient Rome. And then they tell us that an army of citizens will never be called out except for defence! Have we not seen them twice within the last five years pour by hundreds of thousands across their frontiers into a neighbouring country? What chance is there of peace for Europe, of the disarmament which has been talked of so long, if this tremendous military machine is permanently planted on our borders? It is ridiculous to suppose that France, or Austria, or Italy, will consent to disarm and live at the mercy of the North Germans. Are we all to be forced into adopting the same barbarous organisation in order to ensure our independence?

There appears to be an impression that these educated Germans are making war with a gentleness and a consideration for non-combatants never before known, and among other things that they pay for all they take. Of course, individual soldiers are prohibited from plumdering, which is not allowed in any well-desciplined army in modern times, partly because it shocks modern feeling, but still more because it wastes the resources of the country. The Prussian generals go methodically to work, precisely as Napoleon I. did. They strip the country clean by requisitions. They do not even leave the unfortunate peasant enough grain for seed. As for the pretended payment of which English journals talk, it is in the old shape of paper acknowledgments, which it is highly improbable will ever be converted into coin. For the humanity of Prussia, look at the siege of Strasburg. Instead of attacking the fortifications in the usual way, the mild German bombards the houses of the 80,000 helpless inhabitants, in order, as he says, that they may force the garrison to surrender. Bismarck long ago boasted that his was a policy of "blood and iron," and now we may see the full import of that famous phrase.

Germany is not only politically but intellectually backward. France is nominally a Catholic country, but everyone knows how completely its male population is emancipated from superstition. The Prussians are for the most part not only nominally but really Protestants, and an invasion of the country of Voltaire, of Diderot, of Condorcet, of Auguste Comte, by their psalm-singing legions, inspires melancholy thoughts. The very telegrams of the King to Berlin, reeking of blood and slaughter, are garnished with pious talk suitable enough to a contemporary of Luther, but ridiculous, not to say nauseous, in the nineteenth century. Even English generals drop that business.

A strange delusion seems to possess many Englishmen. They have got an idea that Germans are a quiet stay-at-home people, who want to secure themselves against foreign interference, but have no disposition to oppress their neighbours. It seems to be forgotten that they were the scourges of Italy for many centuries, and that though it suited Prussia to form an alliance with that country in 1866, her sympathies with Austria were loudly expressed during the previous war of liberation. The Magyars, of Humgary, have only lately thrown off the German yoke;

E.S. BEESLY

the Czechs, of Bohemia, still groan under it. People who
denounced the Russians for their treatment of Poland
seem not to be aware that Prussia shared in the partition of
that unfortunate country, and that to the present day she
holds the Polish province of Posen, the inhabitants of
which have never ceased to protest against her rule. I have
said that I approved of the liberation of Holstein and the
German parts of Schleswig from Denmark. But Northern
Schleswig, though Danish, has been retained by Prussia in
unblushing violation of the treaty of peace, because it contains a vaulable fortress. And now comes the last and most
atrocious piece of territorial plunder that Europe has seen
since the fall of the first Napoleon. Alsace and Lorraine
have long been provinces of France, the greater part of
them for more than two centuries. Their annexation to
France was no doubt the result partly of war, partly of
dynastic changes. In those days such grounds were held to
be sufficient for alterations of frontier without respect to
the wishes of the inhabitants. The Alsatians still speak a
sort of German, but in sentiment they and the Lorrainers
have long been enthusiastically French. This is not disput-
ed. The German generals now occupying those provinces
have been obliged to publish severe proclamations threatening death to the inhabitants if they show any hostility to
the invaders, and according to the German newspapers
munerous executions have taken place already. There is
not even any small minority of the population to form a
German party. All the misery they are suffering does not
shake their attachment to their country. We thought, and
all Europe thought the day had gone by when a tract of
soil with its inhabitants could be seized by brute force and
appropriated by right of conquest. The cessions of Savoy
by Italy to France ten years ago, was an altogether different matter. It was not torn from Italy by conquest, but
ceded by her in return for services of enormous value. The
Savoyards not only spoke French, but disliked the Italians
and were disliked by them. The annexation was not carried
out until a large majority of the population by universal

suffrage and ballot had voted for it, and not a single whisper of discontent has been heard since. Even under these circumstances, what a cry of indignation went up from England against the rapacity of France! What pity was lavished on the supposed victims! In the case of Alsace and Lorraine, as we have seen, there is not a single extenuating circumstance. It is impossible to imagaine an annexation more outrageous. We know what the Prussian theory is, for it was shamelessly avowed at the incorporation of Hanover four years ago: "The right of conquest constitutes a just title to the acquisition of foreign territories. The idea of strengthening the right of conquest by universal suffrage cannot be entertained, as it would tend to substitute appearances for reality. The people have no claim to be consulted on the question of their incorporation." It is with statesmen who hold this language, and with a people which unanimously endorses it, that we find ourselves face to face. It comes to this, that Europe has to reckon with an outlaw nation, which avowedly rejects right and appeals to "blood and iron." Let it not be supposed that such sentiments are confined to insolent aristocrats and swaggering soldiers. There is in Germany (as everywhere else) a breed of creatures more pestilent than either, the literary tribe—journalists, pamphleteers, song-writers, and professors. For many years past these apostles of mischief have been preaching to their countrymen that every German-speaking people and particularly those of Alsace, should be annexed to the Fatherland by persuasion, if possible, but, if not, by force. Of course, they will not hear of applying the same principle to Danes, Poles, and Czechs, who none of them speak German. But why should all people speaking the same language unite in one aggregate? What good is to be gained that could compensate for all this disturbance? The idea is a thoroughly artificial one, hatched in the smoky brains of professors. The sort of patriotism, or rather partizanship, it gives rise to is on a level, as to rationality and dignity, with the excitement of a pair of rival schools at a cricket match. The soundest and healthiest bonds that can unite a people are old traditions and a common history, provided always that the connection is voluntary. Pedants or fanatics who would disturb it, reviving antipathies that slumbered or creating them where they had never existed, unsettling the minds of the young with their crude theories and furnishing pretexts to scheming politicians, are the pests of modern civilization. Where incurable antipathy does exist, however it has been brought about, whether by real wrongs inflicted and endured, or by the evil activity of literary vermin, disruption had better take place. Anything for peace. Anything rather than this prolonged military hubbub, which throws back civilization, and postpones the dawn of the new era in which the working men. of Europe shall come by their own. But to my mind it is a nobler spectacle when men of different blood and various speech can consent to live together under one polity, subordinating the barbarous prejudices of race to the common ends of civic association. Such a spectacle the Swiss Confederation has long afforded. But alas for Switzerland! The German tongue predominates in her cantons, and Count Bismarck and his professors will soon have leisure to apply their formula at Berne and Zurich.

Perhaps by this time the reader will be ready to say: "You bring a heavy indictment against Germany, but what apology have you to offer for France? Why did she wickedly provoke the war? Why, if she is the model nation, did she accept such a ruler as Napoleon? How is it that she has exhibited such a spectacle of corruption, weakness, and disorder?" I have no desire to shirk the question. To answer it is one of my main objects in writing.

The truth is that France has been for many years in a state of smothered civil war. The burning questions of property, capital, and labour, which are beginning to arrest attention in England, have in France swallowed up all others. The middle and the lower classes glare on each other like foemen about to close in mortal struggle. Upper class there is none; or if there is some shadow of such a thing it is absolutely without political significance; it was ground to powder in the old revolution. The town artizans have for two generations been meditating on such themes as the distribution of property, the remuneration of labour, the increase of wealth and luxury above, of poverty and toil below. They believe some in one form of socialism, some in another; but they are all agreed that the evils of society might be remedied by vigorous governmental measures. They are all for a republic, of course, but they look on it as worthless unless it is the "social republic." Now many of the middle class are republicans, and many more would be were they not afraid that the republic to-day would mean socialism to-morrow. With them, as with the lower class, the economic question takes precedence of the political, and a king, an emperor, or even a Prussian army, is more tolerable in their eyes than the ascendancy of the working class. The lot of these men has been cast by fate in the central country of Europe in which as republicanism made its appearance eighty years ago, so socialism has made its first appearance in our own generation. It has fallen to them to elect whether they will acquiesce in a new order of relations between wealth and poverty, or whether they will make their backs stiff and fight it out. In June, 1848, the midle-class republicans poured grapeshot for three days upon the Paris workmen, who thought the time had come to inaugurate their social millennium; and the blood that then flowed has not been forgotten. In the terror and confusion of that year Louis Napoleon was carried to power by the votes of the peasantry. Established in that position, one might almost say by accident, he profligately maintained himself by playing off the middle-class and the workmen against each other, and the army against both. The leaders of the workmen were massacred or sent to Cayenne. the mass of them were kept quiet by an extravagant out-lay on public works, and the consequent artificial demand for labour. Political life of all kinds was crushed. The Press was silenced. Public meetings were forbidden. Naturally the middle-class, with its republican tendencies, writhed under this system, but whenever it assumed a threatening attitude the Emperor, by a speech like that of Auxerre, or by a measure such as the repeal of the combination laws, or the abolition of the *livret,* intimated that if driven to extremities he would throw himself on the proletariat. The menace always succeeded. It was like a lash cracked over a pack of hounds. The middle-class trembled and subsided. They knew that the blood of June, 1848, was an impassible barrier between them and the people. A new generation of workmen has grown up. But socialism, so far from having been extinguished by grapeshot, is found to be more widely spread and deeply rooted than ever. The workmen remain steady in their detestation of the Imperial system, but they do not care to rise against it for the benefit of the middle-class. They have pulled the chestnuts out of the fire for M. Thiers and M. Jules Favre often enough.

In the meantime twenty years of Napoleonism were bearing their fruit. The object of the Emperor being to cheat and corrupt a great people, he found, as may be supposed, none but knaves to assist him in the work. Honest men of all parties stood aloof from his court as if it was plague-stricken. The whole tribe of functionaries, from the ministers of state to the village mayors, were either corrupt or in process of corruption. Even his army, it now turns out, was a gigantic job. He did not dare to encourage real merit, even of the purely military kind, lest his own name should be overshadowed. So the army was entrusted to parasites, whose only recommendation was that they were ready to shoot down their own countrymen. But this was not all. His pockets were picked by his own confederates, and if he suspected their malversations, he was obliged to wink at them. As everyone knew that France was paying for an army of 750,000 men, we could not make out what had become of them when only some 250,000 appeared to be forthcoming in the first week of the campaign. Even when allowance was made for the armies detained to overawe the workmen of Paris and Lyons, the disproportion seemed unaccountable; and now it is beginning to ooze out, that the money paid by conscripts to purchase substitutes, was not expended on substitutes, but stuck to the fingers of the Emperor's friends; so that companies supposed to be one hundred strong, in some cases mustered no more than thirty.

When the first disasters were announced, every one supposed that it was all over with Imperialism. To our astonishment no steps were taken to depose Napoleon, or to drive from the Tuilleries the wretched woman who was insulting France by presiding at councils and singing proclamations. After a week or two, in spite of new disasters, it appeared that the Emperor was actually gaining ground, and was not likely to be displaced. Now, what was the meaning of this? Simply that the middle-class in Paris had not nerve to face a Republic. Anything rather than give arms to the workmen. The Assembly, a thoroughly middle-class body, after the battles of Metz, refused to repeal the law which makes it penal to possess arms without a license. The Government has been blamed for withholding news, but has not the whole middle-class press of Paris joined in the conspiracy to conceal the danger from the Parisians, lest the workmen should insist on being furnished with arms?

And yet, if Paris is to be defended, it must be by the workmen. The shopkeepers have but one wish, and that is that the city may be surrendered quietly. For years it has been the policy of the Emperor to demoralize the capital. He has laboured by his so-called improvements to efface the memorials of her heroic days, just as he has tried to extinguish in her citizens all serious, manly, and patriotic feeling. His aim has been to make her a sort of gigantic Cremorne or Alhambra, the brothel of Europe. With the middle class, he has probably, to a large extent succeeded. He has imported among them commercial life of the modern English type, which consists in straining immoderately after money half one's time, and spending it in insolent luxury the other half; and a shriek of horror arises from them when it is proposed to spoil their finery for such a ridiculous matter as the independence of their country. But with the workmen it is different. They have no elegant mansions in the Champ Elysées. They do not canter their horses in the Bois de Boulogne, or tickle their palates at the Trois Frères. The splendours, of Paris have meant nothing for them but higher rents and dearer food, and probably they will not break their hearts over some damage to Baron Haussmann's long drawn vistas and stately façades. I should not altogether regret the defeat of marshal's and generals, if our own, yes, I say our own glorious Paris, capital of the west, mother of heroes and martyrs, might recall the memory of her Spartan days, take up the sword which has fallen from accursed hands, and prove herself once more the Paris of '92, '30, and '48. Her palaces may crumble under Prussian shells, and all that is pleasing to the eye may disappear; but, she will be more beautiful to me in the dignity of such ruin, that when bedizened with Imperial gilding to woo the debauchery of Europe.

I cannot conceal from myself that such a resistance would probably be attended with scenes of wild and, perhaps, undiscriminating vengeance on the real or supposed authors of these misfortunes. France has been shamefully betrayed by the Bonapartists. They are even more guilty than the Emperor himself. While wickedly stimulating the military spirit which, if let alone, would have died out of itself; they poisoned the manhood and strength of the nation with mammonworship and luxury. To escape the contempt and discredit which was gathering over them, they rushed into war with a half-recruited army, with a Garde Mobile which, till a month ago, they were afraid to trust even at drill with better weapons than broom-sticks, and with a commissariat which was one huge job. Since the war began, they have been sending the half-drilled Republicans of the Garde Mobile to the front, to be cleared out of the way by Prussian artillery while they have retained veteran troops in the large towns to overawe the Socialists.

They have deluded Paris with false stories of victory, lest she should insist on being furnished with arms, and they have shot, by sentence of court-martial, patriots who were determined to have them. All this they have done, and they have been supported in it by the middle class majority in the Chamber; and when the sad truth is revealed, if the people turn round and take sharp vengeance on the authors of their misery and disgrace, should we be surprised? They may do much that I shall regret, but for my part I shall not judge them too hardly.

The French workmen are not responsible for the war. Their representatives in the Chamber protested against it, but were howled down by the middle class majority. The police had to stop demonstrations in the streets of Paris almost immediately after war was declared, because they were unmistakeably for peace.

In spite of her terrible military reverses, I do not believe that France will ultimately succumb. I do not believe that half a million of Germans can rob her of Alsace and Lorraine. But she must recognise the fact that she is no longer the first military power of Europe. So much the better for her. She will learn at last that her pre-eminence depends not on brute force, but on her readiness to lead the way, as of old, in intellectual, political, and social progress. This is a primacy that no defeats can rob her of. Yet a little while and a word will go forth from her which will thrill Europe as did the declaration of the rights of man in the old revolution. The Reorganization of Labour is a torch which will kindle a flame wherever it touches. It is of this offspring that France is now in labour. It has come to the birth like the Replublicanism of 1792, amid the horrors of invasion and the apparent wreck of her independence. "The martyr country of Europe," as Dr. Congreve lately called her, she bears these sorrows for us, and she shall at least have our gratitude and sympathy.

Shall I say our assistance? Sad and humiliating avowal for an Englishman, we can do next to nothing. *Our* middle classes have tied India, the colonies, and a disaffected

Ireland on our back and Germany laughs, as well she may, at the 20,000 soldiers we could put into the field. But the time must come, and that almost immediately, when we can give her substantial aid. Germany insolently asserts that peace shall be made without the intervention of foreign powers. She deceives herself. The rest of Europe will insist on having a voice in the deliberations, and there we may help France. Let us join with Russia, Austria, and Italy in protesting against, and, if needful, in preventing by force any territorial spoliation.

I have addressed this appeal to workmen. What others may think of it I am very indifferent. I disclaim all intention of offence to German workmen. Many thousands of them as well as of Frenchmen belong to the International, and doubtless endorse the admirable address which that Society issued at the commencement of the war. Workmen throughout Europe are beginning to feel that the ties which bind them to one another are much stronger and more real than those which kings and diplomatists have invented for them. What I desire for the workmen of Germany is that they may have a grand revolution of their own, and sweep away their privileged classes. Now that the nightmare of foreign interference has passed away for ever, I firmly believe they will address themselves to the task.

POSTSCRIPT

Since this pamphlet went to the printer the Republic has been proclaimed. Now I know what London workmen will do. The grand cause is once more before them. The Republic against monarchy and nobles, national independence against foreign domination—it is a simple issue. May our French brothers have the fortitude to continue the struggle to the last gasp rather than surrender a single inch of Alsace or Lorraine.

THE PARIS REVOLUTION

The Bee-Hive No. 493 Saturday, March 25, 1871.

If our newspapers are to be believed, Paris is in the hands of a small body of bloodthirsty, cowardly roughs, bent only on murder and plunder; and all honest people everywhere, whatever their rank in society, whatever their politics, should look with indignation and horror on the new Revolution.

But our newspapers are *not* to be believed. Their articles and correspondence are coloured by bitter antipathy to the workmen of Paris, and have been so throughout the siege. They are in a conspiracy of misrepresentation. On the miserable petty questions of party warfare, on a quarrel at the Admiralty, on a squabble about pebble gunpowder, they are some check upon one another; and from a comparison of their recriminations the truth may be made out. But when it is a question, between poor and rich, between genuine Republicanism and the manifold forms of privilege, they all sing the same song, which they know will please the upper and middle classes. As for the cheap weekly papers, they just transfer to their columns, with scissors and paste-pot, the sensation telegrams, the highly-flavoured correspondence, and the perfidious comments of the dailies, and so, from pure ignorance and carelessness, propagate falsehood and mislead and bewilder the working class.

It is a lamentable thing that the workmen of London have no independent sources of information, no chronicle of events that does not proceed directly or indirectly from the pens of the enemies of their class. I will endeavour, so far as may be attained by the weak and isolated efforts of one who is not a journalist, nor a preacher, nor a stump orator, to supply the need for the moment, and to point out to the readers of this journal, at least, why they should

64

refuse to swallow all the stories they are told about the Revolution in Paris.

First then, I warn my readers not to believe that Paris is in the hands of what our journalists are pleased to call a "rabble of roughs". The Revolution is supported by two hundred and fifteen battalions of the National Guard. It is supported by the whole artizan population; and if the engineers, masons, carpenters, painters, bricklayers, tailors and shoemakers of Paris are "roughs", what are you, my readers? But further, it is supported by the lower middle class. A great part of the industry of Paris is in the hands of small masters, employing five or six workmen, as is the case at Birmingham. These employers are all with the movement. So are the small shopkeepers. Whatever opposition exists is to be found among what the *Times* calls the "best blood in Paris," the wealthiest citizens, the friends of order, waving their shiny silk hats with delicately gloved hands. We thus begin to understand what journalists mean by "roughs". They are men whose hands are not delicately gloved — working men in fact. But strange to say, another correspondent of the *Times* on the same page, makes the curious admission that the Revolution.has the sympathy and good wishes of "a great number of shopkeepers, and even great tradesmen", of people "whom I had thought very sensible, who had a certain rank in the middle classes, and who certainly would be very little pleased to see their shops pillaged and their houses plundered; but the pride of possessing a uniform, and a musket, has been their ruin." So much for the "rabble of roughs" theory. The truth is that numbers of Parisians who are not Socialists, nor even very earnest Republicans, are indignant with the National Assembly for its hostile attitude to the capital, which has for nearly six months set such a noble example of patriotism, courage, endurance, and order; and they are determined not to give up their arms, and so place themselves at the mercy of the reactionists sitting at Versailles. But, we hear it said, they have got a Republic, what more do they want? They have got an Assembly of six or seven hundred members, containing about a hundred Republicans. The majority are rabid reactionists. This Assembly was elected in a hurried and irregular way to decide the question of war or peace, and no other. It presumes to cling to power for the hardly concealed purpose of overthrowing the Republic. This is what Paris and the other great towns will not submit to. The intelligence, education, and patriotism of France, will not submit to be smothered by a squire-archy returned by the votes of ignorant rustics, even though the rustics be numerically in a majority. In the present situation of France, political power belongs of right to the energetic and intelligent. The peasantry have never, in the present century, resisted any Government, whether Republican, Monarchical, or Imperialist. More-over, the Republicans know perfectly well how to endear the Republic to the peasants, as soon as it is firmly established. They will call for six months' service in the army instead of three years, as M. Thiers proposes, and they will permit a delay in the payment of interest on mortgages during the present difficulties, a relief which has already been extended to the upper classes with regard to bills of exchange by M. Thiers. After proclaiming these measures, they may count on the support of the peasantry.

But the insurgents have murdered two generals. It was a cruel and deplorable act, but the Central Committee were not answerable for it. The correspondent of the *Daily News* learnt from two fellow-prisoners of the victims who were eye-witnesses of the murder that the Committee did their best to prevent it. The statement propagated by the *Times* that the two Generals were tried by a tribunal pres-ided over by M. Assi, "a member of the International who instigated the strike at Creuzot", is a gross falsehood. M. Assi is not a member of the International (though his col-league, M. Varlin is) and there was no trial. The victims were murdered by thier captors within a few minutes of their seizure.

Republicans may justly boast that they are, as a rule, merciful in their hour of triumph. They leave slaughter in cold-blood to the Bonapartists and Governor Eyres. With the exception of this solitary act of savagery, the revolution has been conducted with remarkable forbearance and humanity. If the reactionists should in the end get the upper hand, we shall see executions enough.

It seems probable at the time when I am writing (Thursday morning) that the Versailles Assembly will vanish, and that the Republicans will remain masters of the situation. The Central Committee propose to have a Municipal Government of Paris, elected by universal suffrage, today, and then to resign their own temporary power. I do not pretend to predict what course the new Government will pursue. It may be wise or foolish, fair or iniquitous. All I ask of the readers of the *BEE-HIVE* is, not to be swayed by the malignant calumnies published in or extracted from the middle-class press. The one certain fact is, that the workmen of Paris are at the present moment the dominant class in Paris, and that is a fact at which the workmen of London must needs be gratified, until they see overwhelming reason for regarding it differently.

While I am writing comes news of a collision between "the best blood of Paris", represented, I presume, by BARON NATHAN and the National Guards. The *Times* sensation telegram evidently exaggerates the affair grossly. From Reuter's telegram it appears that the "delicately-gloved" gentry tried to force their way through a post of National Guards, who, of course, did as guards generally do on such occasions. I will venture to say it will turn out that not half-a-dozen were killed. If the National Guards allowed their posts to be forced by "unarmed" processions, M. Thiers would have a simple task before him indeed.

THE PARIS COMMUNE

The Bee-Hive — *No. 494 Saturday, April 1, 1871*

Last week, when the London daily newspapers, without a single exception, were loading the workmen of Paris with the coarsest and most violent abuse, and predicting the immediate suppression of the insurrection, I warned the readers of the *Bee-Hive* not to be mislead by the calumnies of writers whose malice is only exceeded by their ignorance. The rapid progress of events has already covered these wretched guides of public opinion with confusion. The *Daily News* was the first to hedge, an operation which it effected with much assurance on Monday last. The *Times* commenced its strategic movement on Tuesday, by an article affirming, with much repetition and cloudy verbosity, that Paris affairs were too mysterious and obscure for any one here to understand. This must have rather startled its readers, who had been assured for a week that the whole thing was perfectly simple, that the immense majority of Parisians were coerced, by "thirty thousand gaol birds," whose only object was to live on fifteen pence a day as National Guards instead of returning to work, and that the salvation of France depended on the energy of M. Thiers and the National Assembly. This morning (Thursday) the *Times* has got so far as to admit that the programme of the Revolution "is not the production of a mere rough; it reveals a whole policy, a new social theory;" and that although the scheme is "a strange anachronism, there is hardly anything more cheering in the prospect of its failure *or in the success of* M. Thiers." The *Pall Mall Gazette,* more bitter and more consistent in its hostility to the working class, is in despair at the peace and order of Paris, and "would sooner hear of barricade and window war than of this peace that comes of the toleration of anarchy."

But enough of the wretched anonymous crew. It is not worth our while to triumph over their discomfiture. Let this lesson, however, be drawn from the latest instance of their ignorance and incompetence — that sensible workmen are more likely to go right by following their own unaided instinct on broad, social, and political questions than if they listened to middle-class journalists.

The Paris Republicans have at length discovered that the dogma of universal suffrage cannot be applied in France without subordinating the intelligent and energetic populations of the large towns to an ignorant and narrow peasantry. They propose to meet this difficulty by two remedies. The first is to withdraw a large part of the administration of the towns from the central authority, and vest it in "communes," or, as we should say, in "municipalities." The second is to arrange representation in the National Assembly in such a way that the towns shall not be swamped by the country districts. Probably this would be effected by assigning to the former a larger number of members in proportion to population. I dare say this will be rather a hard saying for many of our English Radicals and Republicans. But they will have to reconsider their crude absolute dogmas in the end, as the Parisians have done. As for our Conservatives and Whigs, *they* surely will not have the impudence to make any objection as long as they artificially adjust representation in England to maintain *their* ascendancy, as long as two or three little Dorsetshire or Devonshire boroughs are made to outweigh Marylebone or Bradford.

The present movement in favour of self-government for Paris, and the other large towns of France (with a sort of federal union) agrees with the teaching of *Auguste Comte,* and is probably largely due to it. He proposed to divide France into seventeen such groups. The same necessity will arise in time for all the overgrown states of Europe, including our own. English Positivists have not dwelt much on this question, because it seemed remote. But the last fortnight has brought it much nearer; and it is certain that our workmen will gradually come to see that their interests will never be properly attended to by an Imperial Parliament sitting at Westminster.

Workmen of all countries may be proud of the fine qualities displayed by their brothers in Paris. Their courage, patience, order, discipline, good-sense, and sagacity, have been truly admirable.

After the shameful calumnies, spread last week by our newspapers, it is instructive to read the following admissions in yesterday's *Times:-*

I have no sympathy with the movement headed by the Comite; but fair play compels me to state that the discipline observed by their troops seems remarkably good. They have wielded now some time that power which, according to the proverb, shows what a man is, and I have neither seen nor heard of any outrage on their part of a disorderly or wanton character. When they have acted harshly or oppressively, it has been from a deliberately-planned policy, which, wise or unwise, has been carried out in a spirit of strict discipline or organization. The commonest men among them — a far from prepossessing lot, their appearance occasionally suggesting a suspicion that the recent gaol delivery was extended to other than political prisoners — are indeed glad enough to tyrannize in petty ways, and too delighted to show their powers as the sovereign people, by turning anybody whom they take to be an *aristo* off the pavement or out of a railway carriage; but they take care to do so only in obedience to superior orders. Nor have I heard of one solitary case of pillage — for I suppose that in these days of military rule one can't fairly apply so harsh a word as pillage to the requisitions for food made by soldiers, who profess, and perhaps believe, as it is their interest to believe, that they are defending their own city from conspirators and reactionaries of all types, Monarchical and Imperialist, and who certainly go through a great deal of work, in the shape of sentry and partrol duty, that can scarcely be agreeable to men bred to peaceful pursuits. They are, in fact, far superior in point of organization, and perhaps also in pluck and belief in the goodness of their own cause, to the Party of Order, who disgusted with the lukewarmness or faintheartedness of their own friends, and looking round in vain for leaders, can make no solid front. The journals, indeed, representing the Party of Order declare that dis-affection is rampant among the followers and even the members of the Comité — that the latter have taken freely to ordering each other's arrest, and that even on the sacred summit of Montmartre, where stands enshrined the palladium of the Communists, there are two parties, one of which is looked upon as *suspecte* because it is getting weary of the monotonous and barren labour of watching the guns, and wants to return to profitable work. These stories are, I believe, greatly exaggerated as regards the past or even the present, but they probably forecast accurately enough the future.

What the ultimate fate of the Revolution will be, it is impossible to predict. Although its programme at present is strictly political, a certain number of its promoters, and those not the least energetic, aim at eventually using political force for the purpose of effecting changes in the distribution of wealth. As a Positivist, I believe that such interference on the part of the State is improper and mischievous. On this rock the Republic may split. Then there are the Prussians close to Paris, and Bismarck may at any moment throw his sword into the scale. The *Times* has more than once suggested that he should do so, and M. Jules Favre is evidently base and rancorous enough to welcome such a solution. But even then I shall say that it was well done of Paris to make her Revolution.

THE "POLTROONS OF BELLEVILLE"

The Bee-Hive No.496 Saturday, April 15, 1871

One at least of the shameful insults heaped upon the work-men of Paris by our middle-class press has been effectually silenced by the events of the last fortnight. For six months it has been diligently impressed upon us that the sons of the men of '48 are cowards, and the middle-class soul throughout Europe has been cheered with the belief that no example of manhood and generous devotion would ever again fix the eyes of the suffering proletaries of all count-ries upon the metropolis of the West. So fully persuaded of this was respectable society that it treated the guard of the cannon of Montmartre as a farce, and enjoyed by ant-icipation the ludicrous figure which the "Belleville pol-troons" would cut when a few regular soldiers should come to disarm them. For there was one thing which it desired more earnestly than the defeat of the working men, and that was their dishonour. It desired they should discredit themselves and their class before the world, and be taught not only that they were slaves, but that they deserved to be slaves — of which the labouring class of other countries might take note.

This idiotic cackle has died away into blank and chop-fallen dismay. The workmen of Paris, it seems, are what they always have been since 1789 — men who have a faith and are ready to die for it. Without professional officers, without organization, shelled by Mount Valerien (which the Prussians always took care to keep clear of), opposed, as the *Times* tells us, "to a large host of tried mettle and temper, led by experienced officers, headed by columns of picked men, and backed by a formidable array of ar-tillery," this "handful of roughs," these "poltroons of Belleville," these "jabbering chimpanzees," have been fighting for a fortnight outside the walls of Paris, and have inflicted, as well as suffered, heavy losses. The special correspondents in their first reports tried to stick to their old tale, and informed us that the insurgents "fled like frightened hares," "bolted like rabbits," etc.; but, as the stubborn fact remained that the fighting was still going on, they have been obliged to make admissions, a few of which I cull from the *Times* and *Daily News:-*

"The insurgents contested every yard of the ground."

"The Communists are fighting with remarkable courage and tenacity, and have just been sending up reinforcements headed by members of the Commune in person; the moral effect of this display of personal courage was very great."

"The losses of the insurgents are immense."

"All accounts worthy of credit state that the great majority of the National Guards fights with great bravery and desperation."

The *Times,* indeed, now suggests that the desperate valour of the insurgents is inspired by the knowledge that they are fighting "with the rope round their necks." I have no doubt that the Versailles reactionists, if they conquer, will execute all the insurgents of mark — M. Thiers has said as much — and that the *Times* will applaud them for doing so; but they will hardly execute the rank and file, so that this explanation of the courage of the National Guards seems as insufficient as the suggestion formerly offered that they were fighting to keep their fifteenpence a day. Brave as the Parisian workmen are, one may doubt whether they would risk their lives for fifteenpence.

It would be wise of our middle-class friends not to talk quite so much about cowardice. The only cowardice which has been established beyond dispute is middle-class cowardice. The respectable classes of Paris, we have been frequently assured, abhor the Communal movement. They were all armed with chasepots; they had plenty of time to organise resistance; did they fire a shot? Is it a middle-class force which is now besieging Paris? No; but sailors, *gens d'armes* (the military police — wretches who were the instruments of Imperial rule), Breton peasants who cannot speak French, Pontifical Zouaves, nay, even a foreign legion. The well-dressed "friends of order," the men "with shiny silk hats and delicately gloved hands," are not storming the barricade on the Neuilly bridge, but sitting safely at Versailles, and hounding on these poor mercenaries against their own class. The less said about the cowardice the better.

Come what will of this terrible struggle, the workmen of Paris have saved their honour and re-established the claim of their city to the primacy of Europe. In vain have the princes and nobles of Germany crushed the armies of France. She wants no armies. The Commune has proclaimed the programme of the future for France, aye, for Germany too, let BISMARCK and MOLTKE think what they will of it. "The standing army is abolished." Paris is in the van as of old, and she vindicates to herself the prerogative of martyrdom. There are thousands of workmen in Germany who are watching with painful anxiety this contest at Paris, on which the interests of labour are staked for this generation. For more truly is that noble city the heart of Europe in her present agony, than when the foul Bonaparte throned at the Tuileries shook kingdoms with his nod.

And now, on the other hand, consider the humanity and moderation which these poor workmen have shown in the day of their mastery. For a full month Paris has been as the newspapers phrase it, "at the mercy of the roughs." On the first day of the insurrection, before any authority was established, two captives were slaughtered. Since then there has been *just one execution,* and that was for the crime of murder. We were told over and over again that the Guillotine was on the point of being brought out. The Commune did bring it out — to burn it. And all this time Paris is swarming with enemies of the movement, men, as one of the correspondents admits, who, if the reactionist troops enter the city, will probably follow in their rear and shoot down every man they see with a dirty face and hard hands. Even the infamous cruelty of the Versailles Government to its captives has not, as yet, provoked retaliation. Even the *Times* and the *Pall Mall Gazette* are shocked by the wholesale executions carried out and boasted of by the 'friends of order." As I write, news comes that the National Guards are likely to capture three thousand gens d'armes. If they succeed in doing so, it is only to be expected that they will make reprisals, in order to put a stop to further barbarities at Versailles. But it would be for the interest of the Republic in the long run to avoid even reprisals, that the world may see that bloodshed is abhorrent to workmen if it is not to the *bourgeoisie*. If we look back to the old Revolution, we shall find that the names most identified with its cruelties were those of middle-class men. Neither Robespierre, nor Marat, nor Fouquier-Tinville, not Tallien, nor Collot, nor Billaud, nor Le Bas, nor Fouché, were working men.

In conclusion, let me add a few extracts from a *Times* correspondent of this morning (Thursday): "We have been nearly a month under the sway of Belleville, and there has been nothing like socialist spoliations; the poorest and worst fed Nationals pass the jeweller's shops *oculo irretorto* (without a covetous glance). **** One cannot but be struck with the diversity of the composition of this armed multitude. A large number are evidently intelligent workmen or shopkeepers, and, what is very remarkable, elderly men appear in great force in the ranks. **** I believe the tendency is more than ever to acquiesce in the domination of the Commune, and that there is not the smallest chance of assistance being given to Versailles from within this city." When we add to this that several women have been killed, fighting with rifle and sabre, on the side of the people, it may be judged whether this is an insurrection of "gaol birds," or the grand up-rising of the patriotic population.

COSMOPOLITAN REPUBLICANISM

The Bee-Hive No. 497 Saturday, April 22nd, 1871

One of the most striking features in the latest phase of the French Revolution is its cosmopolitan tendency, its disposition to bury and forget the wretched national prejudices and jealousies which have hitherto kept the workmen of different countries apart from one another, and made them the tools of ambitious soldiers and statesmen. The germs of this tendency appeared in the first period of the Revolution during 1792 and 1793, when Thomas Paine sat in the Convention. But the warm affection which France at first felt for the other peoples of Europe, and particularly for the English, was checked when the Monarchs of Prussia, Austria, Sardinia, Spain, and England, sent their armies to crush the young Republic; and it was exchanged for an overbearing national selfishness and insolent contempt for foreigners, when the first Bonaparte had trampled on the Republic, and corrupted the popular sentiment with the poison of militarism. Slow has been the recovery of France from that fatal taint. The restored Bourbons persecuted Republicans and Bonapartists alike, and so caused the rising generation to identify Bonapartism, not only with the false glory, but with the legitimate dignity, and even the liberty, of their country. This mischievous delusion was sedulously fostered by the eloquent writers of the middle-class; and, most of all, by M. Thiers, who not only wrote the panegyric of Bonaparte in his "History of the Consulate and Empire," but was foolish enough, while Prime Minister of Louis Philippe, to bring back the remains of the Emperor from St. Helena.

Without the twenty years of Napoleon III it might have been difficult to divorce Republicanism completely from the Bonapartist tradition.

It is to be noted as a proof of the sagacity as well as the

healthy political sentiment of Auguste Comte, the great founder of Positivism, that so long ago as 1842, just after the people of Paris had been following the coffin of Napoleon I to the Invalides, he denounced the memory of the popular idol with the most energetic language he could employ, accusing him of having made France the tyrant of Europe, and destroyed the fraternity of peoples inaugurated in the early days of the Revolution. In 1854 he predicted that regenerated Paris would "purify herself of" the column in the Place Vendôme, made out of the cannon taken by Napoleon I. from Germany, and would send back the corpse of the enemy of progress to St. Helena.

The Commune has decided upon the destruction of the column as a monument of the military oppression of Germany by France, and it appears that the Imperial coffin also is to be removed from its splendid tomb in the Invalides. If the Commune shall accomplish nothing else than this solemn repudiation of wars of conquest, it will not have existed in vain.

Many other signs have appeared of the fraternal spirit growing up between the working classes of all countries. The middle-class in France has always evinced a pitiful jealousy of foreign merit. But the workmen of Paris placed Garibaldi almost at the head of the poll in the elections for the National Assembly, when the middle-class majority refused to give him a hearing. The National Guards are now serving cheerfully under a Polish general. The newspapers spread a report that the Parisian operatives were refusing to work in the same shop with Germans, and made merry with the difficulty this must cause to the International Association. There was, however, no foundation for the report. A Prussian was even elected to the Commune. There is no rancour between French and German workmen. The cause of labour is the same all the world over, and therefore the operations of a society like the International cannot fail to obtain an increasing support.

Middle-class men may affect to denounce the solidarity

of workmen as unpatriotic; but do they not themselves systematically treat workmen as an alien class? M. Jules Favre, for instance, is on quite confidential terms with German authorities, and bombards Paris with an animosity and spite which they never showed; and our Press, which looked on coolly enough while he helped to conduct a mere national war, sides with him warmly in his attack upon the common enemy. Workmen would be foolish indeed if they did not knit close their bonds of union in the face of this concerted hostility.

I will give in next week's *Bee-Hive* an abstract of the political programme just put forward by the head of the Positivist society in Paris, a copy of which has just reached me.

THE COMMUNISTS

The Bee-Hive No.498 Saturday, April 29, 1871

If I may judge from instances I meet with every day, there are still large numbers, even of educated people, who are not aware that "Commune" and "Communism" are two quite different things; that the former means municipal or local self-government as distinguished from the central or national Government; while the latter is the general name for all shades of the doctrine which condemns private property. I say all shades, because, though some Communists are opposed only to private property in land, others extend their doctrine to property of every kind, while some few, like the Greek philosopher Plato, would go further and break up the family.

Now, from newspaper correspondence and from private information, I have no doubt that the present leaders of the Parisians are Communists. They are, I believe, for the most part, men of good character, of considerable ability, of great energy; and, above all, of a strength of conviction amounting to fanaticism. These qualities are quite sufficient to account for the undisputed authority they exercise in Paris, an authority they have justified by a skill, a firmness, and a moderation such as no revolutionary, and hardly any established, Government has ever exhibited in equally difficult circumstances. They are supported with different degrees of good-will; first, by the Communists, a party which, I believe, makes up by energy and conviction for its comparatively scanty numbers; secondly by Republicans, who, though not Communists, are deeply convinced that political changes are worthless if unaccompanied by a social reformation; thirdly, by ardent political Republicans, who know that the Republic would be immediately discarded and its adherents savagely persecuted if the Versailles Assembly triumphed; and, lastly, by the large majority of Parisians of every or no party who are exasperated at the cruelty of the besiegers and their undisguised intention to deprive the metropolis of all self-government and of its ancient and legitimate dignity.

For the moment, the defenders of Paris, whatever their opinions, are united by the urgent necessity of resisting the common enemy, and the direction of the defence has naturally fallen into the hands of the most resolute and convinced party, viz., the Communists; it being tacitly agreed that all social and industrial questions shall be adjourned till the freedom of Paris has been achieved and the Republic established. This is the reason why Communistic doctrines have not as yet been put forward in any official statement of the Commune, or the Central Committee. But if the Versailles Government should be beaten, my information leads me to believe that there may be a sharp struggle in Parish between the Communists and the rest of the citizens, whether Republicans or Reactionists. It will be the saddest sight that France has yet presented. Let us hope that the Communist leaders who have deserved so well of their country will not force on a struggle in which they must ultimately be defeated; and, on the other hand, that the defenders of property will abandon the absurd and odious attempts of previous Governments, both Royal and Republican, to prevent the free publication and propagation of Communistic opinions, either by the Press, or by public meetings or by associations. Napoleon III is reported to have said, "Communism must be met not with arguments but with grape-shot," and the French middle-class, though not liking his government, kept him on the throne for twenty years because he was ready to suppress the Communist Propaganda. But opinions cannot be put down by grape-shot in these days. If they are ill-founded, nothing but free and open discussion will eradicate them. For my part, as a Positivist, I believe that property and the family are institutions bound up with civilisation, and that they will survive all attacks. The moral pressure which Positivism will eventually put upon the holders of property will compel them to administer it, not for their own selfish enjoyment, as they for the most part do at present, but for the good of society. When that result shall have been reached, Communistic agitation will cease, but not before.

THE DEFENCE OF PARIS

The Bee-Hive No.501 Saturday, May 20, 1871

The working men who have defended Paris with such courage and devotion for two months against the army paid by
the upper and middle classes are gradually being forced
back on their barricades. The ground has been contested
inch by inch. The army of the Assembly consists entirely
of veteran soldiers commanded by professional officers. It
now largely outnumbers the National Guards. It possesses
a crushing superiority in artillery. It has held, alas! the
great fort of Valerien from the first, and it now holds Issy
and Vanves. From these points of vantage it pours a tem-
pest of shot and shell on the lines of the besieged. Its
commanders have preferred to trust almost exclusively to
this method of attack, seldom sending forward their men
till the contested positions had been swept clear by their
superior artillery. Against this iron storm the National
Guards have held their ground with astonishing fortitude.
Where the fire was hottest and most deadly, men have
never been wanting who could endure it. Simple working
men, who have only just learnt to handle their weapon,
have bid adieu to wives and little children, and gone to
face death for the cause of their class as calmly as an
English workman faces a strike or lock-out. Their officers
are only working men like themselves, or, at most, ser-
jeants and corporals who have deserted from Versailles,
because they did not choose to shed the blood of their
own class for the profit of well-dressed people.

Issy and Vanves are taken, and the wall of Paris is
crumbling under the fire of the troops. But there is every
probability that the city will be defended street by street,
with terrible bloodshed on both sides. The working men
have good reason to defend themselves, for they have no
mercy to expect. The Versailles Government has promised

the Assembly that "justice shall take its course," and that blood-thirsty crew were furious with M. Thiers last week, because he was reported to have listened to proposals for an amnesty. *The Figaro* (one of the principal organs of the rich middle class), insists that when Paris falls, "all the Commune, all the journalists who have taken its side, all the Polish generals and their staffs, and all the colonels of the National Guard shall be publicly shot in the Champ de Mars." That these are not idle threats we know from the conduct of the Versailles authorities at the commencement of the struggle. When the noble and gallant Flourens had been taken prisoner and disarmed, a Lieutenant, Desmarets, cleft his head with his sabre, and was promoted for the act. Duval (whom the executives of some of the London Trade societies will recollect as having come here on a deputation from the Paris iron moulders last summer) was summarily executed by order of General Vinoy after the first sortie. This barbarous work was only stopped by the arrest of the Archbishop of Paris and other well known reactionaries, and their detention as hostages. If Paris is taken, it is probable that all the prominent leaders will be executed, that many hundreds of workmen will be sent to Cayenne (as they were in 1848 and 1852), and that large numbers of all classes will be expelled from Paris, and forbidden to return there.

I have already said that there are among the leaders of the Commune men whose ulterior aim it is to abolish private property. While respecting the sincerity and earnestness of those men (who are probably much more free from personal selfishness than the capitalists and economists crying for their blood), I reject their doctrines. I believe that comparatively few of the Parisian workmen would support them if they attempted to carry out their doctrines. But that does not alter the fact that they are defending the cause of labour. Their immediate aim is to preserve the Republic, to secure Municipal Government for Paris, to exclude a paid soldiery from their city, to repeal their Combination Laws, and to withdraw State support from religious sects. In fighting for these objects they are fighting the battle of labour all the world over, and however it may turn out, they will have deserved the gratitude and veneration of all working men.

THE FALL OF PARIS

The Bee-Hive May 27, 1871

On Sunday last the army of the Assembly entered Paris without resistance. The breaches had been swept clear of their defenders by storms of shell. In fact, that has been almost exclusively the mode of attack employed from the first. By universal agreement of eye-witnesses, good troops, whose heart was in the work, would have stormed the crumbling ramparts a week earlier. But the large majority of the rank and file were not to be depended on. They are the soldiers of the Empire — demoralised by defeat; apt instruments for massacre, yet ashamed of their work; ready to slay, but not caring to be slain; just as likely to turn round and fire on their own officers as on the enemy — witness the murder of General Lecomte by the men of his own regiment. The only troops M. Thiers could depend upon were marines and gendarmes, the military police, the sworn foes of the Paris workmen; and he could not afford to waste this precious force in continual assaults. Cannon, therefore, always and everywhere, has been the arm employed.

Behind the walls the Parisians had constructed a second line of strong barricades. For some reason, which we do not yet know, these were not defended. Either the attack at the last moment was a surprise, or the leaders of the Commune despaired of holding so extended a line in a suburb, and thought it better to concentrate their sadly diminished forces in the closely-built streets of the city. However this may be, a large portion of Paris was immediately over-run by the troops, who were poured in at the heels of the sailors and gendarmes, and shouts of triumphant derision were already beginning to rise at Versailles and nearer home over the insurgents who had talked so loudly of burying themselves under the ruins of Paris.

But since Monday the fighting has been desperate. It was much as if an army entering London from Hammersmith, had over-run Bayswater and the Park, and met with determined resistance first on the line from Westminster Abbey to Trafalgar Square and the Regent circus. It appears that the attack was still conducted almost exclusively with artillery, the Parisians replying mainly with rifles and mitrailleuses. This is quite enough to account for the conflagration without accepting the statement of M. Thiers, that the Parisians are deliberately burning down their own city with petroleum. Everybody knows that a city which is bombarded takes fire. As early as Monday evening the Daily News correspondent wrote: "Shells seem to be bursting all over the city. Several fell on and about the Bourse as I was passing." Yesterday (Wednesday) the *Times* correspondent telegraphed: "I have been for some time in the magnificent city which flames and bombshells are fast reducing to a huge and shapeless ruin. Shells from the position of General Cissey are every minute falling close to the lofty dome of the Pantheon. It and the fine building of the Val de Grace near it seem certain to be destroyed by missiles before the incendiary fire reaches them." When M. Thiers is pounding Paris in this fashion, it is sheer impudence in him to upbraid the citizens with burning it.

But if the Parisians, girdled in on one side by a bloodthirsty foe, who openly threatens that in punishment he will be "implacable," and on the other by the Prussians who fire even on women attempting to escape from the slaughter and conflagration — if the Parisians have desperately resolved to bury themselves under the ruins of their houses and monuments rather than submit to the mercy of the ferocious Assembly sitting at Versailles, what shall we say of them? Shall we call them vandals and enemies of civilisation? or shall we not rather remember what judgment the world has passed on men who, in other times, have nerved themselves to the same terrible pitch of resolution? Who has not glowed with generous admiration as he read the story of the burning of Moscow? "When the other events of the Spanish war," says Napier, "shall be lost in the obscurity of time, or only traced by disconnected fragments, the story of Zaragoza, like some ancient triumphal pillar standing amidst ruins, will tell a tale of past glory; and already men point to the heroic city calling her Spain."

> *Then, Saragoza — blighted be the tongue*
> *That names thy name without the honour due!*
> *For never hath the harp of minstrel rung*
> *Of faith so felly proved, so firmly true.*
> *Mine, sap, and bomb, thy shattered ruins knew,*
> *Each art of war's extremity had room;*
> *Twice from thy half-sacked streets the foe withdraw,,*
> *And when at length stern fate decreed thy doom,*
> *They won, not Zaragoza, but her children's bloody*
> *tomb.*

> *Yet raise thy head sad city! Though in chains,*
> *Enthralled thou canst not be! Arise and claim*
> *Reverence from every heart where freedom reigns,*
> *For what thou worshippest!*

If it shall turn out that the historic monuments and the priceless treasure of art which, it is to be feared, some of them contained, were not set on fire by the bombardment, nor even burnt by the defenders for military reasons, but destroyed deliberately in order to rob the conquerors of the prize of victory, we can only regret that a cause which has upon the whole been upheld with so much moderation should have been stained at last by an act of revenge and spite so useless and so irreparable in its consequences. Though, even so, how much of the blame will not posterity award to M. Thiers and his Assembly? They knew that this desperate resolve was possible, and they might have prevented it by offering an amnesty, after they had entered the ramparts, to all who should lay down their arms. But they thirsted for revenge. Victory itself was worthless in their eyes, unless it was attended with a wholesale slaughter. So they stopped all avenues of escape, and announced that "justice should take its course;" and this is what they have got by it.

It is indeed a lamentable disaster, this conflagration, not to us alone, but to posterity. But I must avow that it is not the uppermost thought in my mind, this terrible Thursday. "Blighted be the tongue" that can only prate of bricks and stones when the blood of brave and devoted men is flowing, and the curtain is falling on the first act of the most momentous historical drama of modern times. There is something in Paris nobler than her palaces, more precious than her monuments; it is her breed of men, which even the National Assembly cannot utterly exterminate. Let me be permitted to repeat here what I wrote last September, when it seemed probable that the blow would come from an enemy less ferocious and unscrupulous than Messrs. Thiers and Favre.

I know the howl which is going up today from the class in this country who think that not Paris alone, but all creation, exists simply for their pleasure and amusement. But I am writing for workmen, with whom life is very far from being a pleasure and amusement; and I think that they will distribute praise and blame with a more even hand.

THE PARIS MASSACRES

The Bee-Hive No. 503 Saturday, June 3, 1871

On September 4th, 1870, the People of Paris overthrew the tyranny of Napoleon III. If that revolution had been accomplished ten days earlier, MacMahon's army, instead of being sent on its desperate march to Sedan to fight for the dynasty, would have been concentrated round Paris, and the siege of Paris would have been impossible. The Parisians were ready and able to make the revolution, but the more hesitating unfortunately yielded to the influence of Messrs. Favre, Picard and Co., who hoped to wriggle into office by a vote of the vile Corps Legislatif of Napoleon. The precious moment was lost; Sedan destroyed the last army; and the siege became inevitable. Thus all the miseries France has since undergone lie at the door of Jules Favre and his friends.

When at last the Republic was proclaimed, these ambitious hypocrites managed to get themselves nominated as a Provisional Government. The workmen of Paris had no confidence either in the honesty of their Republicanism, or in their resolution to defend France; but with fatal moderation accepted them, rather than quarrel with the middle classes at such a moment. I described the feeling of the workmen towards Jules Favre in a pamphlet I published on September 9th. The only member of the Government in whom they had any confidence was the gallant and honest Rochefort, now awaiting death from his old colleagues.

The siege began. Trochu, it is now generally admitted, proved an incapable general. But that was not his worst fault. He, like his colleagues, was more afraid of the workmen than of the Prussians. He wished to beat the latter if it could be done without the help of the former, but not seeing his way to that end, he conducted a sham defence, just to keep up appearances. Gambetta from the provinces wrote to Jules Favre, imploring him to supersede Trochu, and show some activity. The National Guards were anxious to fight. In such blundering sorties as were made they fought admirably as was proved by their heavy losses. The stories of their cowardice, so eagerly propagated by our newspaper correspondents to please the upper and middle classes in England, were shameful calumnies. They will hardly be believed in the face of recent events.

Jules Favre at length not only surrendered but concluded an armistice for the whole of France, without consulting Gambetta, and in entire ignorance of the position of the armies. He was forward enough at that time in maintaining that a government with no title, but such as was derived from a Parisian insurrection, had a right to bind France. A National Assembly was convened. Its composition might have been foreseen. Parliaments of all sorts inevitably govern in the interests, not of the people, but of the propertied classes. France is carefully divided into electoral districts in such a way that the town voters are swamped by the country voters, who are very ignorant, and much under the rule of priests, Government officials, and squires. The elections were conducted in a hurry; the only organisation ready was that of the priests and squires; the peasants were anxious only for peace. The Assembly consisted almost entirely of nobles, squires, and rich employers, all detesting Republicanism, and bent on restoring tyranny in some shape, so that they might continue to coin money out of the sinews and sweat of workmen, and spend it in insolent luxury. They knew that the only obstacle in their way was the proletariate of the great towns, particularly Paris; they, therefore, were filled with a ferocious hatred of the heroic city, which had just endured such suffering for France. They threatened Gambetta with impeachment. They hooted the noble Garibaldi when he tried to address them. They protested against the removal of the Assembly to Paris. They looked on Favre and Picard as only one degree less odious than Rochefort and Louis

Blanc. And it was this Assembly that Favre and Picard consented to flatter and serve. Sharing its hatred for workmen, they were ready to be the tools of its vengeance. The Assembly has used them; and now, as I write, is flinging them aside with contempt. Men more irretrievably consigned to infamy do not exist.

But the plans of the reactionists had to be kept in the background till Paris was disarmed. On the 18th March an attempt was made to seize the cannon of the National Guard. Those guns once seized, it would have been comparatively easy to complete the disarmament, and Paris would have lain helpless. But the attempt failed.

Now came the most deplorable mistake that Paris has every made. If the Commune had marched at once on Versailles, Thiers and his Assembly would have vanished without a blow. But by a fatal moderation, Paris for once renounced her claim to act for France. The Commune contented itself with setting an example. It was not, therefore, till similar movements had been put down with much bloodshed in Lyons, Marseilles, St. Etienne, and other places, till Thiers had collected a large army of Old Soldiers of the Empire, till the railways were cut and the first operations of a siege had been begun, that Paris attempted to march on Versailles. Even then the attempt would probably have succeeded but for the unexpected bombardment from Fort Valerien.

Since the first week in April, Paris appears to have had no chance of success. We now understand why Thiers would not allow himself to be goaded by the Assembly into more precipitate operations. He wanted the prisoners from Germany — the demoralised soldiers of Napoleon. These were the only troops he could rely upon to act against the admirable workmen of Paris. The sanguinary old man wished to finish the work he commenced nearly forty years ago by the massacre of the Rue Transnonain. He had made, it seems, his arrangements with Bismarck. Bismarck was to keep the Northern Railway open, and exhibit an ostentatious neutrality, so that all the most active revolutionists in Europe might be tempted to enter the trap, and was to shut the door behind them when the proper moment should come. Thiers began to massacre his prisoners after the first engagement. But the Commune stopped such proceedings for a time by seizing as hostages the principal agents of reaction in Paris — priests and gendarmes. But it was not till long after the Versaillists had begun to indulge in indiscriminate massacre, not till the last twenty-four hours of the resistance that one of these hostages was killed; nor is it shown that even then an order for their death was given by any authority of the Commune.

The total number of persons executed during the "Reign of Terror" in the old revolution was, we are told by Mr. Carlyle, according to the highest estimate, "above four thousand all but a few." How many have been slaughtered by the party of wealth, of respectability, of order, during the last fortnight we shall never know. Some correspondents compute it at 50,000. Not the "Party of Order" henceforth, but the "Party of Blood!" So let it be named.

The ex-Emperor has an organ in London called the *Standard.* This paper is every day calling out for the extradition of any fugitives who may chance to make their way here from Paris. M. Jules Favre has summoned the English Government to render him the same infamous service which Bismarck performed so cheerfully — to force back the unhappy men who may have escaped, upon the bayonets of their butchers. That the writers who defended Governor Eyre should sympathise with the party of blood in Paris is not to be wondered at. Governor Eyre's punishment has not yet reached him, and the stain of his massacres still rests upon England; but I think the workmen of London will have a word to say before we sink so low as to supply victims for the shambles of Thiers.

COMPARATIVE ATROCITY

The Bee-Hive No. 504 Saturday, June 10, 1871

When the news of the conflagration in Paris first reached us, we were deceived in two respects; first, as to the extent of the damage; and, secondly, as to the motives and intentions of those who caused it. We were told that nearly every fine building was destroyed. The Cathedral of Notre Dame, the Luxembourg, the Palais Royal, and the Louvre, with its priceless collection of sculptures and paintings, were particularly specified. We now know that Notre Dame and the Luxembourg are absolutely untouched, that only a small portion of the Palais Royal and the Louvre suffered, and that the art treasures in the latter are quite safe. The only first-class buildings destroyed, after all, are the Tuileries and the Hotel de Ville.

It was studiously impressed upon us that the conflagrations were kindled merely out of spite and revenge. Assuming that view to be correct in the article I wrote in this paper while the struggle was still going on, I deplored and condemned the act, although I felt that much moderation or consideration for the interests of contemporaries or posterity could hardly be expected from men who were being massacred without mercy. But it now appears that the charge was unfounded, and that in kindling the fires the National Guards were actuated simply by strategical motives. This conviction soon began to force itself on impartial observers; but, in proof of it, I will cite an authority which from its very partiality, must be taken as conclusive.

Of all the writers who have assailed the Commune in the English Press during the last three months, the most violent and rabid beyond comparison has been the Parisian correspondent of the *Times.* On Monday last a long letter from this gentleman appeared under the heading "How Paris was Burnt." The writer examines carefully the position of the buildings destroyed. He demonstrates that the fires were kindled to prevent barricades from being taken in flank, and their defenders from being isolated and surrounded.

"It is a strange fact that although these men declared unrelenting warfare against religion, *not one church or chapel has been destroyed* .... It is not mere accident which has led to this result, nor was it a mere desire to work mischief; the Insurgents followed a plan of defence concerted and arranged beforehand, and for which they had prepared instruments and formed special corps .... Those who are familiar with the map of Paris and the points of junction of the great arteries of communication can entertain no doubt upon that head. When one considers what were the sites chosen for the construction of barricades, the fact immediately presents itself that nearly all these sites are in the immediate vicinity of buildings which have been burnt or which it has been attempted to destroy. No attempts were made in lines of communication or districts which the army had not to traverse; and a careful examination will speedily prove that the complete plan of the barricades was closely connected with the scheme of burning certain buildings .... It is difficult to avoid the belief that some military mind was engaged in the work. Incomplete as has been the execution of their plans, yet what has been done and attempted proves the fact. A military man alone could have combined incendiarism with other elements of a formidable defence. Whether he be called Cluseret, Rossel, or Dombrowski, there was, certainly, such a man. Undoubtedly it was not Lefrancais, or Delescluze, nor any of those "civil" commanders, who, however capable of imagining evil, had not the capacity to give it practical effect .... No document, as yet found, has thrown any light on the organisation of the "petroleuses," of which so much has been said. This corps existed only in the imagination of journalists."

94

It is thus proved on unimpeachable testimony that the National Guards burnt buildings for precisely the same reason that the army bombarded them, and with more excuse, inasmuch as they were fighting for their lives. The Hotel de Ville was bombarded with heavy artillery by the Versaillists for several hours; and if the Communals fired it to cover their retreat there must have been little left to damage.

It the Communals had scrupulously respected the public buildings, had dismissed their hostages unhurt, and with their hearts purified from passion and revenge; had calmly met martyrdom for their cause at the hands of their ferocious foe, they would have served that cause more effectually and permanently in their deaths than they had ever done in their lives. The reaction would already, by this time have been weighed down to perdition by the loathing and malediction of every man and woman in Europe who had a spark of virtue or humanity. This would have been, indeed, the more real, as it would have been the nobler vengeance. Individuals there may have been, and no doubt were, with whom, even in that dark hour, this thought was uppermost. But we might search the history of the world in vain for any instance of a large body of men who would have been capable of it. And let it not be forgotten that the responsibility for the execution of the hostages, as for the burning of the buildings, rests largely on M. Thiers. The Communals offered to release the Archbishop, and six other hostages, in exchange for their leader, Blanqui; but the offer was refused. Nay, it is whispered that the priestly party at Versailles were not sorry to be rid of Darboy, who as an opponent of Papal Infallibility, was disagreeable to them; and that they thought he would be more useful to them as a martyr than as a live Archbishop.

The party of blood, whether in France or in England (for we have it here, too, and in great force), endeavours to treat the slaughter of the hostages as a set-off against that of the workmen of Paris. but *we* will not forget that there were sixty-four of the one class, and many thousands of the other, and that the workmen did not take a life except in fair fight until they had been persistently refused all quarter. What the conduct of the victors has been since resistance ceased I will not describe in my own words. I will quote the correspondent of the *Standard,* a paper which has lost no opportunity of calumniating and vilifying the Commune:-

"The wholesale executions of men, women, and children which followed must disturb the consciences of those who suffered them to take place, and of those, who, knowing better, actually, through abject fear, joined the rabble in hooting and illtreating the wretches led away to death. Do not let me be misunderstood; I feel no sentimental compassion for the miscreants of the Commune. At a time when there was not a little danger to do so, I did not hesitate to stigmatise as they deserved the monster Pyatt, the cold-blooded incendiarism of Jules Valles, and all the other members of the gang. I have reason to know that several of my colleagues and myself had a narrow escape of being arrested as hostages; and had I my will not one of the aiders and abettors of the Commune would escape their doom. But I must record my horror and detestation of the wholesale butcheries by which the Party of Order disgraced their triumph, the indiscriminate character of which, whilst it sacrificed scores of innocent lives, enabled some of the very worst miscreants to escape. Take Jules Valles for instance, I have seen his death minutely described in several papers; a great number of friends of mine assert that they saw him shot. But as it so happens that they did not know him by sight, and that everyone of them saw him shot and arrested in a different part of the town, I begin to doubt whether he was shot at all. Now, if before shooting a man, the precaution of establishing his identity had been taken, there could be no doubt on the subject. As for mistakes, they must have been numerous. Imagine the condition of a nervous Frenchman following the crowd, and suddenly set upon with the accusation raised by an unknown voice in the throng that he is a member of the Commune; he has not time for explanations; not time to clear himself; blows from sticks and fists are rained down upon him; he is led along until the nearest detachment is met with. Half-blinded by the blows levelled at his face, utterly bewildered, an attempt at escape, an instinctive movement of the arm to ward off a blow, is construed immediately as an additional proof of guilt; he is forced against the wall, and the next second is stretched on the ground, killed or mortally wounded. No man, whom fury or fear has not deprived of his senses, can approve or attempt to justify such atrocities.

The remembrance of the scenes of horror I have myself witnessed in the way of reprisals makes me shudder as I write; and my only satisfaction is to be able to report that they have now entirely ceased, and that henceforth no one will be put to death without trial. I will give you one out of the many instances of the danger of the precipitate proceedings of the last few days. M. Touzé, a well-known actor of the Threatre du Chatelet, used to perform frequently in the military plays often given at that house; and he had his stage wardrobe in his own house; it included the complete uniform of a private in the line. His house was searched — a pair of red trousers found in his clothes-press was set down as conclusive evidence of his being a deserter; despite his representations he was taken down into his own courtyard, where two bullets at once terminated his earthly and his theatrical career. Got, the excellent actor of the Francais, also is reported to have had a very narrow escape. Before I leave this unpleasant subject, might I suggest to Marshal Macmahon — than whom a more humane and highminded man does not exist — the expediency of his giving orders to his subordinate officers not to act on anonymous denunciations. I am assured that numbers of persons are now awaiting trial at Versailles — and my colleague there will have told you what treatment is awarded to the prisoners — simply because they have some unscrupulous enemy or some debtor who wishes to wipe off his debt, by compelling his creditor to pay that of nature. That such things should be possible is *ipso facto* the condemnation of the system on which the authorities are going to work.

"As to the summary executions, I am glad to find in the *Temps* a protest against them. Our eminent and honest contemporary, while deploring them, views them as inevitable misfortunes; but it is wrong in supposing that they came to an end when the last shot was fired in open hostility. What the Temps, however, is perfectly right in reproving is the disposition which exists 'on the part of the public' to denounce and expose to summary vengeance persons *whose only misfortune may be that they have a threadbare coat* as accomplices of the insurrection. Hundreds of unfortunate people have in this way been dispatched to Versailles or Cherbourg. A week ago they would have been shot. But to many this long journey, and the anguish of being penned up (as is the case at the *organgerie* of Versailles), with thousands of others, or sent off to await their trial on board a pontoon in Cherbourg Roads, is a fate worse than death itself. No words are too strong to express the loathing and contempt every man of average sense, and endowed with a common feeling of humanity, must feel for those persons who keep up and stimulate the popular craving for blood and reprisals. It generally comes from those who have not seen any of the atrocities of the past fortnight. We who have, are but of one opinion — let justice take its course; but we have had bloodshed and wholesale vengeance enough. There are upwards of 30,000 prisoners at Versailles and elsewhere, many of them arrested on the slenderest grounds, and often on no grounds at all. The number of people shot down like dogs will probably never be ascertained with any degree of accuracy, and it is not too much to say that a large proportion of these victims, especially as regards women, had no offence proved against them. It seems to me that the first business of the Government which exists *de facto* — that is the Government of the Assembly — is to proceed to try the prisoners, release those against whom no charge exists, and bring the real offenders to justice. The paltry intrigue for power and place going on at Versailles just now is enough to make one despair of the future of France."

I have quoted from the *Standard* because it is the testimony of an enemy, but there is not one of our journals (all of them more or less hostile) which has not drawn the same or a more terrible picture. What shall we learn when men now hiding in the attics and cellars of Paris shall have leisure and security to give us *their* story of the civil war?

SOME RESULTS OF THE VICTORY

The Bee-Hive No. 505 Saturday, June 17, 1871

When the upper and middle classes of France welcomed with enthusiasm the declaration of war by Napoleon III., last July, the workmen of Paris filled the streets and shouted for peace. Amongst them the mischievous lust for territorial extension and military glory, fostered for the basest ends by the accursed family of the Bonapartes, had died out. The International Associations had taught them that the workmen of different countries have no quarrel with one another; that, on the contrary, they are natural allies in the grand conflict between labour and capital; and that peace is absolutely necessary for the success of the proletariate. The General Council of the International in London, and its branches both in France and Germany, lost no time in issuing protests against the war which was got up by Bismark and Napoleon quite as much with the object of bleeding and chaining their respective proletariates as from hostility to each other. The manner in which the Prussian officers carried on hostilities, and the nature of the terms imposed upon the vanquished, place it, beyond a doubt, that Bismark and his class, far from desiring a permanent peace, deliberately aimed at prolonging and intensifying the old national animosity between France and Germany, in order that the Government in each country might remain upon a military, that is to say, an anti-popular basis. The workmen of Paris fought bravely, and starved patiently during the war, and were ready to make any sacrifice rather than cede Alsace and Lorraine to the Prussians; but when peace was once made, they harboured no rancour against the workmen of Germany. The leagues for non-intercourse with Germans were formed entirely among the middle class. During the second siege no Germans were molested in Paris. One of that nation was even elected a member of the Government. The column in the Place Vendôme was destroyed avowedly because it commemorated the outrageous wars waged by Napoleon I. on Germany — wars of which M. Thiers, the typical representative of middle-class ideas, has been the chief panegyrist. But no sooner is the Commune crushed than we see a revival of those aims and tendencies which have so often and so justly moved the indignation of England and Europe. The restoration of the Orleans family is openly advocated on the ground that it would be "a standing menace to Germany." An anti-German league is renewed at Havre. In military circles a renewal of the war is the common topic of conversation. Nor is Germany the only country threatened. Addresses are being actively circulated amongst the rural population calling for a re-occupation of Rome and restoration of the temporal power of the Pope by French arms, and M. Thiers instructs his ambassador to oppose the transference of the Italian Government to Rome. Such is the return the National Assembly would make to the noble Garibaldi, who not only fought for France, but exhorted his old fellow-citizens of Nice not to add to her difficulties by seceding during the war. How long will it be before Europe learns that peace will never be firmly established until France is governed by the workmen of Paris?

Let us now look at another consequence of the fall of the Commune. An enormous sum has to be paid to the Prussians. The Commune would have raised the money by the only just and, indeed, the only feasible plan. It would have confiscated the property of the Bonapartist ministers, senators, and deputies, who plunged the country into war; it would have withdrawn all State endowments from religion; it would have disbanded the army; it would have dismissed a host of functionaries; finally, it would have laid a heavy income-tax on the rich. By these financial expedients the debt would have been soon discharged with comparatively slight pressure upon the large mass of the population. M. Thiers, on the contrary, hopes to raise the sum by loans, the interest of which will permanently weigh down France, and must be met by taxation. Taxation, lay it on how you will, must as Mr. Mill has shown, fall more or less heavily on the poor. M. Thiers has chosen the mode of taxation which falls most heavily on the poor. The middle class in France has always successfully resisted the imposition of an Income-tax, and even at this crisis the champion of the middle class will not resort to it, but increases the indirect taxes on such articles as tea, sugar, and *matches*.

A third consequence of the fall of the Commune is the re-appearance of insolent luxury and unblushing vice in the metropolis of the West. During the rule of the workmen crime of all sorts almost ceased. This was repeatedly admitted by the most hostile of the English correspondents. The women of bad character disappeared, the higher class of them going to the friends of order, property, and religion, at Versailles, the lower to the Prussians at St. Denis. The Tuileries and the Hotel de Ville were no longer polluted by the extravagance and debauchery of Bonaparte and his gang, but filled with workmen doing the business of the Government on workman's wages. Now Paris is resuming its old appearance. The idle class who enjoyed themselves in London and Brussels during the siege, have hurried back to their old haunts. Luxury and vice rear their heads anew; and the newspaper most read by the middle class, finds time, in intervals between its cries for more blood, to propose that public gambling tables should be established to fill Paris with people of the right sort.

Meanwhile the correspondent of the *Standard* (surely not a revolutionary authority) asserts that notwithstanding the denials put forth by M. Thiers, summary executions of National Guards are still going on, and that no later than last Tuesday fifteen were shot by one volley. If Paris was not unanimous under the Commune, it is unanimous now. No wonder that when the body of the Archbishop was borne to the grave, amidst a dense throng of citizens of all classes, not a hat was raised, nor a mark of sympathy shown. A sullen silence characterised the assemblage, and it was easy, we are told, to see written on all faces the determination to fight the battle over again sooner or later. That day, according to the correspondent of the *Times*, may not be so far distant as is generally supposed, since the very army which has been the instrument of the butcheries of MM. Thiers and Favre contains within itself elements liable at any moment to produce an explosion.

LONDON REPUBLICANS

The Bee-Hive No.506 Saturday, June 24, 1871

The portion of the working classes in London which takes an interest in public questions of any kind is not large. Questions that concern unionism, as a whole, may fairly be termed public. But the affairs of any particular trade society are essentially of private interest, and, while they certainly raise a man somewhat from the lowest depths of individualism in principle and selfishness in practice, it may be doubted whether this good is not outbalanced by the restriction of generous feelings to what is after all but a narrow sphere. The man whose nature prompts him to think of something beyond his own personal satisfaction, and who in France or Germany would turn his attention to the larger interests of his class and his country, in England stops short at the intersts of his own particular trade. The energy and devotion, which assuredly are not more rare qualities among English than among Continental workmen, are here wasted on petty and subordinate movements. It might easily be shown that this is a short-sighted policy, even from the Trades Union point of view; witness the contemptuous refusal of Unionist demands in the present session of Parliament. But this is far from being the worst result. The intellects of our workmen are cramped and their sympathies narrowed. With all their advantages of free public discussion, a free press, and right of association, they are less thoughtful, less informed, less earnest, and less united than the artizans not only of Paris and Lyons, but of Berlin and Vienna. I have the less scruple in pronouncing this judgment because I have for many years advocated the cause of Unions, and often at the risk of great personal sacrifice. Nor have I now any intention of deserting it.

No doubt there are some London workmen who have

more general interests, and who endeavour to direct the attention of their class to the broader questions of politics and society. But in my opinion they show great want of wisdom in the course they adopt. They seem to think that the only way of making converts is to organise processions to Trafalgar-Square, and meetings in Hyde Park, and to send reports of their committee meetings to the daily papers. I will assume that they do all this from honest disinterested zeal; that they are not actuated by vanity and the desire of notoriety. For anything I know to the contrary, they are no more open to imputations of this sort than prominent unionists, or metropolitan vestrymen, or active Members of Parliament. But I cannot understand how they can imagine that any useful result can follow from such proceedings. They aim, if we are to believe their professions, at very sweeping changes; and, I suppose, I am not misrepresenting them if I say that they expect to effect these changes by means not of superior numbers but superior energy. So far, there is nothing chimerical in their expectations. Revolutions have always been effected by energetic minorities. It is true that such energetic proceedings on the part of minorities are liable to be followed by reactions, but with that consideration I do not propose to deal now. I would only point out that the energy required for such a purpose must be of the most determined kind. It must proceed from a strength of conviction amounting to fanaticism. And I would ask our Trafalgar-Square processionists whether they really believe that such conviction was ever yet produced by the sight of a red flag or the strains of a brass band? Those who put faith in such expedients, mistake effects for causes. It is true that revolutions in Paris have often been begun by processions, flags, and bands. But these demonstrations were the outward expression of a deep-seated devotion and long-cherished enthusiasm. The man who espouses a political cause merely from seeing a procession, or even from listening to a speech, must be a very flighty inconsiderate person — not of the stuff from which Paris revolutionists are made. The heroic men who have just been laying down their lives by thousands for the cause they held dear, were not trained after the fashion of our London democrats. For twenty years they had no processions. They could not even form a political society or meet in a room, twenty at a time, for discussion. Yet it was during those twenty years that they grew in numbers, and ripened in earnestness. The man who had strength and knowledge and power of persuasion did not need bands of music or platforms to influence his fellows. Nor did he take refuge in secret societies. He just talked to those whom he knew — his mates in the workshop, his acquaintances in the cabaret. The ground was prepared to receive the seed, for education and public spirit are much more common among the workmen of Paris than those of London, and their energies are not monopolised by trade struggles. A faith so spread was something very different from the frothy sentiment of a London "demonstration".

Even then, from their own point of view, I mean that of forcible revolution, our Republicans and Communists would do well to defer their demonstrations until they have, by a patient and unobtrusive propaganda, got together a far larger body of convinced adherents than they can boast at present. But surely recent events might do something to teach them the mischief that results from trusting to force for the reorganisation of society, rather than to moral and religious means. I am not now condemning the vanquished more than the victors. It is the fault of both alike that they rely on force alone for the creation or the maintenance of the social and political state which they prefer. The Parisian workmen had this excuse in rushing to arms, that they were only anticipating a similar movement on the part of the reactionists. But in England the working class have freedom of the press, the right of public meeting, the right of association, and, if they like to use it, very great influence on the House of Commons. There is, therefore, no excuse for any resort to force or intimidation. There are plenty of Elchos and

Bentincks who would be only too glad of a pretext for employing violence, and sweeping away the guarantees for freedom just enumerated. Let our workmen use their votes to prevent any increase of our army, whether in the shape of regulars, militia, or volunteers, and there will be a fair chance of an ultimate settlement of our social difficulties without any such terrible convulsion as that which is now shaking France. In the meantime let them devote themselves to the cultivation of public spirit among their own order, and particularly among that degraded but formidable portion of it which tills the soil.

POLITICAL NOTES ON THE PRESENT SITUATION OF FRANCE AND PARIS

BY A FRENCH POSITIVIST

EDITOR'S INTRODUCTION

At the end of the *Civil War in France* Marx refers to "an honourable French writer, completely foreign to our Association, (who) speaks as follows:

> "The members of the Central Committee of the National Guard, as well as the greater part of the members of the Commune, are the most active, intelligent, and energetic minds of the International Working Men's Association ... men who are thoroughly honest, sincere, intelligent, devoted pure, and fanatical in the *good* sense of the word.".

The reader of the following pamphlet will discover that Marx secured this passage by running together remarks made on pages 3 and 6 of the original: (pages 109 and 112 in this edition). The pamphlet had neither price nor date, but must have first appeared in May 1871. Positivists treated anonymous journalism as a sin, but under the exceptional circumstances of the time they were prepared to be indulgent. The author was probably Dr. Robinet (1825-1899). This view was first expressed in R. Harrison, "E.S. Beesly and Karl Marx" International Review of Social History,IV, p.216 (Amsterdam) 1959. It was adopted by Abramsky and Collins and by the editors of Documents of the First International. It can be supported on the following grounds: Robinet acted as mayor of the sixth *arrondissement* during the siege of Paris. He was in Paris during the Commune where he saved many lives at imminent personal risk. Robinet was known to be critical of the Commune and yet ready to fight and die for it against the Counter-Revolution: he committed the care of his wife and their children to his fellow Positivists in Britain and America. Two of the other principal possibilities, Messrs Laffitte and Semerie, are virtually excluded by the reference made to them in the extract from the third letter while the French proletarian positivists are excluded by the terms in which both Beesly and Marx describe the writer.

The pamphlet is included in this collection because it was used by Marx and the other defenders of the Commune in England. It serves as a reminder of the important fact that these defenders of Paris were not wholly dependent upon the middle class press for a knowledge of what was happening. Robinet over-estimated the importance of the members of the International, but his pamphlet has an added importance because it draws attention to a small, but under-explored, body of literature in English by French participants in the Revolution. The Story of the Commune by a "Communalist" (1871) pp 43 is another example of this type of writing.

INTRODUCTION TO ORIGINAL ARTICLE

"Political Notes on the present position of France and Paris" were drawn up for the private information of the writer's friends in England, and were not intended for publication. But they seemed to me so valuable, that I have not hesitated to print a translation of them. The writer is a highly educated man, of noble character, and well-tried patriotism.

E. S. Beesly

POLITICAL NOTES ON THE PRESENT SITUATION OF FRANCE AND PARIS

BY A FRENCH POSITIVIST

I

April 1

The Revolution of the Eighteenth of March is much more profound and serious than in generally supposed. Its character is somewhat disguised by the military beginning which still conceals its true nature.

In our eyes, the explosion so incautiously provoked at Paris on the eighteenth by the plutocratic and re-actionary Government of Messrs. Thiers, Favre, and Picard, is only the culmination of a social process which dates from before the fall of Napoleon III.

The members of the Central Committee of the National Guard, which constituted itself after the capitulation of Paris with great skill and courage, and was soon accepted by the majority of the battalions, mostly in the workmen's parts of the town, as well as the greater part of the members of the Commune, are the most active, intelligent, and energetic minds of the International Workmen's Association, working men, small engineers, and journalists.

Their philosophy is Atheism, Materialism, the negation of all religion: their political programme is absolute individual liberty, by means of the suppression of government and the division of nationalities into communes more or less federated: their political economy consists essentially in the dispossession, with compensation, of the present holders of capital, and in assigning the coin, instruments of labour, and land to associations of workmen: their historical theory is that the nobility and bourgeoisie have each had their reign, and that the turn of the proletariate has now come. They exclude all that is outside the working class from society, considering it as socially and even physiologically *effete*.

Such is the doctrine of the Central Committee of the National Guard, and the Communal Council sitting at the Hotel de Ville, which since the Eighteenth of last March have been absolute masters of Paris.

Neither the one nor the other, however, has put forward this programme in an official way, and they defer the execution of it by governmental or forcible means till after the victory which they reckon on gaining over the Versailles party.

I need not point out in what respects this attempt at social regeneration is theoretically and practically vicious, how inopportune is the bringing forward these questions at the time of the Prussian occupation. I merely affirm that it is a popular movement, wide-spread, profound, highly legitimate in principle, honest and sincere, directed by able fanatics, who are in many respects worthy of esteem.

The situation of Paris is, then, a complicated one: for a considerable part of the population, including many even of the avowed Republicans, either does not understand or does not accept this movement, and almost the whole of France, except the members of the International among the workmen of the large towns, rejects it entirely.

This is the cause why we—blockaded on the north and east by the Prussians, cruelly besieged and bombarded on the south and west by the provincial and governmental troops—are on the point of fighting in Paris itself, Republicans and Conservatives against Socialists and Communists. It is a frightful, an unheard-of position, which threatens us with the greatest public and private disasters!

This is what our unhappy country has gained by shutting her ears for half a century to the only voice which could have brought about the reconciliation of order and progress, the satisfaction of all interests, and the fusion of all classes.

II

April 19

Whatever may be the real tendency of the communal movement of Paris (which does not really resemble what is generally understood by a municipal constitution, but is rather in its essence an attempt at social re-organisation), the Central Committee of the National Guard and the Commune have begun and still continue a most important undertaking, which is much more directly political; this gives them their power, and with the immense majority of the people, constitutes their only legitimate action—they are defending the Republic.

In fact it is certain that by its attempt to disarm the National Guard of Paris on the 18th March, the reactionary party had begun the over-throw of the Republic and the re-establishment of royalty, by armed force. If any doubt of this could have existed after the military expedition againt Montmartre, and the placards of the Government, it would have been completely removed by a letter of M. de Clermont Tonnerre to the Minister of War, General Le Flo, published in the *Journal Official* and in the *Mot de Ordre* of the 1st inst., in which the plans and the means of the plutocratic and clerical counter-revolution are plainly expressed, viz.: the immediate and complete disarmament of the National Guard, by force or fraud, and the weeding out of some thousands of the inhabitants of Paris.

As the Central Committee was the only organisation in existence for the direction of the revolutionary party, there can be no doubt that by its preparing, commanding, and directing the resistance against an aggression which it had foreseen, it saved the Republic on the 18th of March; and by persisting, in conjunction with the Commune, in the defence of Paris, it is still maintaining and watching over the Republic. [1] This is a most important and indisputable point.

The Republic is at the Hotel de Ville; at Versailles is a plutocratic and clerical re-action of the blindest and most ferocious kind, whether it conseals itself beneath the name of a Bourbon, an Orleans, or even of a Bonaparte.

Here, therefore, are the *raison d'etre,* the right and the moral prestige of the Committee and of the Commune, which will only cease on the day when they begin to use their authority to introduce social reforms.

Finally I must add, in order to make our situation more clear to you, that the Central Committee of the National Guard, exclusively composed of workmen, members of the International Workmen's Association, has alone taken the initiative, and alone has the merit of the movement; that it gained and keeps its power by means of it direct, organic, and secret connections with the National Guard; that the Commune is, with respect to it, already a miscellaneous body, less exclusively proletarian and federalist; that it has in no degree abdicated its functions, and influences the municipal body through those of its members who belong to it, or who are entirely devoted to it through doctrine or connections; but that sooner or later a conflict may easily arise between the Committee and the heterogeneous elements of the Commune, especially after victory, should they be successful.

III

April 20

With regard to persons I must be very cautious in giving my opinion, for fear of passing an incorrect judgment.

I have already told you in my first note that the Central Committee and the Commune contain many men who are thoroughly honest, sincere, intelligent, devoted, pure and fanatical *in the good sense of the word,* especially in the class of the proletarians and small engineers; less so, I think, in that of the literary men and journalists who have joined them. Citizens Varlin, journeyman bookbinder; Malon, journeyman calico printer; Theisz, workman; Clement, journeyman dyer; Ostyn, working engineer; Vaillant, engineer; Arnold, architect; Jourde, shopman; whom I know personally more or less, are all such men.

Among the workmen, citizen Assi, although a member of the International, of the Central Committee, and of the the Commune, and holding a command in the National Guard, seems to be one of the most doubtful. It is said that his conduct in the struggle at Creuzot was instigated by Rouher, against Schneider, whom Rouher detested and wished to deprive of his Presidentship. He is also said to have defended himself but ill in the trial which followed; and finally he has been suspected lately of dealing with Versailles. This was the cause of his arrest. As, however, he has been set at liberty, and even re-instated in the Commune, no doubt these accusations are false. Still there is little esteem felt in the municipal body for Assi, and he has no influence there.

Among the jounalists citizen Delescluze especially is thoroughly honest and devoted to the Republic, but not emancipated from Deism and the revolutionary non-socialist metaphysics. He is the man of '93, improved by the modern situation.

The party least to be commended is that of the small journalists, which might be represented by Messrs. Vermorel, Paschal Grousset, Valles, &c.; but they have little influence, and submit to the guidance of the Committee, which obey only its faith and principles without recognising perverse or interested action of any kind. Those who bring such charges against it are knaves or fools.

I forgot to tell you that the Central Committee, and therefore the Commune, are in constant connection with the Paris delegates of the International, the workmen's federal chambers, and the socialist committees [2] of the twenty districts of Paris which sit in permanence in the Rue de la Carderie, and which are regularly and unceasingly acting on and being acted on by the Central Committee. You see that the movement is immense and profound, and that whatever may happen it will be necessary to take it seriously into account.

I think, in fact, that the Committee and the Commune have with them, so far as their political action is concerned (viz.: maintenance of the Republic and recognition by the central power of the municipal rights of Paris), at least half of the National Guard, both workman and bourgeois: [3]

among the population the proportion is smaller, because of the women and old men who shrink from war and the arbitrary acts which are rendered necessary by the struggle, especially toward the priests. But if the Communal movement became openly socialist, as for example in case of victory, I believe that the number of its adherents would be enormously diminished, *even among the proletariate.*

In a military point of view, the Committee and the Commune have not distinguished themselves; there has been plenty of courage shown among the soldiers, and still more among their leaders; but the latter, Flourens, Duval, Henri, Bergeret, Brunel, &c., have proved themselves quite incapable. If Cluzeret, Dombrowski, &c., had not taken the direction of the defence, it is probable that we should have lost the game and been soon reduced to a war of barricades in our streets. Instead of this, these brave and prudent generals have succeeded in maintaining until now the southern line of the forts (with the exception, alas, of Mont Valerien) and in limiting the bombardment and the slaughter to the village of Neuilly, and to the quarter between that point and the Champs Elysees. [4]

We have not much fear of the Prussians, who respect the convention and let provisions pass. The Versailles party, besides occupying all the Prussian batteries in order to fire on us, cuts off our provisions and all communications. The Commune has decided to respect all the terms agreed on with the Prussians, and has already offered to pay the share of Paris in the war contribution, which M. Thiers pretends he is unable to discharge.

As to myself, I left the Commune principally on account of my health. I fail and grow weaker from day to day, and could not have endured these new trials. But even if I had been well, I might perhaps have hesitated to take upon myself the responsibility of entering a political body, the greater part of whose decisions would have been formed in contradiction to my views, convictions and advice. For althouth I am *with the Commune* in principle and in fact, there are many of its acts, to say nothing of its grand

114

ulterior design, which I entirely reject.

Amidst our growing disasters, I am more and more convinced that Positivism *alone* can solve the political and social questions which assume such an urgent and menacing appearance with us, and which we are trying to bring to a practical issue by leading advanced opinion to modify universal suffrage in the direction indicated by the accompanying pamphlets by Messrs. Laffitte and Semerie, as well as the various communications to the Deputies and to the Republican journals which I have drawn up, and of which I send you copies with these notes.

IV

April 22

If we now look not only at the particular condition of Paris, but at that of the whole of France, we shall easily see that a struggle exists everywhere between order and progress, and that it is the extension of the revolutionary fever, or the prolongation of the spiritual interregnum and the excessive adjournment of social regeneration which accumulates and keeps up all the disasters with which our unhappy country is overwhelmed.

Indeed the Conservative party, blind .as it is savage, incivic as it is cowardly, can only see its way to preserving the fundamental and necessary institutions of property, family, and government, by the most brutal retrogression, and the employment of force; and is obstinately bent on regarding these institutions as immovable, and rejecting any modification or even any improvement of them. On the other hand the Revolutionary party irrationally pursuing an arbitrary progress, seems to pay less and less regard to order, or to these mother institutions (property, family, and government), in whose gradual growth to perfection, consists the only real progress.

The party of order has at its head the noble, clerical, and plutocratic classes; and supports itself by the mass of the peasantry. It accepts universal suffrage, which, by the overwhelming preponderance of the rural votes, secures to it the possession of power, that is to say the choice of the government, the army, the magistracy, the police, and the control of the finances. Its real tendency is to an absolute monarchy, in spite of the tinsel of the sovereignty of the people with which it has decked its banner.

The Revolutionary party has at its head literary men (publicists and journalists); its body consists of the workmen of the large towns. It believes in the sovereignty of the people, and hopes to correct the too well know vices of universal suffrage by education and by institutions, but above all by force or by insurrection. Its tendency is to absolute democracy.

The Conservative party caused the Second Empire, the *Coup d'Etat* of December, and the *Plebiscite* of May 8th, 1870, the war with Germany and the Capitulation of Paris, the dismemberment of France and the peace *a outrance* in 1871; it is at the present moment bombarding the capital, and its only policy is to exterminate the party of the Revolution by fire and sword, by transportations and by misery.

The Revolutionary party struggled energetically against the Empire, as it is now struggling heroically against the clerico-plutocratic re-action, as it struggled against the Foreign Invasion, which was favoured by monarchical treason, whether Legitimist, Orleanist, or Bonapartist. [5] Full of the great traditions of '93, of generous aspirations of perseverance and of courage, and only wanting in light; with devotion and ardour worthy of a better fate, it is cutting for itself a path without a certain issue, and which may lead to great dangers.

Between these two extremes is a sound and respectable body, the true hope of the future. It is composed of members of the Liberal professions, of traders, manufacturers and independent proprietors, the remains of the old Third Estate, finally of numerous artisans and proletarians, who all feel the need of order and the desire for progress and who only need enlightenment to become a power and save the country.

E.S. BEESLY

Until the light appears, and positivism brings a little
order to this chaos, peace to this combat, light to this
darkness, passion and force crush and grind us down! After
the Prussians come the French, if that name can still be
given to the wretches, who deserting Bonaparte for Thiers
and Picard, have recovered, in order to tear their country
to pieces, the energy and violence which always failed
them when the foreigner was to be faced.

NOTES

1. Neither the Mayors of Paris, nor the Deputies of the Left who
    have shown themselves so irresolute, so divided, and so weak
    during all these events, would have been capable of resisting a
    Royalist *coup d'état* on the 18th March. Before they could have
    agreed and acted, the disarmament would have been effected,
    and the counter-revolution accomplished.
2. All this was formed, developed and organised under the Empire!
    So much for Despotism!
3. There is besides in our ranks a very considerable number of
    regular soldiers, marines, foot-soldiers, cavalry soldiers, and
    artillerymen, who have left Versailles and taken the side of Paris
    and Commune. There are hardly any officers, only rank and file
    and non-commissioned officers.
4. There is also fighting going on round the forts, and for the
    possession of the plateau of Chatillon; but the struggle there is
    less desperate and continuous than at Neuilly. The thunder of
    the cannon is heard day and night.
5. Thiers, Favre, Picard, Trochu, Bazaine, Uhrich, Aurelles de Pala-
    dines, at Tours, Bordeaux, Paris, Metz, Strasburg, and Orleans,
    as well as many other men in many other places, constantly
    betrayed France in diplomacy and in war in favour of Prussia,
    which has, I assure you, had an easy triumph..

III

J. H. Bridges

EDITOR'S BIOGRAPHICAL NOTES

BRIDGES, John Henry, M.B., F.R.C.P., (1832-1906) Doctor, Author, Positivist. Born 11th October, 1832, at Old Newton, Suffolk. The second son of the Rev. Charles Bridges, a celebrated Evangelical, and his wife, Harriet Torlesse. Educated at private schools until entering Rugby in 1845. He met E. S. Beesly and Frederic Harrison at Wadham where he was Senior Scholar in October, 1851. Although placed in 3rd Class in 1854, Bridges won a Fellowship at Oriel in the following year and gained the Arnold prize in 1856. After study in Paris and London he graduated M.B. at Oxford, 1859. In 1860 he married a cousin and emigrated to Melbourne. His wife died shortly after reaching Australia and he returned to England where he became (1861) physician to the Bradford Infirmary. He associated himself with J. R. Stephens in the 8 hour movement although personally favouring 9 as a more realistic demand. With Stephens, he opposed the application of the Poor Law to the operatives during the cotton famine. Unlike fellow-Positivists, he was "neutralist" during the American Civil War. He made a sanitary survey of Bradford in 1862 and lectured incessantly to workers at the Mechanics Institute and to Women and Girls on Physiology and Public Health. He lectured to the B.M.A. on "The Introduction of sanitary teaching into primary schools as an indispensable condition of efficient sanitary reform" (1868). He constantly related Public Health to property relations and morbid fear of Government: his lecture at the Royal Institution on "Civilisation and Public Health" was a pioneer work. (Reprinted in Fortnightly Review, August 1869). He first contributed to the Labour press in 1866 when he insisted on the opposition of working and middle class interests and severely criticised all parliamentary institutions. He supported Beesly's attempt at a Labour Party in 1867. In 1869 he became factory inspector for the North Riding and in the following year moved to London where he was appointed Medical Inspector to the Local Government Board, an appointment which he retained until his retirement in 1898. With Robert Applegarth he was a member of Royal Commission on Contagious Diseases Acts where he "anticipated the measures that were taken nearly half a century later." (J. L. & B. Hammond, *James Stansfeld,* 1932). In 1873 he was co-author with T. Holmes of the Report to the Local Government Board on Proposed Changes in Hours and Ages of Employment in Textile Factories, H.C.; 1873, LV. The recommendation of a 6 hour reduction in the length of the working week and the exposure of the intensification of work since the Factory Act of 1847 aroused the indignation of employers.

In 1879 Bridges became first President of the English Positivist Committee, having sided with Beesly and Harrison against his old Tutor, Richard Congreve. He translated two major works by Comte: replied to J. S. Mill's attack (The Unity of Comte's Life and Doctrine, 1866) and published numerous scholarly works undertaken from a Positivist standpoint.

Bridges was remarried in 1869 to Mary Hadwen. There was no issue from either marriage. He died in Tunbridge Wells, 15th June, 1906.

THE COMMUNE OF PARIS

The Bee-Hive Saturday, July 8, 1871

It is not too late to talk about the Commune of Paris; and it will not be too late for many a long year to come. The 18th March, 1871 is the latest act of a drama which began eighty two years ago, and which is not nearly ended yet. A few yards from where Delescluze fell the other day, a few minutes' walk from the place where the Commune of Paris ended its fierce and heroic struggle, there stood until the 14th of July, 1789, the great feudal fortress which barred the way to revolution. The taking of the Bastille was a day of new birth to Europe. It was the beginning of a society in which every man would be a citizen of a free State; in which governing power would be given to those who were fit for it, not to a few privileged families: in which the wage-receiving class — that is to say, the great bulk of the population, were no longer to be soothed into contentments by statements that God had decreed that the poor should never cease from the land, by doles of well-meaning charity, or by promises of compensation in a future life, but would insist upon their lot being rendered tolerable in the life which now is, and upon sharing with the wealth-possessing classes in the great inheritance of civilisation.

We have not reached this result yet. But from 1789 to 1830, from 1830 to 1848, from 1848 to 1871, the struggle has been going on, and the great object before us has become more and more clearly marked out.

I write, then, in the main, as a defender of the Commune of Paris. It will be seen, later on, that I do not defend it through thick and thin. I shall speak plainly enough afterwards of its weakness, its errors, and the cause of its fall. But this is not the first thing to do. The first thing to do is to shield its memory from the foolish and all but unanimous injustice of the English Press. The anonymous clique of twenty or thirty writers to whom the comfortable classes in England are content to trust the formation of their opinions, form at the present time a far more serious obstacle to progress than any other of the retrograde institutions of the country.

For instance, the phrase "the crimes of the Commune" is repeated by them over and over again, till many people have come to believe that the leaders of the Paris Revolution did really come, as the Pope the other day said that they came, from the mouth of Hell. Now, what are the "crimes of the Commune"?

I deliberately say that the records of history may be searched in vain to find a revolutionary movement, the leaders of which stand out in history more pure from crime that the leaders of the Paris Commune. They are accused of murdering Generals Lecompte and Thomas. Lecompte and Thomas were put to death by their own soldiers in a riot, not by the Paris Commune. They are accused of attempting to burn down the great buildings of Paris. It is now entirely certain that this accusation is an impudent falsehood. Most of the public buildings in Paris were never set fire to at all. The fires that broke out in various places were partly caused by the shells of the Versailles troops, and were partly caused by the burning of barricades, many of the barricades being burnt when they could no longer be held, in order to protect the retreat of the Parisians to the next. They are accused of having imprisoned several priests and other persons as hostages. This is true, and they were perfectly justified in doing so. Their own prisoners were being slaughtered wholesale in cold blood, and the capture of these hostages stopped this slaughter for a fortnight. And if anyone was to be taken as a hostage, it was very natural that it should be a priest, because the priests in France, during the last twenty years, have not confined themselves to their religious duties, but have been active enemies of liberty and progress. The Catholic priest in France has been of late a totally different person from the Catholic priest in England or in

Ireland. In England, the "No Popery" cry is a piece of vulgar and stupid bigotry. The Catholic priest in England is generally a quiet, hard-working, and useful man. The Catholic priest in Ireland has often defended the claims of his suffering countrymen with noble courage. The Catholic priests of France did everything they could to secure the election of the miserable and cruel reactionists of the Versailles Assembly.

To continue. The Paris Commune is accused of having put their hostages to death. Now, what are the simple facts, so far as they are yet known? The Versailles troops entered Paris on the 21st May. The hostages were not killed till the 25th May. All that time, and for many days before, the Commune was endeavouring to get them exchanged for some of their own prisoners. Thiers chose to refuse to enter into any such negotiations. Mr. Karl Marx has been roundly taken to task for holding. Thiers responsible for their death. I have yet to learn in what respect Mr. Karl Marx is wrong.

However this may be, the prisoners were not killed until the Commune of Paris had ceased to have any political existence. That some man or knot of men exasperated by the horrible massacre, not in fair street-fighting, but in cold blood, of their brothers, their wives, and their children should have taken this bloody revenge, is no doubt terrible and tragic in the extreme. But those who would even weigh it on the balance as compared with the enormous mass of cruelty perpetrated on the other side, must belong to that class of persons who regard an attack of the poor against the rich as something belonging to a wholly distinct order of crime from attacks of the rich against the poor.

So much for the "Crimes of the Commune." I have left small space for its virtues. But let the following points be noted:—

1. The Commune of Paris defended the cause of the Republic — that is to say, of social progress and free thought against the Monarchy, that is to say, against stag-

nation and ignorance. And the Commune has in the main succeeded, though itself perished in the struggle. The recent elections show that the Republic is saved; and, but for the strength put forward by the Paris Commune; it would have been inevitably lost. This is why the great mass of the Paris populations, of many different shades of opinion, supported it.

2. Its existence was the most energetic protest that has ever been made against the spirit of national vain-glory and aggrandisement. Its most essential principle was the common interest and well-being of the producing class all over Europe. The International Society and the Commune are not, indeed, to be identified. Many of the most important persons in the Commune held views very different from those of the council of the International. Still this society exercised a very potent influence; and whatever may be said of the theories of some of its leaders, of which I propose to speak on another occasion, it is at least certain that in its conception of European union and European peace it is immeasurably in advance of any other political school, with the single exception of the Positivists. The moment the Commune is suppressed the old talk about standing armies revives.

3. The Commune of Paris showed that workmen, when the need came for it, could govern. By the confession of those witnesses, who were permitted to publish what they saw, in the English newspapers, and from the verbal evidence of the far larger number who were not permitted to do so, it is certain that this vast city was singularly well administered in every way. Let me quote what I believe has before been spoken of in the Bee-Hive, the "English Clergyman in Paris," who wrote to the Spectator on May 20:—

"As to anarchy, never was Paris so quiet and orderly; never were persons or property so safe; you may walk at all hours in any quarter without fear of insult, nay with the certainty of being safe; and this is much more than could be said of the place when, beside the city police and the army of spies, it had 12,000 sergens specially employed in the Emperor's service. There is plenty of freedom of opinion, whereas at Versailles no one dares breathe a word except in favour of the Government. As to personal liberty, you can walk into Paris by the Northern station just as you could into Belgrave-square out of Victoria station . . . . Of drunkenness you see none in Paris . . . . About debauchery, the women have joined the Commune in the perhaps Utopian effort to put down prostitution. The books and prints are mostly decent and serious; it is at St. Denis you see stalls loaded with vile photographs. The Louvre is as free as ever; the Tuileries are open at 5d a head, the money being put into the sick fund. In the Tuileries every room is labelled, and guarded by a sedentaire; no breakage, no scribbling on the walls, nothing of what we might expect from a Paris mob let loose in its late master's palace. In fact, there is no scribbling anywhere; except the text repeated over and over again; "Death to Thiers; respect for property!"

For these and other reasons, the Commune of Paris will live long in the memories of man, and will bear fruit in a speedy future.

THE LATE COMMUNE OF PARIS

The Bee-Hive July 22, 1871

When Paris surrendered at the end of January last, France was left without a Government. There were two fragments of a Government, as there had been throughout the war, the one headed by Trochu and Favre in Paris, the other by Gambetta in Bordeaux. An Assembly was called at a few days' notice, not to decide how France should be governed, but to decide whether France should go on with the war or not. People took very little interest in the candidates for this Assembly, taking it for granted that as soon as its purpose of making peace was ended, it would dissolve. It was thus a good oppostunity for the clerical and aristocratic party to return men of their own choosing. They made good use of this opportunity; working on the selfish craving for peace at any price, which prevailed amongst the ignorant peasantry. A Reactionist Assembly was elected; not in the least representing, as the recent elections have proved, the real political feelings of France. As soon as it met, it began to set up claims to Sovereign power; to coquet with the Princes of the old dynasties; to flatter the peasantry; to insult Garibaldi and Gambetta; and to humiliate Paris. Nothing more foolish, nothing more revolutionary in the worst sense of the word, nothing more subversive of law and order, could possible be conceived than the attempt of this Assembly to set aside Paris as the capital of France. Imagine Dorsetshire, Herefordshire, Suffolk, or the rest of the agricultural districts saying that London was too Radical a place to be the capital of England, and attempting to set up the central Government in Exeter! Yet this is what the Assembly tried to do, all the time having absolutely no authority from their constituents to settle anything of the kind; elected simply to decide on peace or war, having no more to do with the general Government of the country than if they had been a convocation of bishops and clergy, an assemblage of School Boards, or an association for the "formation of social science."

Thiers who had, at least, the instincts of a statesman, though of a very unprincipled statesman, knew that all this was folly, and with great difficulty dragged the Assembly after him from Bordeaux to Versailles. But he could not give it what it did not possess, any legal claim to govern France. He could not turn its members from blind impracticable Conservatives, who wished to restore the Pope to his kingdom, and to hoist the white flag at the Tuileries, to men of sense and sagacity enough to read the signs of the times. Thiers probably over-rated their power and their hold on the country; and being himself perfectly indifferent on what principles France was governed, so long as he was President or Prime Minister, he flattered and cajoled these men, sometimes scolding them a little, but always taking care to soothe them by calling them that which they were not, "the Sovereign Assembly" of France.

What, then, was the issue on the 18th of March? It lay in a nutshell. Was Paris to be disarmed, its National Guard superseded by Catholic soldiers from Brittany fighting for the temporal power of the Pope and for the White Flag? Or was Paris to maintain its just ascendancy over France, to save the Republic, to lead the great cities to municipal freedom, and to keep the question of capital and labour uppermost? The Parisians have been bitterly blamed for raising that question at this particular time. But they had these three excellent reasons for doing so. They were organised, they were armed, and there was no legitimate authority to oppose them.

I promised in the last number of the *Bee-Hive* to point out what seemed to me to be the failings of the Paris Commune. And I will now speak of one, which was this. They failed, not from attempting too much, but from attempting too little. Immediately after the 18th of March, the very day after, they should have marched upon Versailles, where they would have found no resistance of any importance; they should have disbanded the Assembly, and brought back the Republican members of it to Paris. They should then have instantly convoked a Constituent Assembly, returned, not by universal suffrage, for which the peasantry are not yet ripe, but by the universal suffrage of towns of France, including the principal town in every department. It is quite certain that the peasantry care very little for politics. They are perfectly ready to support any and every established Government, whether it be a Republic or an Empire. This being so, it is simply absurd to allow the peasantry to have the initiative as to what is to be the form of government. Their interests must, no doubt, be fairly consulted. On such a question as that of taxation, for instance, they ought to have a direct voice. Ultimately they will see, and all will see, that there is no separation whatever between their interests and that of the workmen of towns. But for the present, the initiative as to the form of government, and as to the men who are to administer it, must belong to the towns. I say, therefore, that in all this the error of the Commune lay — not in doing too much, but in doing too little. Had they shown more energy at the onset, the Versailles usurpers would have been powerless, and their atrocious massacres would never have been perpetrated.

Their second error, so at least I deem it, was that they were so engrossed with municipal and social questions that they did not take into account sufficiently the necessity which still exists for France cohering together as a political whole. Not that thay wanted France to be split up into thirty thousand independent Republics, as has been very falsely and absurdly stated; but they wanted France to be governed exactly like Switzerland, or like New Zealand; a multitude of almost independent communes sending representatives to a Federal Council. Now, there is very much that is noble and admirable in this ideal. I consider it certain that the current of events is tending in this direction. I have no doubt that not merely France, but Great

Britain and every other European country will, at no very distant date, fall into aggregates of smaller self-governing communities, each about the size and population of Switzerland, Ireland, Scotland, Belgium, or Holland; and that the advancement of mankind will be vastly forwarded by such a subdivision. But, *for the present*, it appears to me necessary, though the necessity is most lamentable, that the French Republic should be a great Power in Europe; that it should be "one and indivisible;" that it should be able to hold its own against the new and terrible curse of Europe, the military despotism of the Prussian empire; that it should be strong enough to put a veto on any foolish attempts to restore the Papal power in Italy. I think thus that one of the errors of the Commune was that they were so wholly pre-occupied with the social question (which is, undoubtedly, the most important of all) that the political importance of France, as a European power — of France as a united whole — was not sufficiently present to them. It was a noble error, especially when contrasted with the braggart national vanity of which Thiers is the great representative in France, and with which Germany is now so profoundly infected. It was one of those errors which are only premature anticipations of a splendid truth.

The third failing of the Commune was far more important and more dangerous. The Communals of Paris shared with the whole revolutionary party throughout Europe, the grand want of definite convictions of a Social Faith. And the inevitable result of that want followed: Doubt and mistrust of one another among the leaders; anarchy and insubordination in the ranks. The aspirations of the Commune were most noble. But the clear insight, the sure guidance and the prompt obedience, without which failure was certain, were not there. Petty jealousies, personal ambition, unwillingness to obey, and discord upon fundamental questions — these are the real causes of the failure of the Commune. Take the essential question, the question of capital and labour. Some of the Communals were Communists; some were not. That is to say,

129

some thought that the insitution of private property ought to be abolished, and that all capital of every kind should be handed over to the administration of the State; others, and, I imagine, the great majority, looked upon this theory as wholly repugnant to common sense, and were not in the least prepared to hand over their household furniture or their children to the interference of a majority in the Town Council. Until men are agreed on this essential question, no great success can be achieved in the cause of labour. There can be no great victory without faith. And it must be a faith, like that of the followers of *Moses*, of *Mahomet*, or of the Great Apostles of Christianity — a faith that can inspire the spirit of sacrifice and the spirit of obedience. The Revolutionist of France or England has yet to learn a lesson from the Prussian soldier, and from the Jesuit priest. His faith is nobler than theirs, for his rises above the narrow spirit of nationality, and he prefers, or, at least, is ready to prefer, the religion of humanity to the religion which confines salvation to a single sect. But the Prussian soldier has learnt how to obey. The Jesuit has learnt how to sacrifice his personal vanity to the cause which he serves. Let Republicans learn these lessons.

IV

The Journeyman Engineer

THE ENGLISH WORKING CLASSES
AND THE PARIS COMMUNE

EDITOR'S INTRODUCTION

The following article appeared in *Fraser's Magazine*, July 1871. The author was Thomas Wright (1839– ?) born at Liverpool: a blacksmith and member of the A.S.E. who revealed his identity in 1873 when he republished the piece in *Our New Masters* (pp 194-9).He had already established a reputation as an authority on 'the proletariat from within' by publishing, in the year of the Second Reform Act a volume entitled *Some Habits and Customs of the Working Classes* by "A Journeyman Engineer". He obviously had a shrewd eye for the middle-class market, but the mixture of respect, resentment and contempt with which he treated his clients hardly disqualified him as a representative spokesman of the Labour Aristocracy with which he identified himself so self-consciously. The Superior Person touch, which comes across so clearly in the reference to "those who possess a comprehensive knowledge of political economy," was common to almost all the most articulate leading – and would-be leading – workmen of the time.

Nevertheless, in evaluating Wright's testimony one must allow for his anxiety to secure confidence in his own probity while occasioning a discreetly regulated apprehension concerning the general disposition of his class. He had to earn the condescending admiration of his readers while offering them information of a novel sort. Too much stress upon ignorance and indifference would have put a stop to his employment while too much emphasis upon the advanced character of working class attitudes would have led to his own objectivity as a reporter being called into question. Yet he probably got reasonably close to the truth. The "well-to-do", "pushing", "influential" workmen doubtless dismissed Communism as impracticable. What he has to report about the want of intense political feelings and fascination with "philosophical politics" corresponds very well with Marx's complaint concerning the English lack of "the spirit of generalisation and revolutionary ardour." At the same time there is small reason to question his assertion that politically conscious workmen, without being Communists, would sympathise with the Commune in so far as they saw in it the embodiment of republican and patriotic virtues and a protest against militarism and the presence of a privileged class. The reference to "the most passionate indignation among the working classes of this country at the manner in which Communist prisoners were butchered by the mercenary soldiery" is strong and interesting. The men who sat "round workshop breakfast stoves" did not commit their thoughts to paper. Until we have found means of recovering those lost voices we must attend with some respect to Thomas Wright's assertion that "the sympathy of people was with the Communists."

THE ENGLISH WORKING CLASSES AND THE PARIS COMMUNE

By 'The Journeyman Engineer'

It is somewhat important to know whether, apart from the war, which was only an incidental, and to a great extent accidental, phase of the general question, the working classes of England approved of the broad principles and aims of the Paris Communists, and to what extent. In my opinion the working classes of this country did sympathise with the Commune, though not upon strictly Communistic grounds. In what feelings and beliefs their sympathy was founded we will try to make clear.

Average English workmen are not so political as Continental, and especially French, workmen are. Their knowledge of governmental constitutions is limited to a general idea of the differences between the monarchical and republican forms. Their capability of political feeling is dormant until roused by some incidents, or series of incidents, that at once raises their anger, and points to some person or persons against whom it can be directed. They have not the type of mind for which theoretical or philosophical politics have fascinations, or the habits of life which lead to the interchange of political ideas and the keeping alive and intensifying of political feeling. Of late they have come to know that among the ideas of regenerative social systems there is one of a *Commune,* having as its leading object that of placing the labouring classes in a relatively better **position**, not only towards the non-productive classes, but also towards capitalists, as sharers in the results of productive labour; and that is about the extent of what they do know about it. Of such things as St. Simonism and Fourierism, they have, as a rule, never heard; and in any case they have no knowledge of their principles. Their knowledge of the fundamental principles of general political economy is equally scanty, though in this last respect they are probably not more deficient than the majority of Continental workmen, whose minds are continually exercised with ideas of political panaceas for all the social ills of the working classes. Just at present their chief political wish is to unhorse monarchy in this country; but in a general way their political thoughts and aspirations, though they scarcely recognise them as being strictly political, turn exclusively upon improving the position of labour in relation to capital. And this they seek to accomplish by direct action — as, for instance, by strikes and the strengthening of trades-unions — and not by the establishment of entirely new social systems.

Such men as these, it will be easily understood, could not be, so to speak, *en rapport* with the Paris Communists *as Communists*. This average portion of the working classes is the little educated one, below it is the uneducated, above it the better educated section of the general body. Those among them who take an interest in political matters do understand sufficient both of the principles and details of Communism to be able to form an opinion for themselves concerning its merits, and they are opposed to it as a technical system of society. They believe that, carried to its legitimate conclusion it would make the skilful and thrifty workman suffer for those who are neither. There are thousands of well-to-do workmen, men who own houses, have shares in building societies, and money in banks; men also who, by reason of the 'push' and energy which have, as a rule, enabled them to accumulate money or property, are among the most influential of their class and with their class, and these men are keenly opposed to anything that tends to trench upon the 'sacredness' of individual property, or about which there is any savour of the levelling doctrine. Moreover they are of opinion that, though Communism may be a noble idea and a theoretic possibility, it is not practically workable on any considerable scale.

But while the working classes generally had no particular sympathy with the Paris Commune simply as such, they entertained a warm and very decided sympathy with the Communists on the broader-ground that they believed them to be thorough patriots and true republicans. They regarded them with admiration as being men having the courage of their opinions to the extent of fighting and dying for them, and with gratitude as being the soldiers of the general cause of the unprivileged against the privileged classes, and the boldest foes of the hereditary principle in government. The point, however, on which the English working classes were perhaps most unreservedly and emphatically in sympathy with the Paris Commune was that of the latter's avowed desire to extinguish international rivalries; and their being so illustrates some of the characteristic differences between English and Continental workmen to which we have referred. In seeking to effect this object the foreign workmen have, among their other ideas on the subject, some sublime ones about universal brotherhood and the like; but so have not the English workmen. Their motive in wishing to bring about a 'federation of the world' is entirely a practical, some people would say a sordid, one. Through the agency of the Workmen's International Association the working classes of this country generally, and the trade unionists in particular, are striving to effect this extinguishment; but they took up and are persevering in the object simply as a phase of the question of Labour *versus* Capital. They have arrived at the conclusion — the soundness or unsoundness of which need not be argued here — that only by friendly relations and joint action with 'the foreigners' can they hope to make any permanently better terms with capital. The capitalists, they reason, play off the foreigners against them. The mechanical school-master has been abroad, the mechanical arts have spread and are spreading. Branches of trade of which England had once practically a monopoly are now carried on extensively in various parts of the Continent, where labour is cheaper than here. Some of the more thoughtful among English artisans have of late years come to see that strikes, even when successful for the time being, have proved ultimately detrimental to the interests of labour in this country. English manufacturers tendering for contracts, in the face of wages forced from them by strikes, were cut out by foreigners; and worse still, in some instances English capitalists, after being engaged in contests with labour, have established factories abroad, and employed foreign labour to produce the same goods they had previously done at home. It is in connection with these matters that the English workmen are so eager to extinguish international rivalries, so willing to do their part in sinking them. Knowing that to bring about a common good feeling, conjoint action, and a fusion of interests among the working classes throughout the world, was a chief object of the Commune; that some were well on the way to it, and of the leaders of the Commune were also leading men in the Workmen's International Association; knowing this, they sympathised very heartily with them on that point, and wished for their success as a means to that end.

The general idea of the English working classes with regard to the Communist rising was, however, something like this: when the war with Germany was over, there was the royalty of Germany safe in person and covered with glory; while the ex-Emperor of the French, though defeated, was still in a position to live in luxurious ease, and still evincing a desire to thrust himself upon the French nation again. The people at large had borne the bulk of the bitter suffering of the war. One result of the war, however, they fondly believed, had been to purge the country of the imperialism that could create such wars for purposes of dynastic ambition; and this to them seemed almost sufficient compensation for what they had gone through. But simultaneously with the election of Thiers's Republic came rumours of Orleanist and Bonapartist intrigues, and signs of the Republican ministers having an inclination to the imperial system and particularly to that part of it which enabled the government to use the ignorant priest-ridden peasantry as an instrument for over-

136

ruling the — at any rate comparatively — intelligent town populations.

The Communists might have been wrong; but they *did* believe that, though names might be altered, the old accursed thing of a special governing and privileged class would be forced upon the people again, unless the people themselves could prevent it. To attempt to prevent it was the object of the Communists in taking up arms. They wanted a republic in fact as well as name; they believed they were well on the way to it, and that a determined attitude, and, if need be, a determined fight, at the point they had reached, would enable them to attain their desire.

This, in the opinion of English workmen, was substantially the motive and meaning of the rising; and, despite all that has been said against the Communists, they (the English workmen) hold that they fought bravely and disinterestedly, and that their battle was, as we have said, the general battle of the unprivileged against the privileged classes. When Paris was taken there was the most passionate indignation among the working classes of this country at the manner in which Communist prisoners were butchered by the mercenary soldiery, whom shame at the inglorious figure they made when opposed to the Germans should, if nothing else did, have made merciful to their countrymen, who, whatever may be thought of their cause, fought with a bravery that extorted the admiration even of those most bitterly opposed to their political creed. Though the working classes did not approve of the manner in which the Communists destroyed the public buildings, they objected to the proceeding rather as being bad policy than as being, as others argue, utterly unjustifiable and condemnable. They remembered that, in the minds of the Communists, the churches and palaces would be inseparably associated with the sacerdotal tyranny and monarchical selfishness from which the people have suffered so much and so long; and it was as monuments of these things that they were destroyed, not in a spirit of mere vandalism. The working classes bear in mind, too, that, if the Communists slew those they held as hostages, it was not until their own prisoners had been slaughtered like beasts. It would have been infinitely more noble on the part of the Communists to have left such an act undone, though no credit would have been allowed to them even in that case. It was a stern deed and a bloody one, but, according to the laws governing such evil things, it was a justifiable one. Had it been committed by the hired soldiery of a monarchy, its harshness might have been condemned, but their right to do it would not have been questioned.

The victims of the act were avowedly held as hostages, and were saved alive long after the strict rule of warlike reprisals would have justified their execution. The conduct of the Versailles soldiers in persisting in the wanton slaying of unarmed Communist prisoners was what really led to the death of the hostages. To stigmatise the shooting of the hostages as assassination and murder, while calling the wholesale butchering of Communist prisoners executions, shows partisanship; and the working-class idea on this point is that partisanship and a desire to misrepresent are what the leading English papers have, in varying degrees, shown in dealing with the Commune. Anyone taking the general tone of English public opinion from the 'organs' which are popularly supposed to embody it would have been led to the conclusion that horror and reprobation were the universal feelings in regard to the Commune. But anyone who could have penetrated into working-class circles, who, let us say, could have sat with the men round workshop breakfast stoves, or in workshop dining or reading rooms, who could have followed them into the lodges of their trade and benefit societies and to their own firesides; anyone who could have done this in the Metropolis, and such districts as the Black Country, the Tyne, Clyde, and the manufacturing towns of Lancashire, would have found from the talk of the men that newspaper public opinion was the opinion of a section only; that, as we have been pointing out, the sympathy of people was with the Communists. What is said in this article is no mere expression of individual opinion; it is the generalised opinion of working men as expressed among themselves in the places in which they most do congregate. The intention of the article is not to insist that the opinions are right or dispute that they are wrong, but to point out that they do exist, and are firmly believed to be right by those who hold them.

In the tone of the English newspapers upon the Communist rising the working classes saw a special significance. As we have already said, they have but little knowledge of the technicalities of political systems, but they have a considerable degree of the useful quality called 'rough common sense;' and this enabled them to see that, whatever the rising in Paris might be called, or whatever might be its theoretic details, it was essentially a battle between 'the two parties who still divide the world – of those who want and those who have.' Knowing this, they saw from the tone of the English newspapers that 'those who have' were banding together throughout Europe to give their moral support to those who were fighting the Commune; and so, independently of the instinctive feeling leading them thereto, they argued that it also behoved the party of 'those who want' to band together, and throw in their sympathy with the Communists. At the same time, theirs was not a mere blind party sympathy. What their idea of the meaning of the rising was we have stated, and the monarchist intriguing that has been going on since the fall of the Commune furnishes the most ample justification of the belief of the Communists that the old thing was to be thrust upon them again. What the Communists wanted – what if granted to them would have prevented their rising – was perfectly just. Simply put, the sum of their demands was only that those who had been elected as Republicans should show themselves to be really Republicans. The real traitors to France were not the Communists, but those who, after being chosen by the people as Republicans, lent a too willing ear to monarchist intrigues.

139

In connection with this matter of the sympathy of the English working classes with the Paris Commune, it is a significant fact that the English workmen find satisfaction and consolation in the belief that the Communists, though beaten, have not failed. They hold that

They never fail who die in a great cause.

And to their thinking the Communist rising was a great, even if not a faultless, cause. They believe that the rising, though defeated in its immediate aim, will yet be a material caution to, and restraint upon, the 'right divine' school, not only in France but throughout Europe. If it is, so much the better for the peoples of Europe; if it is not, so much the worse for the party of right divine.

The spirit that in France took the name of Communism is stalking abroad, and it is an evil one — one that, if not exorcised, will mean social disturbance, and may come to mean social destruction. It has entered into the minds of the English working classes, and is sinking deeper, and becoming more dangerous as it sinks. The very concessions that it might have been thought would have laid this spirit have only served to embitter it. Repealed corn laws, and extended franchise, and other things of that kind that they have fought for and won, under the firm persuasion that their condition would be materially improved by these, have in result left matters pretty much as they were — the rich growing richer and the poor poorer. It is not, of course, the fault of other sections of society that such measures have failed to realise the expectations of the working classes, but the disappointing experience has embittered them against the present constitution of society. They say now that these things may be very well in their way, but that it is apparent thay they do not go to the root of things, that it is mere frittering to be struggling for Acts of Parliament, that what is wanted is a thorough change. If asked what was the change they desired, they would be unable to give any definite answer. They do not know, and, still worse, they scarcely care; their feeling is, that no change that would arise out of a disruption of the present state of society could be worse for them, while any such change might easily be better for them. In this frame of mind they are likely to grasp at any specious plan that promised to bring about revolutionary changes beneficial to them; and still more likely to be reckless as to the means whereby it was sought to carry out such plans. One fixed idea, however, they have, and that is, that the present constitution of society is unfair to them, and that the power of regulating that constitution is monopolised by those whose interest it is to make it continue unfair, and who persistently act for their own interests, yielding nothing until it is extorted from them by fear, and even then trying to give only the name, not the substance of the thing. They believe that before they can rise the class which is composed of the rich, the titled, and the privileged must be brought down, and the power of governing and law-making wrested from them. They have come to be of opinion that between that class and their own there is a natural and deadly antagonism. Further, they believe that the other class hold the same view, and act upon it. In justification of this latter belief they point to such facts as the hesitation of English ministers to say decisively whether or not Communists flying to England would be treated as criminals or refugees; the manner in which English newspapers spoke of the Communists as a handful of ruffians, bloodthirsty scoundrels, and so forth, and the cold-blooded murdering of the Communist prisoners without any form of trial.

If the feeling of the working classes of Paris upon this latter point may be judged by that of the working classes of this country, it may be safely said that the deaths of those prisoners will never be either forgotten or forgiven until they are avenged. The soldiers of the Commune, it is held, showed practically that their view of duty was

Like men to fight,
And hero-like to die;

but instead of being treated as prisoners of war, their blood was shed as that of beasts; and if ever an opportunity comes and it will be closely watched for — the shedding of it will be repaid in kind. The 'officers and gentlemen' who ordered or allowed this butchers' work have sown the seeds of a harvest that their class are, in all probability, destined to reap in blood. The Commune has only been scotched, not killed. Its essential elements are left alive, and they will breed and brood, and under that name, or some other, break forth again.

The existence among the working classes of such opinions as those we have been speaking of is a thing that should be heedfully noted by society. Mr. Gladstone has expressed his belief that such opinions had only to be left unnoticed to sink into 'that oblivion which was their destined and their proper portion'. Whether or not oblivion is their 'proper portion' is a question that need not be discussed here; but leaving them unnoticed will certainly not make it their destined portion, and, with the Communist war staring the world in the face, it is wonderful how a really great statesman could think that it would. No person, we suppose, will attempt to argue that the Communist rising was the result of any hasty plot or mere passing impulse. The spirit and opinion that made it possible must have been existing and intensifying for years. As they were shared by millions, they must have been known to those opposed to them; and it can therefore only be concluded that they had been left unnoticed in the hope that they would sink, and ultimately in the belief that they had sunk, into oblivion. Otherwise it is impossible to account for Jules Favre making the fatal condition that the National Guard should be left armed; or the fact of the Thiers' Government being so ill-prepared for the rising, so slow to comprehend its extent after it had taken place. The policy of leaving unnoticed is a dangerous as well as a mistaken one. Those who won't see in such matters become in time those who cannot see, and they mistake the sinking into lethargy of their own perceptions for the sinking to oblivion of the opinions to which they are opposed.

That the views both of the French Communists and the English working classes are to a considerable extent chimerical is, of course, obvious to those who possess a comprehensive knowledge of political economy; but unfortunately for themselves, the working classes have not this knowledge. They do not see that a mere reconstruction of present society on grounds more favourable to the interests of labour is really in the same category with, though upon a larger scale than, those measures which have proved to them, in comparison with their anticipation, a sort of Dead Sea fruit. They imagine that there could be a form of government by means of which the labouring classes could be raised to and maintained in a position of material comfort. They fail to see that *any* form of government can only be *part* of a scheme of social regeneration; that to depend on that alone is to overlook fundamental principles not only of political economy, but of *nature*; principles that would speedily override every temporary expedient in the way of changed forms of government. But even those who can see that the working classes make the disastrous mistake of imagining a part, a mere detail, to be the whole, must admit that there is much in their ideas that to little-educated people must appear plausible; while at least some of these ideas are certainly founded on principles of justice. It is the plausible portions that catch the minds of the working classes. Though there is undoubtedly much that is wrong in their ideas, they do not see it, and consequently the ideas are in their minds practically operative as fully right and just, and in their being so regarded lies the chief point of the whole matter as it affects society. If is the one great reason why the opinions should be made known, and why they should *not* be left unnoticed. To ignore them is not the way to deal with them, or prevent their culminating in violence. Those who would consign them to oblivion should show themselves willing to concede the parts of them that are just, and seek to qualify those holding them to understand that the other parts are erroneous. It is the duty of those in power to so deal with them. If they neglect this duty, or wilfully shut their eyes to the fact that such opinions largely prevail and are still spreading among the working classes, the responsibility will in a great measure be upon our rulers if ever we see such wild work in England as there has lately been in France.

V

Occasional Voices 1

FROM *REYNOLD'S*: *THE REPUBLICAN*
AND THE *INTERNATIONAL HERALD*

EDITOR'S INTRODUCTION

There is room for an intensive study of the 'voiceless' workman's response to the Commune, but it is doubtful whether it would be easy or whether it would afford the basis for reliable generalisations. At any rate, our present concern is solely with voices that were raised and raised in defence.

Gracchus of *Reynold's Newspaper* shows how the tradition of hostility to privilege; sinecures; and Old Corruption could reach up to a positive appreciation of the Commune.

The report of the Republican Meeting in Hyde Park appeared in Reynold's on 23rd April 1871. The International Democratic Assocation was set up by a dissident branch of the I.W.M.A. whose moving spirits were Le Lubez and the German Lassallean, Weber. (Collins and Abramsky op cit p. 195). However, the General Council of the International, defying the advice of Engels, associated itself with this meeting. Mr. Murray, described as "chairman of the chief centre" was James Murray, an old follower of Bronterre O'Brien who went on to become a leading figure in the socialist revival of the eighteen eighties. One of the most striking features of the 'Address' which Radford read was the reference to the Constitution of 1793. Karl Marx himself noticed the continuity although he chose not to dwell upon it. (*Archiv Marksa i Engelsa Vol* III (viii) Moscow, 1934 p.370).

The third item is the editorial from the *Republican* of 1st May 1871 which begins as a commentary upon the demonstration reported by *Reynold's.* The men who spoke on 16 April had indeed received an unfavourable press. The *Graphic* (29 April 1871) described them as engaged in "the war of the penny against the pound . . . . . It is ignorance defying knowledge to try a fall." The *Republican*, after defending the speakers , although in somewhat patronising terms, goes on to show how the Commune might be justified in the antique language of natural law and natural right.

The menacing open letter to Samuel Morley (Paris To-day — London To-morrow) comes from the front page of the same issue of the *Republican*. James Harvey belongs in a tradition that can be traced right back to the seventeenth century: a tradition which joined "true theories of money" to demands for the recovery of the land from the descendants of those who had stolen it. After all, both land and money tended to monopoly. It is ironical that Harvey, who subscribed to such ideas, should have fastened upon that arch bourgeois, Samuel Morley, as a representative of the 'Thing' which had to be over-turned. Harvey's theories, which were not without a certain economic as well as historic justification, worked to conceal the general ascendancy of the industrial and commercial bourgeosie behind the special interests of land and of finance capital.

The *Republican* was a highly cantankerous paper. The proprietor of the copyright was Daniel Chatterton, author of the *Revolution in the Police and the coming Revolution in the Army and Navy (n.d. 1872?)*.   In the eighties he produced a scarcely legible sheet entitled, *Chatterton's Commune*. It had no programme beyond the physical extermination of the bourgeosie to the last man, woman, and child.

THE COMMUNE

Reynold's Newspaper, Sunday, April 9, 1871

To the Editor of Reynolds's Newspaper

Sir, — The monarchical mind has become uneasy and distressed by the extraordinary aspect of affairs in Paris. The working classes of that city, if left to themselves, would prove to the world how easy it is to govern a country without kings or nobles, and how much more cheaply and prosperously a nation can be ruled without such incumbrances. The working men who have been installed in power at Paris by the suffrages of their fellow-citizens showed at once an extraordinary aptitude for government. Even the *Times,* which hates and abominates anything approaching democracy, or any one in the form of a democrat, candidly admits that the working class Government of Paris has displayed more sense, energy, resolution, and purpose than its rival at Versailles, which comprises some of what are termed the most eminent statesmen of Europe.

The Government of the people was not, neither could we expect it would be, inaugurated without some blood being shed. The generals that were executed fell victims to the temporary fury of a populace goaded to almost madness by the recollection of the injuries, sufferings, and wrongs it had so long endured under Monarchical and Imperial institutions, and blinded to any other consideration than the dread of their restoration. The Government of the working classes has been reviled for having demanded money from the Bank of France, and for levying requisitions on many of the rich inhabitants of Paris, who are well able to meet them. M. Assi and his colleagues have been abused for passing a decree to the effect that tenants in Paris shall not be required to pay their landlords the rents due on the quarter ending October of last year, and on those terminating in January and April of this. Of course, the influential and moneyed classes raised an outcry against such a measure, and called it spoliation and confiscation, but it is in every respect equitable and defensible. Hitherto, landowners.and houseowners in France, like those in England, having been all potential in the legislature, framed laws that, whilst protecting at every point their own interests, were extremely oppressive and arbitrary towards the humbler order. Now, however, that Paris has been ruled by a Government of upright, honest, and conscientious men — who make laws for the benefit of the many, and not for the privileged few — things are altered, and justice is done. It would have been the height of injustice to have allowed owners of houses in Paris who left that city during the siege, and escaped the horrors of famine and the perils of bombardment by taking flight to England or elsewhere, to have returned when all danger and hardship was passed, and insist on being paid the arrears of rent that had occurred during their absence. The middle-class Government of M. Thiers was desirous of passing a sort of medium measure, leaning, however, more to the landlord than the tenant; but the working man's Government, viewing the matter in its true light, at once took the bull by the horns, and relieved the tenants of all responsibility contracted during the siege.

Then, again, we find those clever-headed, noble-hearted, patriotic men — Assi, Pyat, etc — disdaining to plunder the public awarding themselves the very modest sum of twelve pounds per month for their services — or less than a clever journeyman's wages What a contrast does this conduct present to that of all monarchical and imperial rulers who by revolution or succession come to the throne! They themselves, with their friends and followers, at once fix upon the nation, and, leech-like, begin sucking its life's blood, its vitals. When Louis Napoleon became the ruler of France, what a scramble there was for the loaves and fishes by his family and his followers! Adventurers of the most infamous character, like De Morny, St. Arnaud, etc., not only obtained enormous fortunes by the corruptest practices, but they were ennobled by their master. His relations at once fastened themselves on the purse of the nation, and every one belonging to, or connected with, the Bonaparte brood in the remotest degree was enriched at the nation's. expense. Indeed, we need not look beyond our own shores to find a striking contrast between royal rapacity here and plebeian disinterestedness and conscientiousness in Paris.

M. Thiers thought to re-establish the old regime of Monarchical extravagance, under the guise of Republican institutions, and was about constituting himself a President, and installing himself at the Palace of the Elysee, with a nice little income of one hundred and twenty thousand pounds per annum, his ministers and followers having proportionate salaries. But even the *Times* admits that the men who undertake to rule Paris for the moderate salaries of twelve pounds per month, have displayed far more astuteness than the old gentlemen who were about bestowing upon themselves comparatively exorbitant stipends. The Parisians, at all events, preferred the cheaper and better article, and, consequently, M. Thiers's pretty little projects were nipped in the bud.

The proposition of the Communal Government to sell the palaces of France, with the lands and forests appertaining thereto, and with the proceeds pay off the German debt, and so get rid of the foreigner, is an admirable idea. If France is to be a Republic, of what use are palaces, forests, and hunting grounds to the nation? These costly establishments are kept up there and elsewhere in order that they may afford amusement to royalty, and shed, as it were, a fictitious halo around that institution. Similar excellent legislative measures, as judicious as they are equitable, and calculated to prevent the pressure of exorbitant taxation being felt more heavily than heretofore, have alarmed all monarchs and monarchists. The press of this country, faithful to its detestable mission of depreciating and reviling everything that is of thoroughly liberal and equitable character, and every one who denounces the rascalities, the rapacity, the iniquities of royalty and aristocracy, are scurrilising all the true-hearted, hard-headed, patriotic men, that are showing to the world how a nation can be well governed by others than those of the patrician and bloodsucking races. The Parisian Government is one elected by the poor for the poor — by the representatives of the masses for the masses. It is cheap, progressive, and would be endurable, if left to itself. But such an example of good and economic government by the people for the people is an eye-sore to kings, nobles, and all those who fatten and thrive in luxury and indolence on the toil of others. Hence it is that nothing will be left undone — no gold spared to uproot such a state of things. The longer it exists, the more striking will become the contrast between good and economical, as typified by the Commune; and bad and expensive government, as typified by empires and monarchies.

The outbreak of civil war is deeply to be deplored, but the blood already shed is upon the heads of Thiers, the Orleanists, and others who have been striving to restore a monarchy of some sort or another. The force of gold and intrigue may vanquish the Commune, and uproot the government of the people. They may overthrow the Commune, but they cannot root out or destroy the idea which originated it. There is scarce a Court in Europe that is not terrified at the existence of a democratic Government, fulfilling some of the noblest missions of democracy — or, in other words, preventing the rich and the powerful from plundering the poor and the helpless, asserting the rights of labour to enjoy the wages of its industry, without being diminished to almost nothingness, in order to support herds of harpies that, clad in imperial purple, in lawn sleeves, in ermined gowns, with coronets on their heads, in broadcloth, with no other title to consideration than their bank-books — harpies such as these that have spread themselves over the face of Europe like a flock of locusts, to eat up the production of the labouring mass. Such as those are the curse of humanity, the affliction of the world. The time must come when, like vermin, they will be extirpated; and the time has come when the eyes of the English, and other working men, are being opened to the fact that kings, princes, nobles, prelates, and millionaires are not needful to the good government of a nation, but precisely the contrary.

Gracchus

REPUBLICAN MEETING IN HYDE PARK

Reynold's Newspaper, Sunday, April 23, 1871.

Notwithstanding the unfavourable state of the weather on Sunday, in response to the appeal of the council of the International Democratic Association, a great many people assembled on Clerkenwell-green at three o'clock in order to proceed to Hyde-Park for the purpose of voting an address to the Commune and National Guards of Paris. The procession left the green headed by a brass band, and the large red flag of the association surmounted by the red cap of liberty. There were numerous other flags in the procession, one bearing the inscription, "Vive la Commune", another "Long live the Universal Republic, Social and Democratic," and others with Republican mottoes. At Hyde-Park there was a very large concourse of persons.

Mr. Murray, the chairman of the chief centre, urged that the meeting was one of the most important ever held upon that ground. Other meetings had been held there for party purposes, but this was for the benefit of the entire human family, inasmuch as the Communists whom they wished to encourage and support were fighting for the rights of the whole human race, and the liberation of labour from the trammels of capital. The persons who at present had the upper hand in Paris were not the bloodthirsty ruffians they had been described by malicious journalists. He deliberately charged the press of England with having done its utmost to bring about the state of bloodshed from which Paris was suffering. Not the Red Republicans, but their enemies were answerable for what was taking place. Former revolutions in Paris had been put down for their virtues by the vices of men who feared that their monopoly of government and emolument would leave them for ever. It was because the ruling classes of the world wished to live as giants by dwarfing their fellowmen — because

152

they wished to live in affluence without working or thinking, that they were opposed to social justice being done, and opposed therefore to revolution. Such persons were never opposed to revolution aimed against the middle classes, of whom they were jealous, but directly it was aimed against themselves, they denounced the movement in the strongest terms. (Loud cheers.)

Mr. Radford read "the address". It was headed, "An address to the members of the Commune, the Central Committee, the National Guards, and the working classes of Paris, adopted by the people of London assembled in public meeting convened by the International Democratic Association, and held in Hyde-Park, on Sunday, April 16, 1871. Its principal points are as follows:—

"We send you fraternal greeting in the name of the Universal Republic. We tender you our most heartfelt thanks for the sublime work you are doing in behalf of human liberty, and in defence of your communal rights. We recognise in you the pioneers of progress and the architects of a new and purer social state; whilst we regard your oppressors, the men of Versailles, as the worthy disciples of the Man of December, and as the cowardly and mercenary instruments of European despots. Mainly 'elected' by the priest-ridden peasantry, with Prussian bayonets at their throats to settle simply the conditions of peace, their mission is ended, and that ignominiously, in the sale of a portion of your countrymen to the German brigands. Nevertheless, they still exercise the 'authority' exacted, and arrogate to themselves the right to enslave you. We salute your proclamation of the Commune, or local self-government, as the resurrection of the glorious era of the first French Republic, which, in the Constitution of 1793, Article 58, 59, and 60, placed direct legislation by the people into the hands of then existing Communes. We wish you success in your heroic defence of the Commune, and trust the other great centres of industry in France will prove true to their Republican traditions, and emulate your illustrious example; for we know that a number of free cities and independent communities would, under the application of the federative principle, develop the resources of the country and constitute an insuperable barrier to oppression and usurpation. We rejoice that amid the many arduous duties you are called upon to perform you are deliberating on important questions relating to organic social reform which are intimately connected with the welfare of the people. We quite approve your project for liquidating the heavy war indemnity by selling the palaces and appropriating the Crown lands to national purposes; and we can only regret that our fellow-countrymen are not yet sufficiently educated to imitate your noble example. The 'Government' of Versailles, if Republican in name, has evinced its monarchical predilections by not having immediately disposed of the 'royal' domiciles; the reimposition of kingcraft is beyond doubt contemplated. We are gratified to learn that you have decreed the separation of Church and State, and hope you will restore the Church property — monopolised by the priests — to the use of the nation; for a *pseudo*-religion which has made itself the willing accomplice of Bonaparte's bloody deeds, whose 'cardinals' have all been decorated and subsidised by that monster, and which has helped to thwart and delay the realisation of the brotherhood of nations, stands condemned .... We mourn with you the loss of the brave Flourens and the many other worthy men who have been so barbarously murdered by the myrmidons of the rebels of Versailles, consisting of imperial gendarmes, police spies, and ignorant Papal Zouaves. They have, in thus dedicating and consecrating their lives to the cause of truth, of justice, of civilisation, of humanity, as against the cause of ignorance, of retrogression, of barbarism, and inhumanity, set us a magnificent example of self-abnegation and disinterestedness, and one to which posterity may not improbably owe their deliverance. They are a loss to us as well as to you. They were part of the army marching to redeem the human race from all sorrow and slavery, and we claim them as martyrs on behalf of human progress. It

154

now remains for us to abjure the impious lies concerning you, and the motives of your enemies, promulgated by our venal and corrupt press, which is the instrument of despotisms that thrive on monopolies of all kinds, and interested in the subjugation and exploitation of the wealth producers of all countries. It is arrayed, as it always has been, with a few honourable exceptions, on the side of might against right. It never fails to calumniate and traduce the real character of all great men and movements. It is enraged at your sublime efforts for self government because it perceives an example likely to increase the love of liberty among our down-trodden fellow-countrymen, and thus hasten the day when the fraud-begotten power of all tyrants shall disappear before the power and intelligence of the united peoples of all lands. And although our unscrupulous and moribund 'Government' may seek, and, no doubt, are seeking, in collusion with the rebels of Versailles, to precipitate foreign intervention in order to annihilate your rights, we the people of London, believing you to be fighting for the liberty of the world, and the regeneration of mankind, hereby express our profound admiration for the grandeur of your enterprise, and tender you the honest, uncompromising hand of friendship and fellowship. Long live the Universal Republic, democratic and social."

A resolution, "That the address just read be forwarded to the Commune of Paris on behalf of this meeting " was carried by a show of hands, only three or four voting against it.

The proceedings ended about a quarter before seven with three cheers for the Universal Republic, and with the singing of the Marseillaise.

THE REPUBLICAN MOVEMENT
AND THE COMMUNE OF PARIS
The Republican, May 1, 1871

On Sunday, the 16th ult., a demonstration took place in Hyde-Park, to express sympathy with the men of Paris, who, in the name of the "Commune," are battling for the "Rights of Man" against the "Might" of men that robs them of their natural inheritance by a craftily contrived system which elevates the few and degrades the many — a system which in this enlightened (?) 19th century impels the *canaille* of the French capital to cast the hazard of the die in a struggle against an agglomeration of well-trained, well-equipped, and "highly educated" traitors, such as Thiers, Favre, Macmahon, Trochu, Ducrot, Vinoy, Canrobert, and a host of other merciless and "bloody philanthropists," whose occupation will be gone the moment the principles of the "Commune" are fairly understood and established. Although the weather was unpropitious and the very elements seemed to be ringing a funeral peal for the fratricidal struggle now pending between capitalists and mere labourers — there could not have been less than from 6,000 to 7,000 people assembled. We do not believe that all those present were sympathisers — far from it — for such a cause, what sympathy can the vacant-minded gossiper, the idling, every day lounger, the base detectives and the baser spies have, for those "respectable" and unknown mechanics who are not "public orators," and who do not come to the front on every occasion to order, from an order given by "the men of order." In London, as in Paris, when certain individuals not known to be political traffickers come to the surface to express convictions, which are only attained by years of perseverance and study — a base and hireling press comes down upon them to malign and misrepresent their every effort and conclusion. This is placing man's destiny in the hands of his fellow-men rather than in the hands of his Creator. Here is spread the wide entrance door of tyranny. What may not the corrupt legislature see fit to declare to be right or wrong, duty or misdemeanour. And what is it that the "Commune" in Paris and its sympathisers in London ask that, like a scare-crow, it alarms the "superficially intelligent" and respectable classes? True, the men who spoke at this demonstration are but little known as public men, and so much the better — for whilst some of these "public men" have *so much "reputation"* to lose, these simple-minded men have nothing of so valuable and weighty importance. Their printed address, too (which is given *in extenso* in *Reynolds's*) does them credit — not perfect, perhaps, as a piece of literary composition, nevertheless we heartily recommend it to the perusal of those refined "intelligences" who occasionally make up the compound known as the "Queen's Speech." Seeing, then, the terrible odds of the powers of Darkness now pitted against our Parisian brethren, — we, too, side with these "Rebels," and ask "If the law forbids that which nature allows, does it not restrain human liberty? If it enjoins a duty which nature does not impose, does it not inflict an act of tyranny upon man? If it confers a right which nature has not ordained, it robs some one or many of that which it confers, and works injustice among men. If we comprehend our French brothers and those of our London brothers aright, it is that their conclusions embrace all human kind. Produce a man, and to them you exhibit a being endowed with the sum of those faculties and dispositions which they have demonstrated as pertaining to humanity. The idea of man, to them, is but the embodying of certain known and well-defined powers, sentiments, and passions in a human being. They know his desires, emotions, and faculties — what he wants, what he wills, and what he suffers. No distance renders his case uncertain. Colour clouds not his observation, nor does time outlaw his claims. He is a Man — *that* suffices to define his certain nature and his ultimate destiny. Climate, country, distance, government, the distinctions of society, can neither change his nature, nor annihilate his rights. The king, the subject, the master, and the slave — each is a man; no more nor nothing less than a man; and in the eye of this philosophy, each is bound to acknowledge the other to be a man, with all the rights pertaining to humanity. This is the science which the men of the Commune and those of their *confreres* who get up the demonstration seek to inculcate. This science does not deny that a very great disparity exists among men in regard to their mental constitutions. On the contrary, it asserts that there are vast individual and national differences in respect to both intellectual and moral endowments, and that this difference is mainly dependent upon their physical organisation. But each man possesses, nevertheless, the faculties and sentiments peculiar to humanity, although, as to each of his natural powers, one man may differ from another, either in the strength, activity, or peculiar combination of his faculties. We assert, therefore, that mankind have one *common nature,* which is now *ascertained* and *well defined,* and to this end the men of the future will inevitably have to direct their attention whether they be Republicans or otherwise — that the Commune may be overpowered and have to succumb to brute force may be its more immediate fate; but the *idea* will again rekindle the fiery spirit which shall ultimately bring it through its seventy times seven heated furnace. From Oxford we learn that a Republican club has been formed by the students of Wadham College, and that the terms of admission to membership is an entrance fee of ten shillings.

PARIS TODAY – LONDON TOMORROW

The Republican, May 1, 1871

To Samuel Morley, Esq., M.P. for Bristol

You are a capitalist, or rather a monied man, – or, to speak correctly, a man who has credit for possessing money – I say credit, for as the law of England is that our only money is the sovereign of the full-weight and fineness, it is preposterous to suppose that you or your bank have the sovereigns, if you were tried on any given morning. Being a capitalist, you stand forth as being *par emphasis* the friend of the working man. You ascend platforms surrounded by Odgers, Applegarths, and Potters, and you advocate emigration, or any other scheme that has a philanthropic twang about it.

Now, Sir, in your position it is impossible that your advocacy of the cause of Labour can be anything but pure dilettantism, for the claims of property and the claims of labour, – *i.e.*, the creator of all property are totally opposed – so opposed, that, as the present state of Paris shows us, there is war to the knife between them.

Let us see what the *Times,* the organ of the monied class – that is, the *respectable* class – says.

"The first remark that the world will make on these events is, that the forces in Paris hostile to the existing structure of society prove to be more formidable than *"French Respectability"* has believed. We see the leaders of this unquiet, hungry population, and can judge what manner of men they are. They are able – they have education – they write well, and publish better proclamations than their opponents. How is it that a few brooding, concentrated men should have succeeded in learning so largely the thoughts of the working class?" I will tell the *Times* it is because the working class, – that is, men who make everything – are, under the cunning devices, law-protected

159

rent, and law-protected *interest,* robbed of their reward, which, by these same devices, are transferred to the speculators of the Bourse; to the class who hold the land; to the class that has got the money, or the credit of having it. These are the classes that supply those crowds of *Flaneurs* who beset the boulevards; those sippers of absinthe, who play in the morning at dominoes, and sit in front of their *cafes* gossipping, and who make little *Thiers* the god of the day.

This outburst in Paris is easily explained. The landlords demand rents for shops and houses which, during the siege, have been unoccupied and unlet. The creditor class have exacted, or tried to exact, the uttermost farthing from the debtor class, though they knew the Prussians were abstracting all the gold out of France.

Is not London seething with the same spirit of discontent? And is not London in the same situation as Paris? Have we not a landlord class, grinding rack-rent from the poverty-stricken Londoners? Have we not money-lenders, bill-brokers, capitalists, loan societies, pawnbrokers, all screwing usurious interest from the debtors? It only wants a combination of circumstances — say a bad harvest, and a run for gold to bring the battle between property and labour to the same issue in this country. The propertied class is the creditor interest, the working-class is the debtor class.

French respectability! — And what is the criterion of respectability in the eyes of the *Times?* Is it not that of the witness in Thurtell's trial, who vouched for the respectability of a man because "he kept a gig." This mouthpiece of Lombard Street; this organ of the monied power, from Lord Overstone and Baron Rothschild, down to the pawnbroker and Scotch pedlar, can see no respectability in arms sinewy with wielding the sledge hammer, in brows bathed in honest sweat, in faces begrimed with the soot of the forge. With the *Times,* the idlers of the *cafe,* and the loungers of the Rue Rivoli, are the *truly respectable,* and the watchers of the turn of the market at the Bourse are the backbone of society.

How long is the present dreadful system to last?

How near are we from "*Shooting Niagara?*"

So long as the annuitant class, those who live on rents, on loans, on shares, on exorbitant usury, can bribe the best out of our ranks to defend their injustice and their robbery; so long as in France they can bribe national guards, gendarmes, and serjeants-deville; so long as in England they can depend on soldiers and police, so long as the system may run. These, these men for a time may be true; once, twice — nay, a third time, they may mow down their brothers, friends, and companions with musketry, but not always. Thomas Carlyle points to the helmeted giant posted at the Horse Guards, and prophecies that, regularly as he is to be seen in his sentry-box, so long things may hold together, but his co-mate at the Tuilleries has disappeared. And how long will he be seen in London?

That is the question.

As to you, Mr. Morley, you cannot possibly be sincere in your assumed devotion to a class whose interests are diametrically opposed to yours. Take your side — stand by your order. You would only desert the working men in their utmost need.

Liverpool, April, 1871.   *James Harvey*

VI

Frederic Harrison

EDITOR'S BIOGRAPHICAL NOTES

HARRISON, Frederic (1831-1923) Lawyer, man of letters, Positivist. Born London, October 18 1831. The eldest, but not the first born, child of Frederick and Jane Harrison. His father, trained as an architect, became a prosperous stockbroker. His mother was born in Ulster: a protestant of Scottish origin. His brother, Charles, was a first member of L.C.C. and an M.P. He attended Kings College School (1840-49). Went to Oxford as a Scholar of Wadham College in 1849. Under the influence of Richard Congreve he advanced to Positivism more rapidly than Beesly, more slowly than Bridges. Placed in 1st Class in Lit. Hum. and in 4th in History and Law (1853). He became fellow of Wadham 1854 and Tutor there until 1856. Called to the Bar at Lincoln's Inn (1858), he was active on behalf of building workers during the 'Payment by the Hour Dispute' 1861-62 and read a paper on Strikes in the Building Trades to the Social Science Association (1862). He taught at the Working Men's College, 1859-62, but was dissatisfied with genteel students and contemptuous of F. D. Maurice's intellectual weakness. From early sixties until mid-seventies he was a prolific contributor to Labour weeklies and radical monthlies as Positivist, Social Investigator and Critic of "plutonomy" i.e. abstract, ahistorical, "Vulgar" political economy. He was offered, but declined, the editorship of the *Bee-Hive* and the *Commonwealth* in 1865. He was a Member of the Committee for the Benefit of Miners, 1864. He was a strong supporter of Polish and Italian Liberation movements and a violent opponent of imperialism in Asia and Africa. He was an active member of the Jamaica Committee (1866) and author of *Martial Law: Six Letters to the Daily News* published as *Jamaica Papers No. V* (1867). Vice President of the Reform League 1866, he contributed an essay "England and France" to *International Policy* (1866) and one on Foreign Policy to *Questions for a Reformed Parliament* (1867)

A member of the Royal Commission on Trade Unions 1867-69; with T. Hughes and Lord Lichfield, he drafted the Minority Report. He prepared a detailed appendix which Hughes accepted and which the Government adopted in its Trade Union Act, 1871 — the foundation of the Labour Law, subject to temporary reverses, from then until now. In 1869 Harrison was appointed Examiner for Jurisprudence, Roman Law and Constitutional History for the Council of Legal Education. He was secretary to the Royal Commission for Digesting the Law 1869-70.

Although never a socialist and increasingly conservative from the eighties, Harrison did advocate the extension of public ownership and control. (See in particular, *Order and Progress,* 1875).

He regularly contributed to the *Bee-Hive* on all aspects of the Labour Laws question, 1871-75. With Beesly he attacked George Howell's direction of the trade union agitation, 1872. He subsequently blew hot and cold on the wisdom of independent labour-politics. 1874-75 he wrote *Tracts for Trade Unionists* Nos. 1 & 2 being *"Imprisonment for Breach of Contracts"* and *"Workmen and the Law of Conspiracy".* He frequently attended and addressed the TUC until the Nottingham Congress of 1883 where the delegates denied him the right to speak against Land Nationalisation. His stock was further lowered in the Labour world by his contribution to the Industrial Remuneration Conference (1885). Although he had declined invitations to stand for Parliament in the seventies, Harrison came forward as Liberal and Home Rule candidate for London University in 1886. He was defeated 2 to

1 by the Liberal Unionist. From 1889-1893 he was Alderman of the L.C.C. A Pro-Boer, he supported the first World War and condemned Bolshevism.

In the Positivist split of 1878, Harrison sided with Beesly and J. H. Bridges. He became by far the best-known and prolific Positivist writer and lecturer in England. In 1870 he married a cousin, Ethel Harrison. They had four sons and one daughter. Harrison died at Bath on 14 January, 1923 in his ninety-second year.

*   *   *

The following articles appeared in the *Fortnightly Review* for May and August 1871. They cost Harrison a great effort. He wrote to John Morley, editor of the *Fortnightly:* "Tyrant, take your pound of flesh. Your copy has gone this morning (24 April) to the printer. It was finished at 2.00 a.m. this morning – with many a groan for my task-master. Go! I feel like Antonio having made his last speech – like the beaver who has just bitten off his own ....s and flung them at the hunter, like Caliban before Prospero – ugh! curses, toads, newts; ah! I feel my bones ache. You are the best of masters and yet the hatred I feel for you at these moments enables me to realise the enmity between workmen and employer all over the world."

"The neutral observers of the spot" whom Harrison declares to be his informants were probably the French Positivists Lafitte, Robinet, Semerie although he may have had other correspondents inside Paris. It is hardly likely that their 'neutrality' would have been recognised by the Counter-Revolution, but that was characteristic of the Counter-Revolution.

"The two chief leaders of the people .... sentenced to death for an old political offence" were Blanqui and Flourens.

The "Massacre of the Place Vendôme" refers to the events of 22nd March: the defeat of a demonstration staged by the Party of Order. According to Lissagary: *History of the Commune of 1871* (1902) p.114 the aggression was so evidently on the side of the Counter-Revolution that none of the twenty court-martials that subsequently searched into every detail ever alluded to the affair of the Place Vendôme.

The reader will notice how Harrison, for all his Positivist crotchets, manages to see the Revolution in its many-sidedness while suggesting that all this diversity was united through the class struggle. He may conclude that there was more merit in this 'instant history' than in many subsequent works of mature reflection. Thus, Harrison struggled to uncover the facts and to relate them within a complex framework of interpretation. He accepted complexity without complaining of "the maddeningly complex problem" of accounting for "mid-Spring madness that engulfed Paris in 1871." He was, however, without the benefit of guidance from Sir Denis Brogan. According to Professor R. L. Williams, *The French Revolution of 1870-71* (1969) p.114 Sir Denis gave us "the fairest brief, and recent, remark about the Commune when he wrote: "The Commune was a folly; some of its leaders were criminals. But the greatest crime of its authors (of whom Thiers was one) was in making final that alienation of the workers of Paris from the official organisation of the French State ... ' ". It was not to be expected that Frederic Harrison, or any other contemporary observer, could attain to the heights of such impartial learning all at once.

The second article, The Fall of the Commune, begins with a story concerning a cook who was suspected of being a petroleuse (communard incendiary). We now know from Edith Thomas; *Les Petroleuses* (Paris) 1964 that domestic servants were almost wholly absent from the ranks of the Commune which knew nothing of the ferocity of a Servants' Republic. On the whole, Harrison deals very effectively with the problem of evidence and exposes those who slandered the communards. It is accordingly, ironical and unfortunate, that he should assert p.135 that: "If any statement whatever is to be believed, it is proved that the explosion in the Avenue Rapp was the work of incendiaries from Versailles ..." Frank Jellinek, whose sympathies are strongly with the Commune, concludes that the explosion may well have been caused by mere carelessness (p.291). However, what is important is not Harrison's mistakes on this or that point of detail, but his correct appreciation that the White Terror was something new and appalling in its savagery; something akin to "the frenzy which seizes a white population when their black slaves grow insubordinate."

THE REVOLUTION OF THE COMMUNE

> "Ultimately, the normal extent of the States of the Western World will contain a population of from one to three millions, as the best limit of States which are really free. For the term free is only applicable to States the parts of which coalesce of their own free will, without any violence, from the instinctive sense of a real genuine community of interest." — *Auguste Comte.*

The genius of France, recoiling from beneath the iron strokes of Germany, has again resumed her task of moulding the society of Europe. Men were still on their knees before the apotheosis of Junkerthum, when the people of Paris struck out from the depths of humiliation the finest political conception of our age. It flashed, with a new light upon a weary generation, leaving us no eyes for the triumph of the conqueror, revealing him as an old-world idol made of brass and clay. Who thinks now of the Teuton man-at-arms, his victories, and his greatness? Who speaks of Berlin more than of Madrid? He and his deeds are now but part of the dismal annals of war. To Paris all thoughts turn. There a political movement has arisen which will make his conquests mere subject for history, which will grow until his new empire dissolves before it, and soon flit back through the ivory portals to its own place — the limbo of historical dreams.

The people have again, as so often in her history, saved France from dying under the errors of her rulers. If the disasters of her arms may be traced back to the internal struggle of classes, those disasters have in turn brought that struggle to a crisis. And from that crisis there has been evolved, in a manner the most unexpected, and by an agency the most marvellous, a new social force — a force in comparison with which, the war and its material results shrink back to the level of an almanack. Paris has again become, in spite of all the soldiery and discipline of

Germany, the true centre of political progress. The principles she has asserted must make the tour of Europe, and ultimately reorganise society from its foundations. The revolution of the Commune, if not the most important crisis of the century, is in one sense the most striking phase as yet of the whole revolutionary era; for it is the beginning of the end. The revolution has now for the first time fully shown its social as well as its merely political form. It makes even the blindest see that no dry modification of the political system can ultimately satisfy mankind. It forces to the front the true problem — a regeneration of our social life; and thus, in spite of appearances, the movement is assuming a constructive instead of a destructive phase.

Let us guard our meaning at the outset, by saying that though sympathising with the purpose of this revolution, we do not justify it indiscriminately. Neither simply adopting its principles or its method, we are certainly not the apologists of all its acts. We deplore its blunders and abhor its crimes. Like every revolution it has both. So far as it seeks a political solution of a social question, so far is it doomed to ultimate failure. It has a strong communistic side; and communism is incompatible with human nature. It has been stained with bloodshed; and outrage we know recoils on its authors. But a revolution may be very great and yet externally fail; very beneficent and yet marred by crimes. The movement of Cromwell was a failure; that of '98 had its terror. Christianity did not triumph without many a crime. And thus, disavowing communism, condemning insurrection, and abhorring terrorism, we may see a great future in the revolution of the Commune.

We must of course put aside the wild stories of the English and foreign newspapers. The true details of this movement are absolutely unknown to us. We must wait for something we can trust. The comments, reports, and prophecies of the Press have been equally ridiculous. No doubt they did their best to supply us with knowledge, and unquestionably, they mean well. But in the electric atmosphere of Paris and Versailles it seems to have been simply impossible to retain one's senses. In war the residuum of fact in the torrent of rumour is usually small; in revolutions there is rarely any; but in a revolutionary war the human mind appears to pass into a phase of actual delirium. We need not believe one syllable of the passionate tales which both sides pour out; and the newspapers have done us a very ill turn in printing this wild stuff. The men who told us that the insurgents were a "band of drunken miscreants," mainly gaol birds and roughs; that the Commune was the idea of a "rabble;" that a few *gendarmes* would drive these "yelping curs" back to their dens; who told us on the 17th of March that the doings of some idlers on Montmartre were merely a bad joke; who told us on the 22nd of March that the Communal elections were held by some drunken roughs; that the National Guards of Paris were a cowardly rabble afraid of the sound of their own guns; the men who assured us of this may be worthy persons, but they were in that condition of mind in which men do not usually expect to be believed.

Anyone who has checked those lurid inventions with the experience of some eyewitness, must have learnt how utterly absurd they were. As the *Spectator* remarked:— "The correspondents seem to rely on the newspapers on each side, which are full of partisan statements. They seldom attempt to be fair, and never give the smallest indication of the motives at work."

But it did not need the correction of sober witnesses to expose the falsehood. Each day succeeding telegrams and letters exposed the untruth of those preceding. The sacking of churches, the murders, the pillage, the gaol-birds, and so forth have all been asserted and contradicted, until the mind simply declines to credit any story at all.

There are few things more sinister to those who watch our own future than the audacity with which, in any class struggle, the facts are distorted on both sides. One of the greatest dangers which await the wealthy and middle classes is their dependence on the statements of those who are simply concocting matter to sell. The tales about "pillage," and "rabble," and "massacres" are mere ribald caricature, got up for the market, like the pictures of "Red Republicans" in the comic newspapers. They are simply coarse inventions, snatched from the lower French prints, or the melodrama of the inferior stage. During the American civil war we used to be assured that Lincoln was a "bloodthirsty monster," the Northern citizens were always "rowdies," and their armies a "cowardly mob". Capital, like slavery, is stupid and savage in its panics. And it is not to the honour of that portion of the English press, which in this, the greatest of all class struggles, thinks only of inflaming this fury with senseless lampoons.

The information on which the present writer relies is drawn exclusively from neutral observers on the spot, men known personally to him, and who have privately and directly given him information, in answer to inquiries. From the only information we can trust, we may fairly believe that the "insurgents" are simply the people of Paris, mainly and at first working men, but now largely recruited from the trading and professional classes. The National Guard form a well-disciplined and enthusiastic army, which fights with extreme desperation. The "Commune" has been organised with extraordinary skill, the public services are efficiently carried on, and order has been for the most part preserved, although the difficulties caused by the withdrawal of the whole staff to Versailles were almost insuperable. Their action, it is true, has been revolutionary, and the Government of Paris has adopted most of the expedients used by other governments in a crisis, and even many of those used by M. Thiers and his ministers. But on the whole, the amount of bloodshed has been singularly little, and, considering the unparalleled difficulties, the violence to person or property has been small. So far from being ruffians, the National Guards, being simply the people of Paris, are really men of more refinement and self-respect than any town population in Europe; and the Government of the Commune, whilst it has been one of the least cruel, has been perhaps the ablest revolutionary government of modern times.

But were the Communal leaders (what they are certainly not) the greatest and the best of statesmen, they would still be the object of calumny, so long as they are simply described as "insurgents." Let us meet this grand objection at once. There are persons to whom it seems enough to say, "The Federals are in insurrection against a legitimate Government, the organ of a sovereign Assembly." Now, to apply to a country in the state of France the ideas of a settled system, is simply to mislead. The legitimacy of the Government of M. Thiers will not stand the least examination. What was its origin? The Government of National Defence arose out of a street riot, the forcible invasion of a national Parliament, and the overthrow of an established constitution. It was a true Government in its way, for it was the only possible Government; but it had not a shadow of legal right. On the surrender of Paris this Government, or rather one of its members, secretly and silently made peace for the nation, and engaged to get that peace ratified by a National Assembly. The elections were held by surprise, whilst one-third of France was in the hands of the conqueror, the capital cut off from the country, and consultation physically impossible. This is the Assembly which pretends to declare itself a sovereign power, and to govern France in perpetuity, for it recognises no one with the right to dissolve it — this Assembly, summoned by a ministry which arose out of a street mob, and convoked at the dictation of a foreign enemy.

What followed was but the parody of national representation. An Assembly like that of Versailles is a farce in France. Cut off by foreign invasion from the centres of thought and action — the active being Republicans broken and divided by defeat — the peasantry were left to the guidance of landlords and priests. A Chamber the most retrograde, the most clerical and aristocratic which France had seen for generations, resulted. Fossil specimens of *ancienne noblesse* emerged from their chateaux — believers in the divine rights of kings, in infallible popes — Don Quixotes of politics, who had never been known in public before. Ordinary men declared that they had never found themselves in such company — "Seven Dukes," said one deputy, "all sitting in a row!" That may seem very natural to us in England; but in France men of this stamp are absolutely impracticable. Had they been merely their grandfathers' ghosts, they would have been as real a national representation. Elect of the nation or not, they did not represent France, or the forces strongest in France, and they could not govern it for an hour.

What were their first acts? They ratified the treaty which they were called to sanction, and then the task committed to them was done. But they set up a claim to sovereign power. At least five hundred of their number were avowed Monarchists. If they did not proclaim the monarchy, it was simply because they could not agree on the monarch. They silenced Garibaldi with insult; they hooted the Republican minority; they suppressed the deputies of Paris; they proclaimed their antipathy to Paris, insisting on transferring the capital; they openly plotted the revival of the monarchy. They put at the head of the Government (avowedly provisional) the most shifty of French politicians. He called to his side the known adherents of the Orleanist dynasty — men whom Paris, the principal cities, and half France repudiate. By every act and word they showed their purpose of restoring the Imperial system, and of governing the great towns by force. Finally, they resolved to sit and to govern away from Paris. Troops of the line were ostentatiously ordered up from the provinces to overawe the city, just as Napoleon drew round him his Imperial Guard. A known Orleanist was put at the head of the National Guard; another was made Commander-in-Chief. The two chief leaders of the people were sentenced to death for an old political offence. It was not concealed that the purpose of the Government was first to disarm the people of Paris, next to restore substantially the old Imperial tyranny under some monarchic form, and then to govern France away from the intelligence, the influence, and the physical resistance of Paris, the natural capital. In a word, Paris was to be a conquered city.

Now this was to declare civil war. From the day that Chamber met at Bordeaux men who knew France saw that civil war was inevitable. To bring back a system which the great political centres abhor and dread, to confront them with arms, insults, and threats, to attempt to govern Paris, Lyons, and Marseilles from the provinces in the spirit of Bourbonism, was deliberately to plunge the country into anarchy. It is easy to say, "Well! but if the elect of the nation choose to do so, why were they not to be obeyed?" It is necessary to remember that France still is, and for generations has been, in one prolonged revolution. No government has ever had any solid legal title; nay, every government has done its utmost to root the idea of legality out of the people, and to claim their acceptance of itself on the sole ground of its power or its usefulness. No government in France is, or can be in our sense, legitimate. Every government is the issue of successful rebellion or conspiracy. And this Assembly, originating from a street riot and hatched in a capitulation, had certainly no legal commission to govern France in perpetuity at its own good pleasure. It was itself openly plotting against that which was the recognised Government of the nation — the Republic.

But it is of less consequence to consider if it had any right to coerce Paris, when we knew that, under the actual circumstances of France, so to govern was to proclaim civil war. In politics we must look at the facts. Paris is not London, or Berlin, or Vienna. Paris is to France what no other city is to any other country. Politically, Paris is France. We may like the fact or not, but there the fact stands. In political force, in moral influence, in historical prestige, Paris outweighs a score of provinces. French history is such that for generations Paris has exercised over France that fascination which Rome had over the West.

Socially the whole of the intelligence and force of France has been concentrated into that city. And, above all, it has, as a city, an organic personality of its own which is one of the most magical facts in social philosophy. There are cities, and cities large and small, but Paris is not a mere city, but is a special social organism, animated with the nature and passions of men, but of a nature not precisely homogeneous with man's. Right or wrong, such is the fact. At any rate all Frenchmen feel it. It is useless to quarrel with it, to ask why it should be, or whether it ought to be. It would be as wise to ask why the eye does all the seeing and the brain all the thinking. And no man can long judge truly French politics who does not feel that in Paris is the head and heart of France. In intelligence, in strength, in vital force, it weighs as much as all the provinces together. We see that now as a hard fact at the gun's mouth. And if in obedience to your formulae you choose to put the legal power in one place, whilst the real power is in another, your political system will be torn in pieces. France is so constituted that Paris is become its natural head; unless it lead, the genius of the French race is eclipsed; and if France seeks to enslave Paris, anarchy is the result. Such are the facts; and in politics you must accept the facts, or they will destroy you.

Whether this supremacy of Paris over the rest of France be a good, or not, is a very different question. It is part of the present movement to abdicate the material and to retain only the moral power. But if the ascendancy of Paris over France has often been used oppressively, the ascendancy of France over Paris has become an intolerable tyranny. The history of France for generations has been the oppression of the cities by the country. It is clear that M. Thiers and his ministry dreaded the attitude of the Assembly towards Paris. And yet M. Thiers and his ministry themselves had deeply alienated Paris, the Parisians as a body, men of all classes alike. When the workmen determined to resist they had the sympathy of many a Parisian who in no sense belonged to their party. The *Debats,* one of the least corrupt of the French newspapers, the organ of the Orleanists and the rich bourgeois, was thoroughly disaffected to the Government of Versailles. In short, the reactionary parties parading the figment of national sovereignty declared war on Paris, and the people of Paris took up the challenge.

For generations the history of France has centred in the struggle which at last has come to a crisis. The singular concentration of the whole activity of the nation in Paris, united to that wonderful personality of the city itself, and especially from the peculiar conditions of the working classes there, have stimulated in Paris a political advancement far beyond the rest of France. In Paris, owing to peculiar conditions, political, social, and industrial, the questions which are in embryo elsewhere are the living faiths of masses of men. Amongst these principles are the Republic, the importance of social questions over political, secular education, the abolition of standing armies, social equality. It is now clear, perhaps, to the least observant that the active population of Paris is ardently and definitely Republican. It is clear that they will not submit to the oppression of priesthood, soldiery, and police. It is plain they seek a changed political state only as a step to a changed social state. In these great points the people of Paris are more resolute and more united than any other single population whatsoever. And for generations the people of Paris have found themselves, in their ardent pursuit of a social future, dragged back and crushed down by the ignorance and the prejudices of the country. The Bourbons, when restored by foreign bayonets, held down Paris and the cities by the aid of the country nobility. The days of July, 1830, came; and Paris, freeing itself again from the Bourbon reaction, set up the Orleans dynasty, which offered itself as a compromise. But the House of Orleans soon swayed round to reaction, and again governed the cities by the aid of two Chambers, both recruited from the rich and the provinces. February, 1848; followed: and again Paris set up a Republic, which again the retrograde deputies from the provinces succeeded in discrediting. The expedition to Rome, the work of the rural deputies, prepared its fall. Napoleon followed; and at once men saw how universal suffrage in a country, agricultural and clerical, like France might contrive the triumph of ignorance, of superstition, of priests and landlords, and end in the tyranny of the administration. There was some genius in the idea of turning one of the weapons of the party of progress against progress itself; and the device succeeded to a marvel. The Empire was one long struggle of Paris with the peasants, Paris crushed, silenced, and degraded by 100,000 bayonets, ultimately based on the votes, the conscripts, the taxes of the country. For twenty years the intelligence and spirit of Paris writhed under the yoke, but at no one moment of that twenty years did the workmen acknowledge the tyrant, or submit to the dictation of the peasants. At length their resistance grew formidable; and the Emperor at bay sought escape from revolution in war. Sedan came: and for a third time in this century Paris made an effort to be free. This time she was crushed by the cannon of a foreigner whom the Emperor of the peasants had brought down on their country. And the foreign enemy, who well knew his business, stipulated that Paris should continue to be held down by a rural National Assembly, for he fears Paris more than he feared all the armies of Napoleon. The Assembly hurried to the welcome task, and for a fourth time the country sought to gag and subdue the capital. But this time Paris was armed. The whole of Paris, including men of all classes, was outraged and alarmed by the reckless policy of the Assembly, and their avowed hostility to the capital. And in the midst of the general discontent the workmen resolved to act. They seized the cannon that they might not be disarmed. They put themselves on the defensive. The *coup* attempted by the Government failed. In twenty-four hours the workmen were masters of Paris. They proclaimed the Commune.

Now what is it that this means? If we are to believe the

newspapers, it was the most wanton and purposeless revolt in history. But not to say that revolts organised and fighting like this one are never purposeless it is not very difficult to discover most important purposes in it. The whole history of France we have seen turns on the excessive centralisation in the capital, and the oppression in turn of the capital by the authority which possesses the support of the country. The people of Paris have been taught by long experience that this unnatural centralisation is as oppressive to Paris as it is injurious to the provinces. They saw that the tension of the bond between them was becoming unbearable to both. And they struck out the idea of loosening it by making Paris and the principal cities locally self-governing communities. They did not seek to detach Paris from France, but to enable Paris to work out its own civic existence without the task of governing the provinces, and without the degradation of being governed by them. The social condition of the great cities is not homogeneous with that of the rural districts. Paris has one religious, political, and social ideal, and the country people another. The attempt to force either to submit to the ideal of the other has ended in bitter struggle. Let then Paris become for political and social purposes a self-regulating society, united with other city communities and with the provinces in definite federal bonds. Paris would thus become what Geneva is in the Swiss federation; more distantly what Rome, or Frankfort, or Strasbourg were in the mediaeval Empire. Such is the idea of the Commune in its simple form, as they said in their really noble proclamation, "a free city in a free country." "Paris," they said, "does not want to reign, but she will be free; she has no other ambition to dictate than by example. She neither aspires to intrude her own will, nor will she renounce the same. She does not care any more to issue decrees than to submit to *plebiscites;* she represents progress by marching ahead herself, and prepares the liberty of others in founding her own."

Now this idea is so just, so honourable, so perfectly

adapted to the position of France, that it is strange men here should not have welcomed it with applause. For a generation our writers and speakers have insisted, as indeed have all the true thinkers of France, that their country was eaten up by centralisation. Their revolutions, we have been told, have been due to the domination of the capital, followed by the reaction of the provinces. And here, in a situation apparently hopeless, the people of Paris throw out the only solution by voluntarily ceding their claim to dictate on condition of receiving the right to be free. One would have thought that a people of practical sagacity like ours would have hailed this singular adaptation of the old doctrine of local self-government to solve a hopeless problem — a solution which is at once so apt and yet so unexpected as to reveal true political genius.

As so perhaps in England, had this the first purpose of the Commune been its only one, we should have approved it. But there was, and was felt to be, something more beyond. We have been told, indeed, in the inveterate spirit of vestrydom, that the people of Paris wanted their own municipal liberties — local self-government as understood in Farringdon Without. In the midst of these horrors one cannot withold a laugh at the idea of the workmen of Paris dying for the right of electing their own lord mayor, aldermen, and common council and the noble pleasure of bearding Mr. Bruce, or trying a fall with Mr. Ayrton. Sublime as may be these civic rights of a liveryman, people do not fight for them, at least in Paris.

In truth, the Commune meant something more than this. There was something beyond. It was this. The workmen of Paris had found by bitter experience that not only was their political, but their social, future impossible whilst the bonds of centralisation between city and province remained. They found that their great industrial movement was crushed by a Government resting on the country. 'They saw that economic and social development as they conceive them can only be carried out on a smaller area, and in a more prepared society; that the vast national unit forms a field too complex and too multiform for their growth; that, in a word, their social emancipation depends on the being able to deal with Capital and Government, apart from the resources both can command in the numbers and ignorance of the peasants. They therefore came down to the root of the matter. With consummate instinct, with that genius for politics which masses of cultivated workmen possess, they came back in spirit to the problem of the middle ages when the municipalities arose. They felt, like them, that true civic life can only be worked out within real civic limits, that a commonwealth of equal citizens can only flourish by withdrawing it partially from the feudalised peasantry; that in order to deal with Wealth and Ambition they must bring them down from their strongholds in the country, and make them citizens within the limits of the city.

But as some people saw in the Commune nothing but the right to elect one's own common council, so others see in it nothing but the mediaeval free town. The Commune may be compared with the old municipality, but it is a very different thing. The old free city was the incarnation of jealousy and narrow civic patriontism. Now nothing can be less narrow than the spirit of the Commune of Paris. Paris, they say in their fine appeal, desires only to be the elder sister of France. The very fact of the movement towards the Commune is an abnegation of rivalry. It disarms jealousy. Paris voluntarily cedes its exclusive rights and authority. What city of Greece or Italy would have willingly laid down its sceptre and given up its subjects? Besides, the civic rivalries of the past are impossible now: the great national aggregates have silenced them for ever. Paris, Marseilles, Lyons, have for centuries formed cities of one nation. They desire still to form cities of that nation. But in seeking a new civic life, they give to and claim from each other a greater freedom; whilst ceding power they retain influence, and whilst asking civic freedom accept national duties. They seek in the past a vivifying idea in the free self-ruling cities which were parts of an aggregate

Empire. Their ideal is far more that of Frankfort than that of Florence, and far more that of Geneva than either. What is there here of the Italian Republics and their feuds? Away, then, with historical sophisms good for nothing but to fill a column for some jaded journalist.

The Commune has itself explained its own mission in a series of State papers more distinct, vigorous, and frank than any of our time. It is quite reasonable to find in a true Government — even though a Government of workmen — men who can state their purposes without the evasions of trained diplomatists, and with the point of true earnestness. One of these vigorous preductions explains the entire programme, and is well worthy of record and of thought, albeit but the language of "drunken miscreants." It runs thus:—

"It is the duty of the Commune to confirm and ascertain the aspirations and wishes of the people of Paris. The precise character of the movement of the 18th of March is misunderstood and unknown, and is calumniated by the politicians at Versailles. At that time Paris still laboured and suffered for the whole of France, for whom she had prepared by her battles an intellectual, moral, administrative, and economic regeneration, glory, and prosperity. What does she demand? The recognition and consolidation of the Republic, and the absolute independence of the Commune extended at all places in France, thus assuring to each the integrity of its rights, and to every Frenchman the full exercise of his faculties and aptitudes as a man, a citizen, and a producer. The independence of the Commune has no other limits but its rights. The independence is equal for all Communes who are adherents of the contract, the association of which ought to secure the unity of France. The inherent rights of the Commune are to vote the Communal budget of receipts and expenses, the improving and alteration of taxes, the direction of local services; the organisation of the magistracy, internal police, and education; the administration of the property belonging to the Commune; the choice by election or competition — with the responsibility and permanent right of control and revocation — of the Communal magistrates and officials of all classes; the absolute guarantee of individual liberty and liberty of conscience; the permanent intervention of the citizens in Communal affairs by the free manifestation of their ideas and the free defence of their interests; guarantees given for those manifestations by the Commune, who alone are charged with securing the free and just exercise of the right of meeting and

181

publicity; and the organisation of urban defence and of the National Guard, which must elect its chiefs, and alone watch over the maintenance of order in the city. Paris wishes nothing more under the head of local guarantees on the well-understood condition of regaining, in a grand Central Administration and Delegation from the Federal Communes, the realisation and practice of those principles; but in favour of her independence, and profiting by her liberty of action, she reserves to herself liberty to bring about as may seem good to her administrative and economic reforms which the people demand, and to create such institutions as may serve to develop and further education. Produce, exchange, and credit have to universalise power and property according to the necessities of the moment, the wishes of those interested, and the *data* furnished by experience.

"Our enemies deceive themselves or deceive the country when they accuse Paris of desiring to impose its will and supremacy upon the rest of the nation, and to aspire to a Dictatorship which would be a veritable attempt to overthrow the independence and sovereignty of other Communes. They deceive themselves when they accuse Paris of seeking the destruction of French unity established by the Revolution. The unity which has been imposed upon us up to the present by Empire, the Monarchy, and the Parliamentary Governmnet is nothing but centralisation, despotic, unintelligent, arbitrary, and onerous. The political unity, as desired by Paris, is a voluntary association of all local initiative, the free and spontaneous co-operation of all individual energies with the common object of the wellbeing, liberty, and security of all. The Communal Revolution, initiated by the people on the 18th of March, inaugurated a new era in politics, experimental, positive, and scientific. It was the end of the old official and clerical world of military supremacy and bureaucracy, of jobbing in monopolies and privileges, to which the proletariat owed its slavery and the country its misfortunes and disasters. The strife between Paris and Versailles is one of those that cannot be ended by an illusory compromise; the issue should not be doubtful. The victory fought for with such indomitable energy by the Commune will remain with the idea and with the right. We appeal to France which knows that Paris in arms possesses as much calmness as courage, where order is maintained with as much energy as enthusiasm, who is ready to sacrifice herself with as much reason as energy. Paris is only in arms in consequence of her devotion to liberty, and the glory of all in France ought to cause this bloody conflict to cease.

"It is for France to disarm Versailles by a solemn manifestation of her irresistible will. Invited to profit by her conquests, she should declare herself identified with our efforts, she should be our ally in the contest which can only end by the triumph of the Communal idea or the ruin of Paris. As for ourselves, citizens of Paris, we have a mission to accomplish, a modern revolution the greatest and most fruitful of all those which have illuminated history. It is our duty to fight and conquer."

The central principle, then, of the Commune, is simply a protest against over-centralisation, an effort towards basing society on smaller units without destroying national cohesion. Whether the Commune, as organised by the workmen of Paris, is precisely the form which this decentralisation should take, may fairly be open to doubt, and we need not accept their attempt as a final solution. But the principle of decentralisation is one peculiarly necessary to France, and is ultimately applicable to western Europe. The vast and heterogeneous forces concentrated in the single head of the great modern States are becoming hostile to progress, and especially to true social and industrial development. The great problems of the industrial centres are cruelly complicated by the backward condition of the great rural areas. And the vast power wielded by the Governments of these national aggregates are hostile to free development and true social life. On these grounds it was urged by Auguste Comte twenty years ago that the first great step towards a true reconstruction of society, must be found in the easy dissolution of the great nations of the West into smaller political areas. The first step would be the establishment of local self-government, not necessarily democratic, over areas about the extent of an old French province, grouped round the seventeen principal cities, and all united in the nation by a federal bond. The second would be the actual autonomy of these groups with the national bond, exchanged for, or expanded into the grander national bond of the Western Republic, cemented by a moral and intellectual unity. Without pretending that the Commune is based on this ideal of Comte, or that it exactly expresses it, it does, in fact, accord with it. It shows how truly he saw the instinctive tendency of France, and points to their ultimate realisation. It has long been a necessity for France. It is the idea of the provinces as much as of the cities. The social and political life of the future requires more real publicity of action, more personal responsibility, than is attainable in the vast wilderness of modern nations. The men of a city or of a province can estimate a right, and effectively influence the citizens of their own area. But when government is carried on by men hundreds of miles off, personal influence ceases, and it becomes government carried on through the instrument of the press, and of the talking chamber. And since both of these instruments are liable to special abuse, it ends in being the government by the art of manipulating these — that is to say, ultimately the government of the powerful and professional classes, who alone have the means of learning this art.

An objection on the threshold must be honestly faced. This decentralisation, they say, is the loss of national greatness, the surrender of glory and power. The answer is an easy one. Undoubtedly it is so. There is a point, and we have reached it, at which national greatness and glory pass into national tyranny and pride. The idea of imperial grandeur is a simple evil — reactionary, oppressive, and demoralising. This pride in vast State aggregates which do not correspond with true political and social units, made up of dissimilar parts bound together by force or craft, is not a good thing, but an evil. The grand State systems having done their part in Europe, like the Roman Empire, like it are growing oppressive. These empires, cemented by "blood and iron," have no true vitality. They gratify the ambition or the vanity of the professional classes, but the people throughout Europe abhor them, and they are doomed. The imperial spirit is the Nemesis of patriotism. Look at the history of the late war, and of its authors on both sides, and judge how profoundly hostile to civilisation this pride of imperial greatness has become. Events have given this sentiment a momentary strength, but the people do not share it in France, in Germany, or in England. It is the honour of the Paris workmen that they definitely repudiate this coarse ambition. They look forward in the future to a nation greater than any — the

people of the West of Europe. They repudiated the league
of the bourgeoisie against the Germans. A Prussian sits on
the Commune. Their dream of a universal Republic means
no absurd extension of national territory. It means the
union of men in their true political aggregates, bound
together as a nation in a federal bond, forming for many
purposes but one people, without the barriers of jealous
nationality or the oppression of centralised states.

Such is the idea of the Commune, destructive it may be
of jealous nationality, only to rise to a civic union more
real, and a national unity more great. It is a crying want in
France. And if it seem to expose France for a season to the
nations adjoining her, it releases Europe at last from all
fear of French imperialism, and the contagion of her example must shortly spread to surrounding nations. It is a
need for Italy, for Germany, and England as much as for
France. We see the spirit working in France in the heroic
efforts of Paris to free itself from the tyranny of the provinces; we see it even in the very movement of the provinces
to free themselves from the authority centralised in the
capital. We have seen it even during the war in the repudiation by Lyons and Marseilles of the Government of
Paris. It is visible in the strong municipal spirit of the old
Italian cities, forced together for a time by a military
monarchy. It is the great problem of Germany seen in the
resistance of the separate free towns and states to the
oppression of Prussia. We see it amongst ourselves in the
hostility of our workmen to the spirit of imperial aggrandisement, in the protest of our economic reformers against
our colonial empire, and lastly in the undying resistance of
Ireland to the domination of England. The idea of the
Commune, the idea of the gradual dissolution of nations
into more similar aggregates and truer political unity is the
idea of the future. It lives deep in the instincts of every
people of Europe, and now that 200,000 workmen in Paris
have taken up arms to conquer it its ultimate triumph is
assured.

A principle so just as this, and so obviously grateful to

the suspicions of neighbours, could hardly have driven capital into a panic, and journalism into a rage, unless there had been much beyond. But there was much beyond. To withdraw politics within smaller areas is to settle politics in a certain way. To govern from centres in which the workmen have a clear preponderance is certainly to govern in the workmen's sense. And thus the struggle for the Commune is virtually a struggle for that social system to which the workmen look. In a word, the Commune really involves a series of political principles over and above the primary one of substituting municipalised provinces for a centralised empire. What these are we may briefly consider.

1. The first of these principles is that of the Republic. Indeed so strong is this principle in the movement, that the original insurrection proclaimed its task to be the maintenance of the Republic. And undoubtedly the frank acceptance of the Republic by the Assembly for the time would have checked the movement. What does the Republic as understood by the Parisian workmen mean? It means that government, as the highest of all functions, must be nothing but a responsible public duty, and not the property or privilege of any family man or class; that is to say, the sole condition for ruling must be personal capacity, and the sole object of rule the public service. When the interests of a certain family (as in a monarchy), when the prerogatives of certain orders (as in an aristocracy) are considered first, and the convenience of the public comes second, then *pro tanto* the Republic is overridden. And even where, under the forms of parliament and suffrage, a popular government exists, still if the privilege of governing is retained by special orders, and the interests favoured by the government are those of proprietary classes, there you have not a Republic but a disguised aristocracy. Now the workmen in Paris are not content, as ours are, to submit to this; and having arms in their hands they resolved to secure a true and real Republic. And by this they mean not

a government differing only in name from one of the old regimes — with Republic on its lips for a season, but monarchy in its heart and aristocracy in its acts — not a government reserved for special classes and existing for the rich; but a government animated from top to bottom of the scale by the spirit of public duty, and looking on itself as the servant of the people, existing solely for the sake of the people. Such a government was not what M. Thiers, with all his life protestations, intended; and it was certainly not what the Chamber would tolerate. They meant to govern France from the proprietary point of view, and ultimately as the symbol of the system to make France the property of a dynasty. The way in which they treated the question as to rents and bills (*i.e.*, so as to place the poor under a hopeless load of debt to the rich) was the proof of their temper. Nothing can be futher from the truth than to say that the people of Paris rose against the Republic, or were the worst enemies of the Republic. Republic with them does not mean simply the absence of a grand llama supposed to exist in a distant mountain. It means something very real which M. Thiers and his Chamber had no intention of giving them. It means the absence of any proprietary spirit in state action. This principle they insist upon as the axiom of civil society, the corner-stone of national union. And as all societies proclaim certain things as above discussion — the principles on which they rest — as the institution of property, family, and the like — so these Paris workmen insist that society is to them not worth maintaining unless on the principle of the Republic — the honest devotion of the whole public forces to the sole end of the public good. And to my mind it is their peculiar honour that alone of modern communities they have preserved from compromise or corruption the principle which is now the life-blood of all human society.

2. The second principle which the Commune involves in the repudiating of the dogma of universal suffrage. It is a protest against the oppression of a majority. The pretended appeals to the people by universal suffrage in France

have long been known to be an organised fraud. Bodies of ignorant peasants have been cajoled by priestly artifice or driven by official audacity. These vaunted results of universal suffrage have in no sense expressed the true opinion of the nation. They have expressed the purposes only of knots of men who have learned the art of manipulating masses of voters. And thus universal suffrage in France has become one of the most dangerous, as well as one of the most degrading artifices of the conspirator. As a protest against this ignoble superstition, the action of the Commune is invaluable. It is but the first step, but it leads inevitably to the second — the protest against appeals to the suffrage altogether. It has long been a cardinal doctrine of the Positivist system that government by the suffrage — the election of the superior by the inferior — the basing of authority on the nomination of a majority — is inherently vicious. One of the most curious instances of the studied misrepresentation of which Positivism is the object is the attributing to it an ardent faith in universal suffrage; whilst it really regards every system of election as irrational, and universal suffrage in certain societies as a mere system of cajolery. Indeed, Comte is the only philosopher who discards on strict principle everywhere the election of the superior by the inferior, and insists on the selection of inferior by the superior.

Yet more droll than the denouncing Comte as the apostle of universal suffrage is the indignation of English Conservatives at this latest protest against it. For sheer hypocritical self-condemnation, few things have been more complete than the outcries in England over the enormity of men who refuse to submit to the divine right of universal suffrage. "What!" cried Conservatives in horror, "rebel against the Elect of the Nation!" "Defy the will of the people!" cried Whigs in pious grief. As if any one of our politicians or parties accept the dogma of universal suffrage themselves, or mean by the will of the people anything but a parliamentary cabal. Have we got universal suffrage in England whist the electors even now are a minority of the adult males, and even that minority is coerced, cajoled or bribed by an organised system of electioneering? Would these indignant people be ready to abide by the verdict of universal suffrage in Ireland, or India, or Jamaica? No! they would reply there are certain classes only whose intelligence entitles them to vote, and there are only certain things which it is wise to put to the vote. Exactly so; and that, perhaps, is the meaning of the Parisian workmen when they refuse to bow down to the idol of universal suffrage.

3. The third principle which the Commune proclaims is the system of direct instead of indirect government. They threw off at the first step the incumbrance of a huge representative assembly. Instead of electing a chaotic chamber of talkers, they formed a simple executive council. The tribune they said is abolished. The council is a committee for action, not for the displays of advocates. Nothing so completely shows the political sagacity of the working class as their true estimate of that demoralising nuisance, the unwieldy talking parliament. Political progress and civic life are impossible so long as men invest with a superstitious importance this very secondary institution. If the suffrage affords a ready field for the arts of the rich and powerful, the parliament supplies an arena for rhetoricians and intriguers. In parliament, the workmen and their cause are easily overborne. Professional politicians develop in them an art which, by analogy with "electioneering," may be called the art of "parliamenteering". It is the art of manipulating an assembly by rhetoric, tact, or manoeuvre; an art more or less testing practical skill, but perfectly distinct from political genius. Government, by the parliamentary system, is government without real responsibility, without efficiency, and without simplicity. All of these are lost in the meshes of divided authority and personal rivalries. Government, in a word, breaks down under the tangle of machinery which it has to work. What we need is, as the Commune proclaims, a responsibility of the governing body, real, direct, and personal, the greatest simplicity of

authority, and the utmost supervision of opinion. The age of parliaments is passed, and the 24th of March rang their knell. And of all parliaments in history one would think the most foolish and the most vile is that chamber of intriguers at Versailles, where reign loquacious vanity in its dotage — the very demon of conspiracy, distrust, and imbecility; flatulent cowardice alternating with impotent ferocity. It is not at the Hotel de Ville that we can see the lowest depths of political decay. It is at Versailles that one may see of what folly, treachery, apathy, fury, and selfishness man is capable, all seething in hopeless confusion — in the elected wisdom of the nation, in the worst and the last parliament of France, whose true king is Anarchy.

4. The next principal which is involved in the Communal idea is the abolition of that curse of modern society — the standing army. Their movement originated in the National Guards, and their first act was the abolition of the conscription. They decreed that no military service should be longer than six months, and that the army of France should be limited, so far as they could effect it, to a mere militia. The gain to France, to peace, to civilisation, if this grand movement could be carried out, is incalculable; and it will ever remain the honour of the workmen, that whilst the Assembly were dreaming visions of armies vaster than Napoleon's, to exact a vengeance which might eclipse his worst orgies, they gave the first direct death-blow to the detestable system of war.

5. There is another principle which grows out of and is but the application of the Republican idea — that workmen may be called on fitting occasions to the functions of active government. The idea which the wealthy and professional classes have so carefully fostered — as did the patricians at Rome — that the whole system of administration from top to bottom is a peculiar mystery, in which they alone have been initiated, is a dogma so irrational, that it could only obtain so long as fitness for government is supposed to depend on rhetorical skill. In sober truth, the practical sense of an active workman is often the most

useful quality in the politician of a crisis. And nothing in this movement is more promising, and certainly nothing has more angered its enemies, than the high measure of success with which mere workmen have conducted the government of a vast capital. Placed in a position of unparalleled difficulty by the old parties withdrawing the entire staff of administration, confronted by a resistance which makes ultimate success hardly possible, the workmen who, for the first time in the history of modern Europe, assumed the functions of government, have shown extraordinary energy and singular skill. Every act of theirs has been reported to us in a travestie, falsified, ridiculed, and mystified, but they have wrung, even from their enemies, the acknowledgment of its vigour, its directness, and its honesty. Man for man, these working shoemakers and printers have shown out well beside the chattering crew at Versailles; and whilst the first advocate of France was wailing in the tribune, and the first orator of France was prosing and temporising, the workmen have shown how emergencies are to be met, and how it is possible to be a statesman without academic adroitness, and to be a minister without the ostentation of courts.

These were the principal aims of the Commune; and they all spring out of the fundamental idea of the Republic. There were also many minor principles which, though natural consequences of the former, were not inseparable from them. Amongst the first acts of the new power were decrees to establish secular and gratuitous state education, the entire separation of Church and State, the resumption by the State of the spiritual endowments, and the transformation of the police from a political engine into a civic protection. The election of officers by the National Guard and the exclusion of the regular army of France from the capital, were obviously expedients to guarantee the independence of Paris from the oppression of the provinces. The proposal to throw the burthen of taxation upon capital, is only a step towards the dream of our own financial reformers. The scheme of meeting the exceptional demands of the war by using the vast stores in the hands of the State and the national domains, is a scheme in accordance with sound policy. Their plan for relieving debtors from the arrears of rent and the liabilities of bills, is one which can only be fairly judged after an intimate study of special facts. In general character the situation of the people of Paris whose debts had accumulated during the siege, curiously resembled that of the plebeians in the early Roman Republic. A war in which all classes were equally liable had brought about a state of things in which the poor saw themselves in danger of being bound hand and foot to the rich. And thus a common disaster, for which all were equally responsible, would be endured in very unequal degrees. It was the old problem which so often troubled antiquity of the *nexi ei addicti*. What was called for was a new *seisactheia* — a new *lex de Nexis*. The question is far too complex and obscure to be now discussed; but there seems nothing in the decree of the Commune on rents and bills which is incompatible with justice and policy, or which may not find justification in the action long recognised as the duty of government in France.

It is far from our present purpose to defend or excuse the acts, as distinguished from the principles, of this movement. That it opened with the murder of two generals, that resistance in Paris has been crushed by force, and in one instance by massacre, that repeated acts of violence and confiscation occur, is what I neither pretend to doubt or venture to palliate. The insurrection of a capital against a nation, which is also the insurrection of a class against another class, has never been, and is never likely to be, an affair without crime or disorder. That acts of terrorism, brutality, and pillage have been committed by certain gangs of men, actually, or professing to be, National Guards, is very probable; that the Guards as a body, or the Commune officially, have encouraged this conduct, I have satisfied myself to be a wanton calumny. That the police has been utterly disorganised is partly the act of the Gov-

ernment of Versailles, which wilfully threw the whole
administration of that vast city into confusion, and partly
that of past governments of France, which deliberately
converted the police into agents of their own tyranny.
They had practically effaced the distinction between
ordinary crime and political disaffection. If the clergy have
been ill-treated, and the churches deprived of their valu-
ables, about which the facts are too uncertain to ground
any opinion, it is clearly due to the course which, during
the whole Napoleonic tyranny, the clergy have chosen to
pursue, as its agents, abettors, and supporters. The Church
for a generation has left its spiritual function to become
the tool of a cruel and infamous tyranny; and the priests
who have consented to be the spiritual, as the *gendarmes*
have been the political, police of a merciless oppression,
can hardly escape being objects of the bitterest popular
hatred.

As to the arbitrary acts of the Government, it will be
time to denounce them when we know more precisely
what they are and how far they exceeded the acts of every
government in a desperate emergency. They certainly
never came near the seizure of the Orleans property by
"our firm ally." If they have seized eminent persons as
hostages, or retain them as suspected, it must not be forgotten that the Versailles troops (in spite of the denials of
M. Thiers) commenced by shooting prisoners, and Mr.
Thiers even now asserts the right to shoot their leaders,
and to convict every Federal as a rebel. A party which in a
civil war resorts to the atrocious practices of Russia in
Warsaw can only be brought to its senses by reprisals. We
must remember, also, that the Commune is surrounded by
Government spies — that every disaffected resident in Paris
regards himself as an authorised conspirator, bound in
duty to embarrass and overthrow the *de facto* government
under which he chooses to remain. As to the massacre of
the Place Vendôme, it is perfectly well-known now,
though the newspapers have never frankly admitted it, that
it arose from a concerted and partly-armed attack on the

key of the military positions held by the National Guards.[1] It was a terrible and deplorable catastrophe, accompanied, doubtless, by acts of brutality; but it must be looked upon simply as part of the general scheme to get possession of Paris by force. In a word, I know no proof yet that the official action of the movement cannot favourably compare with that of other revolutionary governments, or that the popular passions it arouses are nearly so savage as those of the party at Versailles.

Words cannot describe the insane injustice with which every feature of this movement has been related and judged. Every one knows how much blacker the case of the Commune appears in our newspapers than it does in the private conversations of well-informed persons. It is impossible to acquit the journals of suppressing the truth on system, in deference to the prejudices of a majority of their readers.[2] As to their comments and judgments, their own pages display self-contradiction of the most ludicrous kind. "The Commune has disarmed the loyal National Guards!" they cry in horror. Well, did not the movement commence in Thiers' attempt to disarm the disloyal National Guards? "The Commune has ordered numerous arrests on suspicion!" — exactly as M. Thiers orders the police throughout France "to arrest all persons whom they may have reason to suspect." "The National Guards were fighting for their thirty sous a day!" The Deputies, however, were patriots upon their twenty-five francs a day, and M. Thiers was a patriot on three million francs a year. "The men are too lazy to return to work!" exclaimed, in moral indignation, the effeminate idlers of London or Versailles. The Assembly scraped together to satisfy the conqueror has a sort of divine right to perpetuity the Commune elected by Paris is rank usurpation. To condemn Blanqui and Flourens to death, to shoot Cluseret or Duval, is wise and just; to kill Le Comte and Thomas is a horrible murder. To declare war on Paris is admirable policy; for Paris to resist is wild anarchy. The defence of the capital against the nation is the "orgy of the rabble;" the helpless malcontents on the boulevard are the Party of Order. The Commune which passes three prudential laws a day is all division; the Assembly which wrangles over tombstones and cockades is the collective wisdom of France. The Commune, they say, "is making forced levies of troops." As if M. Thiers were fighting, as if any government in France ever fought, with anything but conscripts, dragged from their homes by force. "The wretches killed two generals!" — just as M. Thiers began the movement by condemning two politicians to death, and continues it by shooting prisoners and sending them to the galleys. "The Vandals are destroying the Column of Napoleon!" — just as Thiers is bombarding the Arc de Triomphe. "The miscreants," they say, "would kill every decent man in Paris!" They have not, however, done it as yet; but in the meantime cries for extermination and vengeance are re-echoing from Versailles through the provinces of France, are caught up by our parasite press, and drop with atrocious coolness from the lips of our cultured and wealthy class. It has developed a hatred as horrible and as blind as the hatred of race — the hatred of dominant race in a panic.[3]

It may be well to point out the relation of this Revolution to the principles of Comte. His existing followers in France, though their opinions are perfectly familiar to the chiefs of it, have in no way whatever taken part in its action. In some respects the movement is utterly opposed to their principles — in the first place, as a violent attempt to solve social problems by force; secondly, as having Communistic tendencies which they utterly repudiate; and thirdly, as being based on the doctrine of rights and the dogma of democracy. Yet notwithstanding, the movement in effect coincides with some of the cardinal principles of Positivist politics. Its central idea, the restriction of the community to smaller areas, in outline agrees with the scheme of Comte for the peaceful disintegration of France into seventeen separate and federated republics. France, he said in 1852, must be relieved from the material oppression of Paris, as Paris must be freed from the incubus of the provinces. In discarding the crude appeal to universal suffrage, in rejecting all pretence of parliamentary government, in the principle of direct government under the constant control of the active citizens, in suppressing the standing army, in a system of gratuitous secular education, in separating Church from State, even in the destruction of the Column of Napoleon, and the removal of his remains from Paris to wipe out the memory of that inhuman career, the decrees of the Communal leaders have been in too close agreement with the counsels which Auguste Comte publicly advocated in Paris twenty years ago, to leave any doubt that both have strong common grounds.

After all, the precise form in which this Revolution embodies its purpose is a matter of small moment. The manifestation of its spirit may fail, or change, and the spirit remain. There is in truth a deeper phase, which underlies it all; and that is the social. Primarily the Revolution is a political, but really and mainly a social movement. And the first is but the manifestation of the second. This struggle of the capital against the provinces, of the great cities against country, of the Republic against Monarchy, of Communal against Parliamentary government — what does it mean? There is one thing which inspires and causes these. That one thing is the struggle of the workman against the capitalist. It is because the workmen in the great cities, and especially in Paris, by their numbers, by their intelligence, by their social unity and intensity of purpose, are strong enough to insist on a government in their own interest, that the capital represents the cause of the workman, as the peasants of the country, whom the fatal blunder of the Revolution converted into proprietors, represent the cause of wealth. So, too, the Republic has become the symbol of government in the interest of the people, as Monarchy is the symbol of government in the interest of privileged orders and proprietary classes. And the Commune represents responsible action in the interest of the public, as the Assembly represents artificial administration and the rivalry of "interests."

196

And so all these contrasted systems virtually spring out of the grand contrast of all society, those who live by their labour, and those who live by accumulated capital. And the transcendant importance of this crisis is this — that for the first time in modern Europe the workmen of the chief city of the Continent have organised a regular government in the name of a new social order.

That social order as yet is most vaguely apprehended; but it is not to any sensible extent a system of Communism. There may be an element of enthusiastic Communists amongst the leaders; but the people are not, and never can be, in a body Communists. It is one of the vulgar calumnies against Comte that his system countenances Communism, of which it is the most resolute opponent. It is, as he proved, the very starting-point of all society to recognise property under proper conditions. He showed that to be logical, Communism must extend to the family — to wife, children, home, and all the domestic surroundings. He showed that to exercise over the individual that amount of control, and to exact from him that amount of social devotion, which is essential to every system of Communism, it would be fatal to leave him in possession of his own family, to the individualist influence of his household. Thus, far from shaking the foundations of property, it is the purpose of Positivism to add to its power, and to increase its freedom. But if it increase the freedom of property from material trammels, it is to subject it to real and effectual moral control. And hence in preserving the institution of property its power must be moralised and its uses consecrated by a constant sense of social duty.

Thus, though the mass of the workmen in Paris, like the mass of the people everywhere, who cling with intense love to their personal and domestic belongings, are not and never can be Communists, they passionately believe in the spirit of which Communism is the gross and extravagant expression. The people of Paris believe not in any god, nor in any man. But they have a religion of their own, for which they are ready to die. That religion is the faith that capital and its holders must adapt themselves to nobler uses, or they had better cease to exist. A society in which generation after generation passes away, consolidating vast and ever-increasing hoards of wealth, opening to the wealthy enchanted realms of idleness, luxury, and waste — laying on the labourer, generation after generation, increasing burdens of toil, destitution, and despair; a society in which capital has created a gospel of its own, and claims for the good of society a divine right of selfishness, the right to exert its powers at will indefinitely for the indulgence of its own desires, rebelling against any social control, and offering up "with a light heart" the misery and degradation of the poor as a sad but inevitable sacrifice on the altar of competition — such a society these workmen of Paris will not for ever tolerate. The war and the siege had rudely broken the splendid flow of the established order of things. For once luxury, pomp, and accumulation had been arrested in mid-career. For six months they had all stood, rich and poor, side by side on the ramparts. They had seen themselves all brought down to the simple worth of man. They had seen the millionaire unable to buy a loaf with his hoards; they had seen the master of factories as poor and as helpless as Crusoe on his island. They had been called on to serve in arms, and they had served. They had been ill-led, ill-governed, distrusted, and eventually stung by a crushing and unexpected surrender. And now they were told it was all over. Their idle season was ended. The workshops in time would open; in the meanwhile, they must shift for themselves, and in the first place pay the arrears of rent and debt which had grown whilst the war had suspended trade and cut off their earnings. It was hard, but they must submit to the law of competition, and supply, and demand. They must shift for themselves; the great god Competition would, somehow, bring them out at last. In the interval, numbers might starve or rot; but soon trade would revive; capital, if they were quiet, would timidly return, and condescend to send for them; the gaiety and life of the city were even now recovering; luxury, wealth, self-indulgence, and gilded vice were hastening back to their old haunts after their tedious absence in foreign capitals; pleasure would come back to her wild satyr dance, and enterprise to her grand mill, by whose myriad wheels colossal fortunes would be reared, and through whose gates the poor might crowd and crush for their pittance. The old familiar world had been suspended; but was not dead. It was about to restore its wonted triumph; and whilst the poor scrambled and struggled for bread and life, Competition and Riot should renew the spectacle of selfish and pitiless ostentation.

And this, the workmen of Paris, with arms in their hands, this, they said, should not be for ever. Little knowing how to end it, or what it might be that could save them, they have thrown up this tremendous yet wild veto on the absolute reign of capital. It is their protest against the selfish anti-social independence of wealth — a protest which now may fail of effect, which has but a small programme of its own, which may soon be silenced and crushed for a time, but a protest which nothing can stifle for ever. The evil, it is true, is deeper than can be reached by any wild protest. Man cannot be forced by law, nor by revolutions, to be just, generous, and right minded. As a political and violent remedy of profound social disorders, the Revolution of the Commune is abortive, and must fail. These disorders need a true education, a new morality, and an organised religion of social duty. But as a political solution of a profound political disorder, the oppression of the cities by the rural suffrage, the cause of the Commune has triumphed, however cruel the reaction it may suffer. Their great political programme is effectually founded in France; is sufficiently suggested to Europe; and the bloody vengeance of the Monarchists will not blot it out from the memory of the future.

Frederic Harrison.

(1)   I have this on the authority of an aminent (foreign) eye-witness.
(2)   I have reason to know that the editor of an English newspaper,

on being urged to correct certain statements hostile to the movement, replied that it would never do to say anything in favour of the Commune.

(3)   The ordinary language of British Respectability reading its newspaper has been: "Would to God the Prussians would go in and exterminate the whole lot of them." A curious instance of this blind rancour was seen in the published letter of a person who signed himself an "English Officer," and writing from Paris. After conferring with the Versailles generals, he inspected and minutely described the exact posts of the Federals, and pointed out the weakness of their position, though, as he said, "it would not be right to explain the positions of the Versailles troops." Here was an officer and a gentleman, to whom it seemed quite natural to play the amateur spy in a war which did not concern him, and against a Government which admitted him as a neutral, and whose protection he was himself claiming. But then it was the government of the common enemy — the workman.

THE FALL OF THE COMMUNE

The Fortnightly Review

During the massacres which followed the entrance of the Versailles troops into Paris, a friend of my own was the eye-witness of the following scene:— A woman, speechless and bleeding, was being dragged through the street to be shot as a *petroleuse;* a furious mob were assailing her with imprecations and blows. She was on the point of being shot by the troops, when a bystander stepped forward to proclaim her innocence. The fury of the mob was at once turned upon him, and both he and the woman were in imminent danger of their lives. At length, almost by chance, it was recognised that the woman was the cook of a neighbour's family, who had crossed the street to buy a bottle of salad oil.

One who attempts to discuss the recent events in Paris does so to an audience almost as little prepared to listen as those who were on the point of murdering this woman. An attempt to prove that certain crimes were not committed at all is regarded as the same thing as the justification of them. No one who has not himself sought to trace out the evidence for any particular act in these events can conceive the cloud of false witness in which the whole is involved. During the early days of the Commune I tried to explain what appeared to me, after investigation, to be the true character of this movement. I was not as has been assumed or insinuated, the unhesitating apologist of its acts. Believing as I do Communism in all its forms to be a dangerous dream, I unhesitatingly condemned all that was Communistic in the movement. Repudiating as I do every attempt to settle social problems by violent means, I distinctly condemned its acts of violence. But I saw that, in spite of this, a great and fruitful purpose was in it. I justified it as a defence of the legally-established Republic of

France against a conspiracy of deputies. I insisted that its administration had been marked by striking success; and, on the whole, by few crimes. During the delirium which accompanied its extinction in blood, I expressed no hasty opinion. The facts were involved in such a chaos that no serious writer, speaking under his own name and looking to more than the opinion of to-day, could consistently stake his character upon any complete view of the circumstances. There is no man living who, from every principle that he has professed and from every accidental interest of life, could feel more appalled than I at such an act as the deliberate burning of Paris. Of all men we, who look on the living as but trustees for the coming generations of the labours of the dead, are those who feel most deeply any wanton destruction of the common inheritance of mankind. I need not add that the murder of unarmed prisoners would not meet from me with one word of palliation. It was necessary, before speaking of events so tremendous and so wildly misrepresented, to satisfy one's self by a patient and personal investigation of what has actually taken place. This I have now done. I have examined many men, both English and French, who were present and eyewitnesses of the scenes which marked the fall of the Commune; I have critically studied, I believe, the whole of the journals which appeared in Paris during those weeks; and I have most carefully compared the statements of those who were the earliest to enter the city.

No one who has not examined into it for himself can conceive the delirium into which the human mind may be thrown by events such as these, or the degree to which misstatement can be carried by crowds of infuriated writers and speakers repeating with variations what can be ultimately proved to be a deliberate invention. Historians have frequently shown us how in times of public excitement the wildest and most meaningless belief is propagated under the combined influence of terror and hatred. Given a state of society in which two orders, two races, two parties, find themselves brought face to face with mutual

202

loathing and fear, and we have that phenomenon which has puzzled after generations — when wholesale cruelties are perpetrated by entire populations under what has been eventually proved to be a childish invention. During the Middle Ages, it was quite a common thing for a wholesale massacre of the Jews to be preached as a duty towards God, and carried out with unrelenting ferocity, under the idea that the accursed race had crucified a Christian baby. Under the Roman Emperors, the calmest statesmen and the most philosophic historians saw and approved the extirpation of Christian sects by endless barbarities, under the idea that they were the enemies of political society, who met for the purpose of celebrating horrible rites. In our own days we have seen how, in questions of race, the wildest stories of mutilation and bloodshed, said to have been committed by native Hindoos and by African slaves, have been passionately believed by the white races on the spot; and how years have scarcely sufficed to dissipate what we now know to be an invention. Where social or race hatreds are so deep, anything is believed on the one side or the other, and the human intellect becomes the prey of extravagances which are in the true sense of the word actual mania.

Let any one read for himself, as I have done, and compare one with the other the newspapers published in Paris during the week which followed the entry of the Versailles troops. He will find there statements about the same matter repeated with every circumstantial detail, and with a curious appearance of accuracy, day after day, in fifty contradictory ways. He will find every leading member of the Commune captured or killed under fresh circumstances every morning. And these tales are repeated oftenest about men like Cluseret, Pyat, and others, whom we now know never to have been captured at all. They were all sheer forgeries. Circumstantial accounts of the destruction of various public buildings of Paris are repeated day by day — are written, printed, published, and read by men who were standing within half a mile of the uninjured building. Half the newspapers in Paris on Saturday, the 27th of May, when almost the whole city was in possession of the troops, repeat that the Palais de Justice, the Sainte Chapelle, and the Theatre of the Chatelet (to mention these instances only) are reduced to ruin. It is known to every one now that they are untouched. In a word, no one reading the French newspapers of that time with the light of our present knowledge, can fail to see that they are filled from beginning to end with unadulterated fiction. It is not news which they give us, but wilful lying.

There is a feature about the Paris press which is not sufficiently known in this country. A portion of it, and that by far the most widely read, is made up of paragraphs which, professing to be statements of fact, are nothing but idle invention. We are apt to imagine, when we see in a newspaper a statement of this or that having happened in some part of the city, that, if not quite correct in its details, there is some foundation for what is alleged. The contrary, however, is the case with the Paris press; and with many of the best known Paris newspapers the staff of so-called reporters are simply romancists, who, sitting at their desks, evolve these statements from their own inner consciousness. When we read, for instance, how Delescluze was taken at Villers-le-Bel disguised as a beggar, and attempting to escape, and what he said, and how he looked when he was captured (the said Delescluze lying all the while dead upon a barricade in Paris); when we read at least in ten different versions, all of them contradictory, how Courbet the painter fought for his life and was killed by the troops (the said Courbet being for weeks after this in his own house) — we are not to suppose that this is a mere mistake of person, place, or circumstance, but simply that the story from beginning to end is due to the brain of some petty follower of Eugene Sue. Circumstantial accounts of how the petroleum was spread upon rags, and curtains, and carpets; how the Archbishop looked when he was shot, and what he said; *fac similes* of orders for the

burning of certain quarters or particular buildings; proclamations, documents, and statements said to have been
found (where, we are not told) by a soldier (name not
given) on the person of a dead member of the Commune
(not further particularised) — we must remember that
these are all due to the ingenuity of a few practised pens
working at a desk. A large portion of the Boulevard
journalism is devoted to simple forgeries. A case in point is
the long letter of M. Thiers to the Pope, now officially
asserted to be a fabrication. Another is a letter pretending
to be written by Dr. Karl Marx. This is now known to be a
forgery. The same is the case with various proclamations
and addresses of the *Internationale,* letters and orders of
leading Communists, and professed statements of theirs.
Forgeries all — wilful idle lies, which goaded the fury of
the public, and earned for the writer a few francs.

Let us take a single instance of this work. In the history
of these events there is none more completely worked out
than the story of the disguised firemen pumping petroleum
on the burning buildings. If we are to believe anything at
all, it appears certain that scores and scores of men were
shot for this supposed offence. The newspapers are full of
circumstantial details, how at a particular street, at a
particular building, some ten or twenty men were found
thus adding to the flames. It is quite certain that men were
put to death on this ground. Now if any one will look at
this story with a moment's calmness, he will see that a
more outrageous absurdity was hardly ever suggested to a
people mad with panic. From a mere mechanical point of
view it is ridiculous, and a moment's thought might con-
vince any one that men, whose object it was to spread fire
through a city as widely as possible, would occupy themselves with setting fire to untouched buildings, and not
with pouring petroleum upon buildings which were already
in full blaze. Nor, indeed, is the story now believed by any
rational person who has had any opportunity of inquiring
into the facts; and this grotesque invention will take the
place of the Christian baby who was believed to have been

crucified by the Jews in the Middle Ages. Again, if there is one feature of the scene which is more widely believed in than another, it is that women spread themselves through the city in organised bands for the purpose of burning down private houses with bottles of petroleum. The idea having been once started by some ingenious brain, was worked out with every variety of suggestion. Young children, we were told, were the favourite agents. The women carried about the petroleum in their chignons; demure market-women were found with their baskets just emptied of explosive material. Certain it is that, in the panic of the moment, the Parisians sedulously covered up the air-holes of their vaults, down which these demons were believed to be pouring inflammable oil. Men who have passed that week in Paris, Englishmen, perfectly well known, of the highest intelligence and honour, have assured me that the whole idea was a wild absurdity, that not a single authentic case was established, and that the pretended mode of setting fire to houses is a simple impossibility. The hundreds of wretched creatures who, in the madness of the hour were torn to pieces, or shot without the chance of explanation, were victims, like the woman of the anecdote just mentioned, of the mere madness of the moment; and the people of Paris gave themselves over to that same delirium which we read befell the Athenians after the mutilation of the Hermae, or the Romans when they believed the Christians had burned Rome.

Yet this was the state of the public mind, and these were the sources from which all our information has hitherto been derived. The correspondents of English newspapers, many of them men of the highest acumen, courage and good faith, were themselves more or less under the influence of the Parisian press, which may be described not so much as mendacious in relating facts, as busy solely in inventing paragraphs. The English reporters could but tell us what was the belief of the men amongst whom they lived, and naturally had no time or opportunity to verify what on the face of them were authentic documents. More careful investigation, and the personal examination of those who were on the spot, must lead any man who undertakes the task to the conviction that the whole story of the fall of the Commune, as at present known to the English public, is little better than a nightmare. Let any man accustomed to deal with historical evidence attempt to verify any single incident and really to satisfy his own mind — how, when, by whose order, for instance, the Palace of the Tuileries was burnt — and it is certain that he will find no foothold of sure ground. Having patiently sought for these proofs myself, I most urgently ask that the judgment upon the facts must be suspended; for I am certain that no impartial mind can satisfy itself that there is any evidence whatever upon which to form a judgment. With a full sense of the responsibility which I incur, I most distinctly insist that there is no evidence whatever of any concerted plan or organised attempt to destroy Paris as a city, or wantonly to injure private property or houses. I am not about to undertake — what I assert is at present an impossible task — the establishing in detail the truth about these tremendous events. Much, however, is already certain. It is certain that the supposed plan of the Commune to bury itself under the ashes of Paris is a gratuitous invention. It is certain that the stories about petroleum are one and all wild calumnies. It is certain that the Versailles army, if it did not actually destroy the principal public buildings, by pouring a storm of shells upon them, did that the almost inevitable consequence of which was to set fire to them. It is certain that the destruction of houses and property in the suburbs, caused by the shells launched by the orders of M. Thiers, exceeded tenfold that in the houses burned in any way by the order of the Commune. It is certain that the private houses destroyed in the streets of Paris suffered from the ordinary effects of a desperate street warfare. A mere catalogue of the barricades and of the houses destroyed will show that in almost every case the ruin is due to the proximity of the house to an important barricade. English eye-witnesses of the most undoubted good faith saw with their own eyes shells pouring on public buildings without intermission for hours consecutively; and we know, from the experience of the Prussian War, that when a city is systematically shelled a conflagration is inevitable. The most bitter enemy of the Commune, the "Parisian Correspondent" in the *Times*, has shown by elaborate proofs that the whole of the conflagrations resulted from the strategic system of defence. If the Communists desired to destroy Paris, why did they not do it? And why is it that the richest quarter, from the Madeleine to the Porte St. Martin, including the two Opera Houses, is practically uninjured?

Let us now follow for a moment the course of events. The late elections have proved to the world that the Bordeaux Assembly was in no sense the representative of France, but was simply a conspiracy of Bourbonists and priests. They have also proved to the world that Paris, after all that has taken place, that France herself, is unalterably Republican. I repeat what I wrote in April, that the movement of the Commune was in the first instance the effort of Republican Paris to defend the established constitution of the country against the machinations of a cabal of deputies. The 150,000 bayonets that Paris at one time mustered were in fact Republicans, determined to defend the Republic. The attempt which is made by the Romish priesthood and the Bourgeois journals throughout Europe to make out that these 150,000 men were the enemies of human society, and were in arms to rob good people of their property, is a suggestion as silly as it was malicious. Indeed the majority of them were not Communists, but Republicans.

The insurrection of Paris, in spite of all that has been said, was not in any sense an abnormal or incomprehensible outbreak against the established institutions of society, family, and country, but was as clearly a political movement as any in history. Its immediate occasion was a belief, for which we now know there were only too many

FREDERIC HARRISON

grounds, that an Assembly got together by a few priests and landlords during the spasm of the capitulation of Paris was about to overturn the established order of things. It has now been made known — for the account was published in the Versailles newspapers, and was signed by an officer on the staff of the War Office, who was himself an eye-witness of the fact — that the murder of Generals Thomas and Le Comte was effected by some of their own soldiers, against the efforts of the National Guard and their officers, who were present on the spot, and had scarcely been carried out before an order arrived from the Central Committee for their release. With regard to the affair of the Place Vendôme, it so happened that there were two distinguished foreign generals, who saw the incident from the windows of their hotel, and who have positively proved that it was an armed attack upon the most important military post of the National Guard. It is now certain that the administration of the public offices, in spite of the unparalleled difficulties of the situation, was never more efficiently carried on than after it had fallen into the hands of the men of the 18th of March. Order was better preserved in the street than it had been in the days of Napoleon, with his thousand of gendarmes. It is now ascertained that neither public nor private property was plundered by the authority of the Communal Government; that, though surrounded by implacable enemies, and attacked by ceaseless conspiracies, no single life was taken whilst the Commune remained an organised body. The government which was absolutely obeyed by a city of two million inhabitants, which carried on with regularity its complex administration, which could call into the field 150,000 bayonets, which failed in none of the functions of a regular government, which had received the sanction of more than 200,000 votes in a single city, and which maintained its vitality for two months, was in every sense a real, though it may be a revolutionary, authority.

Yet the first act of the Versailles Government was to cover the origin, principles, and acts of this authority with furious abuse, to treat the entire population of the capital as felons, and to massacre in cold blood those whom it captured. For a time the seizure of hostages checked this act of wanton barbarity, but as the siege went on, and the hopes of the Versailles Government rose higher, and as the creatures of Napoleon returned from their German captivity, it became obvious to all who were watching events that a deadly vengeance was being planned. During the closing weeks the reappearance of the monster Galifet, and the wholesale butcheries of unarmed men at Clamart and Moulin Saquet, prepared us for the worst. If any statement whatever is to be believed, it is proved that the explosion in the Avenue Rapp was the work of incendiaries from Versailles, an explosion by which hundreds of innocent persons were killed and mangled. The delay with which the Versailles troops conducted the ultimate attack was inexplicable to those who were looking on, and who were not aware that M. Thiers was relying upon the work of treachery, and had a very sinister understanding with the German army. The vendetta of Versailles was preached by the clergy, it was urged from the tribune, it was gloated over in the press; its aim was not so much to crush the insurrection of Paris as to catch the whole body of the insurgents in one vast net. At the appointed signal the Germans on their side closed the city behind, whilst treachery opened it to the Versailles troops in the front. From that moment a scene of massacre began, such as in recent ages has never disgraced the soldiers of any regular army. I have it from an English witness of the highest respectability that quarter was refused to the prisoners taken with arms during the whole week. "The incendiarism," he adds, "is always quoted as a justification of this, but the 'no quarter' began on the Monday morning, and the burning did not begin till Tuesday afternoon, and it was Wednesday night before the poor Archbisop suffered. During all that time every person taken was shot." "Petroleum is another justification," he says, "but there is clear evidence that the *petroleuses* never existed, and that they never burned anything." A reference to the English newspapers will show that the English correspondents saw the execution of prisoners taken in arms before a single building was fired in Paris, and heard from Versailles officers the parts that they had taken in this butchery. It was eagerly proclaimed in the Assembly, it was the avowed policy of M. Thiers, and it was the boast of the leaders of the army, that every one connected directly or indirectly with the insurrection of the Commune, and that all who had attempted to defend it in arms, should suffer. In a word, the workmen of Paris were to be treated like wild beasts, netted and smoked out of their lair.

I deliberately say, that crime so infernal in its cruelty and so vast in its area has never, in recent ages, been committed by any political party whatever. It was the victorious party in a civil war proclaiming war to the knife against their opponents, with the avowed purpose, not so much of establishing their own authority, as of exterminating the other side. Nothing in the acts of the old revolutionists of France, nothing in the story of modern political warfare, bears any parallel to it. We must go back to the times in which hatred as furious was at work — the massacre of St. Bartholomew and the capture of Magdeburg. The party which has deliberately assumed the weight of this enormous crime, the party of Order in France, are not the men who have a right to bring any charge against their opponents, or to pretend that any such crimes whatever justified their own, which in point of time plainly preceded them. The attempt to cloak this system of extermination by charging their victims with every possible and every impossible crime, was worthy of the original design; but the statement that every man who bore arms within the city of Paris — ay, and every woman too — was, to use the phrase of the hour, "a fiend in human shape," was simply a repetition of the type of calumny in which civic hatred veils its atrocities. It must not be forgotten that down to the Sunday night when the army of Versailles effected an entrance in Paris, and re-commenced on system a massacre of prisoners, no single life can fairly be laid to the account of the ruling power in Paris. We, at any rate, cannot forget that it was the Commune which had publicly burned the guillotine, which had abolished the conscription, which had repudiated the doctrine of national retaliation, and was a living protest against the whole system of war. If of these rival parties either must be counted as outside the pale of humanity, it was certainly not the people of Paris, guiltless of the blood of a single citizen, and who had laid down their lives for the cause of independence, but rather that so-called party of Order who were in league with the foreign enemy to crush their domestic rivals, who had introduced into regular warfare the savage practice of murdering disarmed men, and who, for the first time in modern political strife, had determined that their victory should mean not so much their own restoration to power as the butchery of their opponents.

What passed during that week in Paris when, the national enemy stopping up the earths in the rear, the soldiers of the Versailles Government had free licence to slay any citizen of Paris, and when the principle of death to every Communist had proved to be a bloody reality — what went on, I say, is not yet known, and may never be completely known. When men who had headed a successful revolution saw the cause for which their lives had been spent trampled down by a party in league with a foreign power, and the citizens who had elected them and maintained them in power butchered in cold blood — saw themselves pursued and treated like mad dogs — there is no limit to what they may have been driven in their desperation. I do not pretend to say what mad purpose may have been worked by individual men so sorely tried as these were, but I do say that it would be folly to wonder much at anything they might have done. For my part I can find not a shred of definite evidence — nay, I will say, not a grain of resonable probability — that the public buildings of Paris were deliberately or wantonly burned in sheer revenge. As to the deliberate destruction of works of art and national monuments, however deep the offence, it is impossible to forget that most modern nations, and most assuredly the English, are open to a similar charge. When the British army burnt the Summer Palace of Pekin it was an act of destruction as wanton as can possibly be conceived. That was done for the sole purpose of wounding and humiliating an enemy after a desperate conflict. It was chosen as being that particular national monument which was most surrounded with national pride. From the point of view of art there can be little doubt that ten Tuileries and their contents would not to the true artist and historian be a loss so irreparable as was that of the Palace of the Emperors of China. And when another British army wantonly burnt the Capitol of Washington, it was the destruction of a famous national building for the sole purpose of humiliating the pride of an enemy. If even it were true that the public buildings of Paris were deliberately destroyed by the Commune, it would be an act which, however we might condemn or deplore it, is such as, under similar circumstances, has been often equalled in crime, and which assuredly is a crime immeasurably less than that to which a blood-thirsty faction drove the Government of Versailles. But, as I have said before, I can find no reasonable proof, or even probable ground, for believing that the fires of Paris were the result of a settled plan. If in the midst of fighting, continued for a week, during which a storm of shell was poured night and day across the city, in which every great building was the scene of a separate and bloody engagement, buildings had not been set on fire, it would have been little short of a miracle.

It must not be forgotten that, in order to charge with incendiarism the entire people of Paris, to justify the massacre of every supposed Communist or of every National Guard, it is necessary to show that this incendiarism was in the nature of a distinct purpose, planned and carried out by public authority, and generally known and approved by the body of the people. The fiercest denouncers of the

Parisian Guard would hardly venture to say that if, at the time of a general massacre, in the midst of a hundred unconnected street battles, in the paralysis of all authority and the disappearance of all governing power, orders had been given and executed by a few irresponsible men — it matters not how criminal or savage — that this would be sufficient to make the population of a city, its men, women, and children, equally worthy of death — that this could justify their entire extermination. Now I challenge any one fairly to read through the Parisian newspapers of the week preceding the capture, and to believe that any such violent design was present to the mind of the people, or had been broached in the councils of their leaders. The debates of the Communal Chamber have been published up to the last day of their meeting and it is plain that up to the hour of the entrance of the Versailles troops the Government of Paris were thinking only of the administration of the city. It is an argument resting mainly on negative evidence, but in a case like this negative evidence is all-important. If here and there an ingenious correspondent has detected in a newspaper a paragraph about "Moscow rather than capitulation" (and such paragraphs were not one-tenth part as numerous as they were during the siege of the Prussians), no one with an open mind can come to any other conclusion that neither the National Guard, nor the people of Paris, nor the Commune as a body, nor its leaders in office or in journalism, had ever conceived a plan remotely akin to that of burning Paris, or even destroying its monuments.

I am not about to shirk the case of the murder of the Archbishop and the other hostages. Under whatever circumstances it was done, and by whomsoever it was ordered, it was in my opinion, as in that of every right-minded man, a wanton murder; but it is certain that on the Wednesday on which it was accomplished all organised government in Paris had come to an end, the city was one scene of battle and of massacre, no responsible authority existed, and the leaders of the Commune who survived

214

were engaged either in directing isolated street fights, or escaping the fury of their pursuers. It has now been ascertained that the execution of the hostages was, up to the last moment that the Commune existed as an organised body, opposed by the principal leaders, and most signally by the chief of them, Delescluze himself. It has now been ascertained that it was a wild act of fury carried out by some irresponsible men, without the knowledge of their colleagues, and certainly without the knowledge of the people of Paris, and under circumstances which must make such an act hardly a cause for astonishment. It was a retaliation for the wholesale murder of captured Federals. But on this subject I will quote an authority, in whose high character and good sense we can thoroughly confide. One who personally went to see the Archbishop at the prison, and who inquired into the circumstances of his arrest and detention, writes as follows:—

"There is no disposition to punish them as criminals. On the contrary, they receive in some important respects a consideration and indulgence which could scarcely be accorded them if they were not formally recognised as innocent of any crime. They are kept merely as hostages in order that their safety may be a guarantee of the safety of those Communists who fall into the hands of the Versaillais. I am not prepared to justify their detention, though, unless the whole theory of hostages be indefensible, I don't see how it can be altogether condemned; and there is, at least, this much to be said for it, that it was to a great extent provoked by the foolish ferocity of some of the military leaders of Versailles. It is highly probable, too, that the ostentatious detention of such men as the Archbishop of Paris, or the President de la Cour de Cassation, may have prevented undue effusion of blood, shed not in a calm spirit of policy to avert wider calamity, but with vindictive fury which would only have led to still more vindictive reprisals. When leaders of high rank like the Marquess de Galifet are ready publicly to encourage their soldiers to shoot down like mad dogs those citizens who, however erroneous and mischievous their views, are many of them thoroughly honest and well intentioned, sincerely believing in the goodness of a cause for which they face death, there is no slight excuse for the leaders on the other side who threaten that for every life thus taken they will take the life of some one whose exalted position ought to make his party anxious to save him. The lives of the political prisoners are not, I believe, in the slightest danger if M. Thiers can make his party consistently carry out his own wise policy of clemency and reconciliation."

Thus wrote at the end of April an able and well-informed correspondent of the *Times*. What he says comes now with double truth when it is known that subsequently, upon the very eve of the capture of Paris, the Communal authorities even offered the Archbishop and six of his companions in exchange for the single person of Blanqui. But the Government of Versailles, who cared less for the safety of the Archbishop and the hostages than for the satisfaction of their own plans of vengeance, contemptuously rejected the proposal, and, leaving the Archbishop to his fate, continued their career of hemming in Paris, and of putting to the sword all who adhered to the Communal side. The blood of these victims does not rest against the Commune as a body, but against some individuals connected with it; and they must be singularly constituted who are prepared to say that the death of some sixty men, whose lives were distinctly taken in retaliation for thousands of unarmed prisoners put to death, is a crime so deep as wholly to put out of sight the inhuman vengeance of those who devoted the armed defenders of a city to summary execution, who massacred in cold blood twenty or thirty thousand of their fellow-citizens, and hunted down the leaders of a rival political party as if they were wild beasts.

We who live under a more favourable political atmosphere do not easily conceive with what ferocious tyranny the Republican leaders of France have had during life to contend. Almost every one of the men who were returned by the City of Paris at the elections which closed the war, were known chiefly as having been the victims of an unrelenting persecution; as having passed the best years of their life at Cayenne and Lambessa; as having been hunted by the Imperial Police; as having wasted in the prisons or in exile. After the *coup d'état* which established the Empire, some twenty thousand men, the flower of the workmen of Paris, were deported to die in different stations. Blanqui, Pyat, Delescluze, Vermorel, Rochefort, and the rest, were known to us of old as having fought the battle of true civic life against that unforgiving despotism. Let us take the life of such a man as Delescluze himself — a man of high training, of great powers, and, in spite of the calumnies of the party of assassination, a man of inflexible honesty. His first entrance into public life was a familiarity with a royal prison. He defended the insurrection of June, 1848, and subsequently escaped to England; but on his return to France, in 1854, he was instantly arrested and tried upon the old charge, arising out of events before the *coup d'état* or the Empire, and again sentenced to unlimited transportation. For two years they kept him in the docks of Toulon — this great and heroic spirit chained with a cannon ball to a common felon — then they thrust him into the hold of a transport and sent him to Cayenne. The voyage recalled the worst horrors of the middle passage of the old slave trade. There was neither light nor air, and scarcely food, in this foul dungeon. When the ship reached Cayenne, he was found, contrary to expectation, to be still alive. Instead of landing him on the coast, with a devilish refinement of cruelty, he was put in the hold and returned back to Toulon, with the obvious purpose of putting him to death. Still he lived. Five times backward and forward across the Atlantic he made that horrible voyage, without ever leaving his dungeon in the ship's hold, until it seemed almost as hard to kill the life in his body as it was to crush the spirit in his soul. In sheer despair at the end of the fifth voyage he was taken out of the ship, and passed the best years of his life at Cayenne. The story of Delescluze is in one sense the story of the rest. Persecutions, imprisonments, exile, transportation, calumny, suborned witnesses, and forged documents, every device of unrelenting tyranny, had been brought to bear upon these men for twenty years. Scenes such as these do not improve the temper, and may sometimes deteriorate the character, and it would not be strange if they who had borne and lived through this were not prepared to quit their place and power with the well-bred grace which sits so well upon our English statesmen on a change of Ministry or the downfall of a party. Tried as they were, and brought to bay at last with political opponents thirsting for their blood, the enemies of their country on one side and an army of 100,000 men on the other stopping up every avenue of escape, struck down by a system of extermination more sweeping than anything which history has seen since the days of St. Bartholomew, I assert fearlessly that these men will be proved to have been singularly free from crime, to have abstained in a striking degree from the natural acts of the last despair, and will stand out in the future beside the butchers of Versailles as political, ay, and as religious martyrs. English eye-witnesses of undoubted good faith have described to us how the high-minded Delescluze — who from the first had seen that ruin was inevitable — remained night and day at his post, until nature sank exhausted with the strain, and then with a few kind words to those around him, utterly unlike the melodramatic folly which calumny has put into his mouth, took up his walking stick, and, uncovering his grey hairs and baring his undaunted breast, walked feebly but manfully to the top of a barricade. The figure of that noble old man will remain in history, though the bestial *Figaro* heap calumny on his memory, and the Government of Versailles has destroyed his very bones.

Now that language has exhausted its resources in denouncing the supposed acts of the Republicans of Paris, there remains for Englishmen to pronounce their judgment on the other side of the picture. They have not yet done so. Two months have passed and in our current judgments there is still a strange miscarriage of justice. We have had brought before our very eyes the picture of a vast, wild, and yet concerted massacre, by the victorious party — a massacre on a scale as great as any recorded in history, as hideous in its details, and as blind in its fury — and we are still denouncing the burning of palaces. Nay, there have been found men who in the midst of this new reign of terror, had no thought but how they might assist in feeding the shambles. A heavy responsibility rests on those who direct English opinion. They must show us that they hate a massacre at least as much as they hate incendiarism. They have still to show us that their antipathy to political vengeance is something like honest humanity, and not the mere expression of political feeling. If men are found dealing tenderly with a reign of terror when they happen to detest those who suffer in it, they must make up their minds to face results. What they are doing is, in fact, to make massacre one of the instruments of political warfare, and to teach us that our horror of bloodshed can be reduced to a simple question of party.

It has often been falsely asserted that to defend the popular cause is to justify every excess of revolution. No revolutionist of character has ever spoken of these with any language but abhorrence. It is now our turn to remind conservatives of their rule. Let the party of Order condemn with no uncertain voice the atrocities committed in the name of order. A reign of terror to punish revolution seems to meet at their hands with a very different treatment from a reign of terror to maintain one. The professions, indeed, of Englishmen have always been that political massacres were evil in themselves and for whatever end. Politically speaking, the Vendeans of '93 were committing the very same offence as the Parisians of today, with this difference, that it was they, and not their opponents, who were in league with the foreign enemy. But it has always been our faith and boast that we would suffer no political offence to justify wholesale massacre. We denounced the butcheries of Carrier, not because we sided with the Vendeans, but simply because it was butchery. Yet there is not a crime committed by the terrorists of '93, which has not been surpassed by the terrorists of Versailles. The old revolution can show no massacre in the same area, and within the same period, so enormous as that which the Government of Versailles inflicted upon the population of Paris. They commenced with the fusillade of prisoners on a scale which surpasses Fouché, Carrier, or Tallien. English eye-witnesses have told us how they showed the same ferocity to the captives, to the wounded, and to the dying; how men and women were smashed to death by muskets, or ripped up with bayonets; how prisoners were chained in gangs and shot in heaps along the line of march. They have reproduced for us the very court-martial of the September assassins, sitting in the Chatelet Theatre. They have told us how the very hospitals were ransacked for the maimed, to add to the piles of slain. Throughout more than a week regular slaughter-houses were set up in various parts of the city, in which the captives were butchered in heaps. Englishmen by scores have seen and told us how every outrage was inflicted on gangs of prisoners on their way to the poisonous dungeons of Versailles — how old men and young women were driven in by bayonet thrusts, and shot as they sank down from exhaustion. They have seen officers with their own hands mangle their prisoners and leave them writhing in agony; they have seen them slash off a woman's shoulder for a defiant word; and they tell us of lines of young girls dragged off to be hacked to death on the fallen altar of Imperial Moloch, "after first being publicly disgraced."

There is this difference between the crimes which are charged against the Commune and the massacre of which we are now speak. There is no evidence whatever, there is not even a probable suggestion, that the burning of Paris was a meditated act of revenge. The massacres rest on the most undoubted testimony — on the authority of English eye-witnesses, many of whom are well known, and of most unimpeachable character; and, if in this scene of bloodshed there is one feature which has been authenticated better than another, it has been the mode in which the captured prisoners were put to death. It seems too horrible to dwell on; yet horror was never held as a ground for forgetting the acts of Carrier; and there is one loathsome feature in the story which even exceeds the worst of his crimes. It seems that the ferocity of Algerian commanders had called for a new engine of massacre to which the guillotine is a toy. We are told, incredible as it sounds, but in a manner which it is impossible to distrust, unless we distrust every other statement whatever, that the mitrailleuse has been used to destroy whole gangs of prisoners at once. Just before the war began, in July, 1870, a loathsome story went round the press. We were told how at the trial of these new machines of death a group of knacker's horses had been chained together as a target; how for some minutes, under the exulting eyes of imperial chiefs, the storm of bullets poured into the quivering mass which writhed in a heap of crushed flesh. It made one sick to hear of, though the target then was but one of worn-out horses. But in these latter days these devilish engines, we were told, have been heard shrieking hour by hour in all quarters of the city; their targets now were chained men and women, some of them noble enthusiasts, some of them young girls — all of them, at least having sought certain death for their cause. The imagination faints as it tries to recall the scene — how into this target, into this mass of intense human life, the leaden hail was driven, crushing the bone and flesh of hundreds into one horrible pulp, till it grew into one shapeless mass of splinter, blood, and quivering muscle, writhing, and slowly stiffening into such a gigantic pile of human agony as Dante may have seen in hell, but such as surely this earth never saw before.

This was not the licence of a maddened soldiery. Suppose that we put aside and count as nothing what was done in actual fight. The organised massacres I speak of were effected by responsible officers, on a regular system, in parts of the city which were perfectly conquered. It was continued for a whole week. It was not madness, for it went on a system. It had no military necessity; it did not even terrorise, but added to the desperation. It was not caused by the difficulty of guarding captives, or in holding the city. The Germans had easily guarded 175,000 French prisoners at once, and in such a city as Paris it was easy to secure any number of prisoners in any sort of groups. This barbarity was not necessary to conquer Paris. It did not aid, but seriously impeded its conquest. It is trifling with us to pretend that it was caused by the fury of the contest, or by any military object. The Marquis de Galifet (the Carrier of our time) is escorting a gang of prisoners to Versailles; he halts them at the Arc de Triomphe, selects eighty, and, to refresh himself, shoots them in cold blood. We know this for a fact, for there chanced to be an Englishman amongst them, an innocent and accidental victim, like so many there. Four or five different shambles are set up in various parts of the city, over which staff officers preside, and where whole battalions of prisoners are shot by the mitrailleuse. All this was after every pretence of contest was over. It is stupid hypocrisy to pretend that this was the fury of the combat. Let us give it its true name. It was simply an organised attempt by one political party in a civil war to exterminate the rival political party. This butchery was no sudden frenzy, but was a determined plan. We all saw it coming. We were told day by day how the partisans of all the monarchic factions were brooding over a vengeance upon their common enemies, the Republican workmen, which should out-do every act of the old reign of terror. Every English observer rehearsed the tale of the murderous temper of Versailles. An English clergyman, who returned during the siege, assures me that he heard at Versailles but one language — "Wait till we take Paris, and you will see La Vendée amply avenged!"

Revenge has been its one object — revenge deadly, vast, and final. Does the language of Marat, or of any Jacobin, exceed that of the organs of Versailles? "Forty thousand Communists only have been killed," cries one leading journal; "why have the other 60,000 escaped military justice?" "There shall be," cries another journal, "but one end for them all — death." What number have actually been slaughtered no one can truly say, or will ever perhaps know. In certain quarters of the city the English eyewitnesses tell us simply "there are no men." It is certain that in many quarters men, women, and children were indiscriminately killed, whether they had been taken in arms or not. Calmer estimates say that 20,000 have been killed, with 30,000 prisoners. And what of these 30,000 men and women? A large portion of them, it is now known, wholly innocent of any act whatever, chained on the fetid mud of Satory, crowded in hulks, stifled in dungeons in Versailles, or more slowly done to death in foreign settlements. The details matter little they think. Order is triumphant, and 50,000 of the most determined Republicans in France rot in the blood-stained trenches, or, still more slowly, in poisonous dens.

Now, I ask plainly, is English society prepared to welcome this result? Do they call this political justice, or is it a true reign of terror? Do they mean to make common cause with those who are responsible for it? Do they shut their eyes to it? Do they extenuate it? Do they think of it merely as something which it were best to forget? If they do they need never display indignation again. They will have simply handed over political and social struggles for the future to one plain issue — that of extermination.

Are they sure that these 50,000 are all morally guilty of the blood of the Archbishop? Is it proved to them that each of these 50,000 conspired to burn down Paris? Are they sure that the slaughter of the hostages was ever known to more than to a few? Do they know which buildings in Paris were burnt by design, which from military necessity, and which by the shells of Versailles? Do they know what the design was, or whose design it was? And if they know all these things, about which we have still but a mass of contradiction, will Englishmen calmly tell us that the murder of some venerable men, and the burning of some historic buildings (authors of both acts, it is true, yet unknown, taking place, be it said, in a war waged without quarter), are crimes so unparalleled in human history that the massacre and deportation of 50,000 men are but a fair equivalent and penalty?

The balance hangs thus: Against the Commune the

execution, in retaliation, of sixty-four hostages, and the alleged burning of certain public buildings, the circumstances of both being still doubtful. Against Versailles, the waging a war without quarter, prisoners shot in cold blood, an organised massacre, dungeons, hulks, and Cayenne, and a population of 50,000 souls swept away. And to be just, we must remember that the atrocities certainly committed by Versailles preceded those alleged to have been committed by Paris; that the latter were carried out, if they were carried out at all, in the last delirium of despair. It is just also to remember that whilst against Versailles must be set this accumulation of vengeance, against the Commune, as an organised government, no slaughter whatever could be charged but that done in fair warfare. The Commune as a body did not exist until after the street riots of March the 18th and 20th. On the capture of the city walls it ceased to exist. Whatever isolated or irresponsible members of the body may have done, as an organised government the Commune has shed no blood. As the *Times* very truly said, they would have shed no blood if they could have had their way. Of Versailles this cannot be said, for their very aim was to exterminate.

It has been the special feature of our national abhorrence of terrorism, that we have always denounced vindictive bloodshed for itself under whatever circumstances and for whatever end. We have held massacre to be evil in all its features and in all its consequences. As a people, we have never faltered or compromised with persecution. It has been to us the one indelible brand on Catholicism. All the lustre of the revolution has not effaced the memory of its horrible revenges. Our creed has been, that massacre is something which must be everywhere and for ever accursed.

And now? Now wholesale butcheries and organised vengeance find us only execrating the victims for what, in their death struggle, they are hastily supposed to have done. It is easy to pile up accusations against the memory of the dead, to believe the cowardly calumnies with which *litterateurs* feed the passions of the party; to scrape sentences from long-forgotten publications, or from the idle forgeries of the Parisian press, that this was a great insurrection against society which must be dealt with in a way that political crime has never been dealt with before. Hitherto the voice of Englishmen has been plain that the political offences of the victims should form no justification for a reign of terror; and we have condemned terrorism not on the ground of party, but in the name of humanity.

It is not likely that politicians in a country like this, whose pride has been to avoid all desperate issues, will be prepared, on cool reflection, to identify the cause of order here with the cause of order in Paris, or will shut their eyes purposely to a new reign of terror because they hate the principles of those who suffer in it. The party of Order in France will be hereafter known in history as the party of blood, and terrorists will be a name that will describe no longer the Republicans of '93, but the Monarchists of '71. Nor is it likely that a people, which still loves to call itself Protestant, will continue long to re-echo the cry of the Roman priesthood, and see in a policy of massacre the triumph of the Gospel, the return to Christ

It is singular that this new system of persecution should have failed to raise more public indignation here, when we remember with whom and with what it is so closely associated. Natural sympathy with the fate of the aged Archbishop of Paris should no longer be suffered to blind us to the part which his Church has played in recent events. Rome gains largely, and hopes yet more, from the extinction of the Commune; and it is eager to use its opportunities. But it is right to recall how deeply it is responsible for all that has been done. We have seen it again, as of old, fanning political animosities by appeals to religious bigotry. The spirit which taught Charles IX., Alva, and Tilly how to crush rebellion, is still at work in our days. The vengeance which has just been recked upon the people of Paris was slowly and in cold blood prepared by that fanaticism which throughout France, in a million homesteads, has preached unwearyingly to the peasants that the people of Paris are accursed of God and man. The Romish priest-hood has proclaimed and insisted on war to the knife between the Church and the Republic. Prelates as amiable as the late Archbishop deliberately tell us, and told us before the fall of the Commune, that Paris is a nest of pirates who must be burned and smoked out of their dens. The Pope himself, in that language which so well becomes the Vicar of Christ, tell us that the Republicans of Paris are "men who have issued from the jaws of hell." That rural Assembly which has just triumphed at Versailles was nothing but a priestly conspiracy. The Bretons and the Vendeans, who were the mainstay of the army of Thiers, were taught that they were engaged in a new crusade; and they who have fanned and organised this spirit of exterm-iniation are now making homilies over the massacres by which they profit. No word of moderation to the butchers or pity for their victims escapes them. For them this unparalleled massacre (wrought as usual by the secular arm) is one of the brightest days in the history of their Church; and over the corpses of 20,000 citizens, with hosannas to the returning conscience of France, they are plotting to restore their "anointed" king, and to regain temporal power for the Pope.

It is a singular proof of the slough of formalism into which our Protestantism has fallen that scarcely a voice is found to repeat that to which it was once our boast to bear witness, that the Papacy is incompatible with human society and order. We have put aside, and rightly put aside, the worn-out invectives against the errors of Romanism as a religion, until we are in danger of forgetting that in the state of modern civilisation it is an intolerable curse to human society. Those truths which inspired some of the greatest characters in our history, and some of the noblest passages in our literature, are now as good as forgotten. Has class sympathy with those to which that Romish Church has attached itself really caused us to forget how little its nature has altered? Is not that religion still what it always was — a religion of lies, with imposture for its creed and servility for its object? Have not advancing ages and the growth of civilisation widened rather than narrowed the breach between that Church and a healthy society? Its head in solemn conclave has recently uttered his idle but malignant curse against every principle that men of sense hold dear, and every belief that men of intelligence hold true. In that arrogant and silly syllabus the Pope has formulated for us, as it were, all that makes the institution which he guides the implacable enemy of all good men. To cripple the intelligence, to spread falsehoods, which the very propagators themselves scoff at, to play into the hands of any tyrant, however mean, to invoke the blessing of God upon any conspiracy, however unscrupulous, to divide nations one against another, and classes in nations against each other, to fight for every abuse, to resist by means, fair or foul, every improvement, and to do all this, if need be, by wading through blood; this is the political character of that Church in its decay. When men of sense refuse to listen to them, they crawl into the confidences of women, working not upon their intelligences, but upon their more excitable nature; when the grown-up would have none of them, they intrigued to get possession of the education of the young, that they might poison manliness and good sense at their very roots. When the intelligent workmen of cities cast them off, they betook themselves to a peasantry, from whom they withheld education in order that they might inspire them with a blind and selfish antipathy to their fellow-workmen of the cities. And when the whole of the middle and working classes had broken through their yoke, and governments and governing classes were treating them with ill-concealed contempt, they played one last cast for power, and offered in return for their possessions to preach a bloody vengeance on the workmen. They it is, these servants of the Reconciler, who have compassed sea and land that they might set peasant against citizen, teaching the world that the workmen of Paris, the

most intelligent, the most unselfish, the most truly religious class in Europe, are fiends in human shape and the
enemies of human society. For twenty years they have
served the tyranny of Napoleon, and have become but a
mere spiritual police. For twenty years they have poisoned
the mind of all French society with the belief that the
workmen of Paris, the men who had most completely
thrown off their yoke, were the enemies of every government and every class. The Archbishop of Paris and the
Curé of the Madeleine, however amiable their natures, and
however respectable their lives, were two of the chiefs of
the alliance between the French Church and the Corsican
dynasty. We see them with the same policy in Spain maintaining to the last the bestial despotism of Isabella. Italy
still rocks and heaves with their plots. The Catholic Church
in Italy is an organised conspiracy against the established
government. In Germany it is tearing society to pieces in a
wanton attempt to enforce by persecution the most
grotesque of all its grotesque doctrines.

We have heard much of late of institutions which are the
enemy of human society. There is an institution of which
this may be said with truth. It is that same Church of
Rome which every year grows in its creed more false, in its
policy more despotic, in its system more inhuman, which
has introduced into political strife the maxims of extermination and the hatred of religious fanaticism which has
now no other hope but to crush out in blood those who
reject it, which is now in unceasing insurrection against
modern society. Are there those who think that any good
cause can gain by the help of such a Power? which is seen
ever ready to sell its support to any party or any leader
who will offer it its wealth and its privileges; which makes
the cause of morality the same thing as the retention of its
endowments; which invokes the name of heaven to pursue
its end without submitting to the check of mere human
considerations; which raises the standard of God that it
may provoke men to discard the pity and justice of man.

It is difficult to see in what the principles of good

government are to gain by the extinction of the Commune in the way that we have seen. The evil which of all others Englishmen have most deplored in France is the extent to which a centralised bureaucracy has crushed all the life out of its people. No sooner has the Government of Thiers triumphed than we see again in all its glory the Imperial system revived; a Chamber which is the mere tool of the chief of the State; elections carried by the will of prefects under the dictation of the government of the day; the old system of an organised police, whose energies are concentrated on maintaining the government in existence; and an administration which entirely centres round the great function of government, the repression and punishment of all political parties opposed to it. Now, the Commune was in the first place a protest against this, not as was ridiculously pretended, with a view to divide France into an infinite number of Communes, but for the purpose, as was well said in one of their official documents, to found a free Paris in a free France. It was well said, in one of the admirable articles in which the Communal leaders endeavoured to enlighten their fellow-citizens, "that to attempt in a great country like France, with thirty-eight millions of inhabitants, to apply everywhere the same rule was to crush the many centres of intelligence throughout the country, and to condemn it to an indefinite succession of bloody revolutions or of intemperate despotism;" or, in the words of Alexis de Tocqueville, "It is in the Commune that the force of a free people rides," or, as Sismondi says, "The Commune is the true country;" or, as De Bonald says, "The Commune is a body more real, more solid, and more visible than either the department or the kingdom." The Commune is crushed, and with it for a time in France all prospect of local independence and life.

Among the leading ideas of the Commune was certainly that of putting an end to the era of national contests, and of founding a state of society such that all Western Europe might gradually form one great country, made up of many independent communities. The Commune had not existed a week before all trace of the hostility to the Germans was at an end. A Prussian, indeed, was a member of the Commune; and amongst its last acts was the destruction of the Column of Vendôme as a signal that the age of war and of military glory was gone for ever. The Commune was scarcely crushed when Imperial Chauvinism in its worst form raised its head. The hatred to Germany is preached as a duty. The Government, the Chamber, and French society resound with dismal cries for military revenge. All parties vie with each other in the grossest flattery of the army; and in this race of infamy it is but fair to say that the Government of M. Thiers and M. Thiers himself end the undoubted winners. Ordinary Englishmen can with difficulty conceive a degradation of nature such that in sight of the triumphant foreign conqueror, over the smouldering ashes of a city which he had deluged in blood, the old apostle and now the mimic of Imperialism, having wriggled into the Imperial throne, could parade his army of ex-prisoners still fresh from the chains of their captivity and yet reeking from the shambles where they had butchered their own citizens.

Order reigns they say in Paris, and the city we are assured is returning to its wonted aspect. Under the Commune it is true that the public administration was carried on by men who served it with enthusiastic devotion, and received but moderate salaries. The wanton extravagance of idle life had retreated to the congenial shades of Versailles, and the city no longer presented the extremes of human misery and reckless ostentation. Vice, too, we were assured, had followed the party of Order. The richer quarters of Paris had ceased, we were told, to be the brothel of Europe. The Commune had even officially attempted the suppression of prostitution; and, though it had not succeeded in this, it had unquestionably done something to mitigate the extravagance of vice. The members of the Commune, it is true, had once met together at a public dinner, and their act was received with shouts of ridicule. But, on the whole, their administration

had been one of stern work. It was essentially a Republican Government, and their lives had been the lives of the
ministers of the public. The Commune has fallen, and we
are now told that Paris resumes her ancient ways. M.
Thiers, to ape his great ideal, must be restoring the feasts
and the splendours of the Empire. As the *Times* well said,
it is the Empire under another name. The train of cooks,
dancers, and harlots has come back from Versailles; and
the foulest literature in Europe is pouring forth again its
feculent deluge.

A writer we were told in a leading journal can scarcely
contain his transports. He writes ecstatically:—

"The *Vie Parisienne* is about to appear, and I already see severe
moralists drawing long faces, and commencing a litany of lament-
ations upon our incurable frivolity and the decay of our manners.
'C'est qu'en cette *Vie Parisienne* se sont résumées, durant sept ou
huit années, toutes les fausses élégances, toutes les vices capitaux
et charmants, toutes les spirituelles immoralités de ce demisiècle
de cocodettes et cocottes. Que de tableaux voluptueux et piqu-
ants tout ensemble! Qu'elle désinvolture à mepriser les préjugés du
vulgaire! Qu'elle ironic légère et de bon ton! Qu'elle persiflage
hautain et amusant!' "

He then goes on to say how much the world at large is
indebted to Paris for *La Belle Hélène* and *La Grande
Duchesse,* and for the peculiar class which are its *special-
ité:—*

"C'est une manie à présent de crier contre Paris et ses vices —
mais si Paris n'existait pas, savez-vous que l'Europe s'ennivrait
joliment? J'en suis conaincui pour mon compte; la moitié de
notre force et de notre courage à nous autres Français est dans
notre gaieté. Tristesse est chez nous abattement d'esprit, et d'âme.
C'est Meilhac qui a dit le vrai mot de notre caractère dans sa jolie
chanson de *Barbe Bleue,* 'Soyons gais! je suis gai!' "

Such is the *Vie Parisienne,* to which Versailles has
waded back through blood, which the workmen died in
resisting, which the Catholic priesthood flatters, inflames,
and consecrates!

Order is restored, and with it the reign of parliamentary
intrigue. In place of the noble aim of the Commune to
abolish national jealousies and enormous taxation, the

party of order are preparing to abolish free trade, and to vie with the Empire itself in burden-some extravagance. To raise again the old Imperial army, to grind the bone and sinew of France in that ghastly mill, to fawn on it, and pamper it, and fling the country at the feet of a new praetorian guard — such is the aim of the old man who now rules France. Recent history records no more repulsive character. In literature, the greatest living master of falsification; in politics, the greatest living adept in intrigue; without a scruple, a conviction, or a purpose; as sanguinary as Robespierre, without the excuse of his fanaticism; as Chauvinist as Napoleon, without the excuse of his genius — he has managed to wriggle himself into power for a time, simply because he is known to represent nothing but himself.

To those who watch with anxiety the future, there is something appalling in the spirit with which the movement of the Commune has been judged. It is true that it was something new in political experience; but at most its ideal was that of government by and for the working classes. An ideal one-sided and extravagant it might be; but when we reflect for how many centuries, and in how many societies, all power has been wielded by the rich or the great in their own exclusive interests, it is an ideal not so entirely preposterous. Yet the attempt, even before a single act by which to judge it, was looked on by the respectability of Europe with transports of rage. Language was exhausted in flinging epithets at the leaders, and literature hurried forth to drown them in calumny. Some of the most honourable, cultivated, and, indeed, some of the richest men in Paris, were spoken of only as "obscene miscreants." That men who had once been working men should undertake — nay, even succeed — in the affairs of State was received with a howl, in which amazement struggled with rage. Before a building had been burnt, or a hostage shot, before the Commune had committed a single act of violence, the friends of order throughout Europe were devoting them to destruction with a hate that was simply fiendish. It was as

FREDERIC HARRISON.

if the horses had made an insurrection against men, had harnessed human teams in their carts and ploughs, and successfully established a Houyhnhnm Government. Our Yahoos howled with rage. It was the frenzy which seizes a white population when their black slaves grow insubordinate. That wretched workmen should set foot on the Elysian fields of luxury; that they should disturb the very gaieties of the season; that, in the pursuit of a more moral and just world, they should disarrange the charm of the pleasantest city in Europe — all this, in the eyes of the silken puppets who call themselves Society, was an outrage worthy of death. That in their mad death-fury they should destroy the very scenes of revelry, and leave for years to come a black spectre looming over the gay procession of Fashion, marked them to be fiends in human shape, for whom death was too good, who should be reserved, said one of our army organs, "for vivisection in the interests of science."

Few things of late have revealed how inhuman is the principle of our modern distinctions of class more clearly than this Satanic outburst of rage which the rich have shown towards the poor. It is the character of the refined luxury and the selfish power which are the modern result of wealth, to breed indifference to mankind, till it passes into utter cruelty of nature. At the decline of the Roman world under the influence of luxury and slavery, this spirit had reached its perfection. The gratification of every whim at any cost of human suffering was the mark of the fine gentleman or the fine lady. An emperor fattened his lampreys on live slaves. A great lady would have her slave-girl flogged for misplacing a curl or breaking a vase. We have seen this same temper to-day. They who have met an insurrection against the selfishness of wealth with the malignant hatred of the slave-owner, are the legitimate heirs of the corrupt Roman society. For them any who break their dream of enjoyment are the enemies of God and man, and the destruction of their tapestries and their crockery is scarcely avenged by the massacre of a whole population.

It is melancholy to reflect how the great and noble name of Art has been degraded by those who oftenest use it. True Art is a social, humanising, and purifying power. That only is worthy of the name which unites men in one common enjoyment, abolishes the barriers created by brute wealth, soars beyond the separations of class, nation, or language. Its mission is to make the whole world kin, and its dignity is that all that is human is akin to it. It is the very degradation of Art to be the mere lackey of wealth, to embitter and not to brighten the contrasts of life. A turn for *bric-a-brac* is not Art. The knowledge of a Jew broker is not culture. A craze after upholstery and tapestries, the collecting of unique pots and rare carvings, if it but minister to the self-love of luxurious living, if it instil a contemptuous antipathy towards those who know not these things, if it make men and women more selfish, exclusive, and idle, is not a blessing but a curse.

To conclude. This great crisis had stated though it has not solved the social problem. What, in a few words, is this problem? It is this. In this complex industrial system wealth has discovered the machinery by which the principal, in some cases the whole, results of common labour become its special perquisites. Ten thousand miners delve and toil, giving their labour, risking their lives; ten masters give their direction or their capital, oftenest only the latter. And in a generation the ten capitalists are rioting in vast fortunes, and the ten thousand workmen are rotting in their graves, or in a workhouse. And yet the ten thousand were at least as necessary to the work as the ten. Yet more. The ten capitalists are practically the law-makers, the magistrates, the government. The educators of youth, the priests of all creeds, are their creatures. Practically they make and interpret the law — the law of the land, the law of opinion, and the law of God; they are masters of the whole social forces.

A convenient faith has been invented for them by moralists and economists, the only faith which in these days they at all believe in — the faith that the good of mankind is somehow promoted by a persevering course of selfishness. Competition is, in fact, the whole duty of man. And thus it comes that in ten thousand ways the whole social force is directed for the benefit of those who have. Habitually, unconsciously, often with what they think is a religious sense of duty, they work the machinery of society for their own objects. In this favoured land, whilst the owner of the soil knows no other toil or care but that of providing fresh modes of enjoyment, the peasant, out of whose sweat his luxury is wrung, lives like a beast of burden, and dies like a dog in a ditch; whilst the merchant-prince is courting society for a peerage, a thousand lives of seamen are lost, decoyed in rotten ships to sea; whilst mine-owners can still paralyse the legislature, a thousand lives are lost each year in pits, "chiefly, it is said, from preventible causes;" and whilst fortunes are reared by iron-masters, a hundred thousand workmen are ground to the dust by truck. Let us reflect what is implied in this mere finding of the late Commission. One hundred thousand families in England are cheated, insulted, and oppressed by being forced to barter portions of their wages for some fraudulent equivalent in goods. Now all this makes up in gross that which they call in France "l'exploitation des ouvriers." They say that where in a common work labour is no less necessary than capital, and labourers are as worthy of the profits as managers, the system by which the gross result is appropriated by capital, and under which the self-indulgence of wealth soars to yet unimagined heights, whilst the area of misery, ignorance, and exhaustion sinks ever deeper, is a system which is doomed to end. And this their claim is good.

Let us turn to the remedy they propose. The whole social force which so long, they say, has been directed by capital in its own interest, shall be directed by workmen in the interests of workmen. The laws shall no longer be made and administered so as to handicap the labourer in the race of industry. The power of the State shall step in to neutralise competition, and to restrain the selfish abuse of capital. The land, at any rate, they say, must be resumed by the State for the benefit of the whole community; and farmed on social, and not on proprietary, bases. Ultimately, in short, the whole existence of capital, and the ordering the lives of the community, must be subject to the will of social authority.

Such is the faith which, in spite of its extravagance, has seized the foremost minds of the workmen of Europe, which in some form or other receives the devotion of a religious creed. Can any one doubt its strength, compared with the conscious corruption of the opposite creed? Does the selfish cunning of competition in its heart think it can stand a social energy like this, with all its errors and all its dangers? Does a society which lives in its equipages, and toils only in amusement, match itself seriously with men who are ready thus to die for a cause however mistaken? Poor gluttonous fribble, whose cares are divided between the coming battue and the last new dish, the roughest of those who went to death in Paris in the hope of a better time to come for his children, was a hero and a man of honour in contrast with you!

The claim of capital to amass wealth by what means it chooses, and to spend it how and when it pleases, is so vile, the claim of the workman to have his part in the social result is so unanswerable, that in the end the issue is not doubtful. And since this social problem must some day be faced by all, it seems time for serious men to reflect what other solution remains. Communism stares them in the face; it grows and deepens. Whatever it may suit a journalist to say, no sensible man believes that the 200,000 men who voted for the Commune are bandits and fiends in human shape. They who think that such a story as that of the Commune of Paris is explicable on the "miscreant" theory are unfit to discuss political questions. It has a great purpose, and it has great leaders. For every man who died on the barricades, ten will spring up hereafter. The cry of Millière as he died, "Vive l'humanité!" will not be unanswered. The bones of Delescluze may be burnt in quick-lime, but his spirit lives. He and his followers have a purpose. They have sworn that the "exploitation of the workman" shall end; and end it must.

They are not so clear about a substitute, but, so far as they have a scheme, it is Communism. There is but one alternative — the answer of Positivism. In one sense Positivism is akin to Communism, for it heartily accepts its belief in social reorganisation; in another it is the opposite of Communism, for it exalts instead of abolishes the exercise of property by individuals. Positivism teaches that the highest uses of society are best served by massing capital in aggregates, and by entrusting these masses to the free control of individuals. It teaches that the dignity of domestic life and of public action, that moral as well as intellectual energy, demand the existence of capitalists as a class. It shows that the highest functions of social life and the noblest powers of the character would cease to exist without the free control of capital. It insists on this freedom in no grudging or unreal spirit. It looks on capital simply as power, and the wise exercise of power as the noblest function of man, and the trustful respect of power as the most generous of human instincts.

And if Positivism insists that Communism would dwarf and unman every side of human nature, by destroying the infinite sources of nobleness inherent in individual property, it asserts as strongly as Communism itself that individual property can no longer exist on its prevalent conditions. It insists that the use of property must again be made a religious duty — that capital arises from the combination of many efforts, and must in justice minister to the common wants. It would, by an education prolonged through life, teach the workmen of every grade to trust and aid the owner of capital, and the owner of capital to look on himself as the minister of a free community. It would train the rich to rely on their own resources, and compel them to use their full responsibility in so ordering the common industry that the fewest disasters and the least suffering befell the labouring community. Such is a picture of capital not extinguished, but moralised; not cut in pieces, but raised to new functions; not harassed by the fetters of law, but strong in the noble consciousness of a public office. Let capital, shrinking from the fires and the shambles of Paris, choose which of these two it will have. Communism is a not impossible future. Positivism is a not impossible future. The *status quo* is impossible. The alternative is Communism or Positivism.

Frederic Harrison.

VII

Thomas Smith

EDITOR'S BIOGRAPHICAL NOTES

Thomas Smith: *Letters on the Commune, The Law of the Revolution; or the Logical Development of Human Society*. Reprinted from the Nottingham Daily Express, by the Nottingham Branch of the I.W.M.A. March 1872.

Unfortunately there is little that one can add to what has already been said about Smith in the Introduction. The fullest account of his activity will be found in Peter Wyncoll: the First International in Nottingham, *Marxism Today* December 1968 pp.372-379. The dates of his birth and death are unknown and nothing can be said about the nature of his occupation beyond the fact that he described himself to Marx as a working man. He sought a London publisher for his pamphlet and assured Marx that he would be happy for any surplus to go to the Communard refugees. He founded a branch of the I.W.M.A. in Nottingham and it was sufficiently successful to encourage the British Federal Council of the International to select that town as the setting for its Conference of 20-21 July 1872. Smith presided at the Conference which resolved to create an independent workers' party. The Nottingham Internationalists were soon subject to oppressive proceedings. Two of their leaders were victimised by employers. Publicans in Nottingham, as in London, who let rooms for meetings to commemorate the Commune or discuss socialism were liable to have their licences suspended. Besides, "Citizen Smith"being "a worthy man and earnest" could not spend much time in public houses "him being a total abstainer". By 1873 the International in Nottingham was all but broken. Yet the Commune was not wholly forgotten nor were the ambitions which it had aroused among its English defenders doomed to a lasting neglect. In 1887 the town's secular Hall was decorated with a red banner inscribed 'Vive la Commune' and the names of Delescluze and Dombrowski appeared alongside those of H. M. Hyndman and William Morris.

De Paepe was being extravagant when he told Smith: "your defence of the Commune will afford another light by which posterity will view and form its judgements upon the supreme efforts made by the martyred heroes of that really classic commonwealth." Yet Smith deserves to be remembered. He was perhaps the closest English equivalent to Joseph Dietzgen. He was one of the few workers in the nineteenth century who sought, not merely to master a complex intellectual tradition, but to promote its further development.

INTERNATIONAL WORKING MEN'S ASSOCIATION

At a meeting of the Nottingham Branch of the International Working Men's Association, held at Lesters Coffee House, Hounds-gate, it was resolved:—

"That this Society will advocate and promote the principles of the political and social revolution, as being the only principles that will advance the welfare of society as a whole, as being the principles on which alone just and equal government is based, and to which all civilisation tends." These principles we hold to be:—

First. Politically, the rights of conscience, freedom of the mind — the unlimited right of the individual to proclaim his or her convictions on all subjects; and socially, the right of every child to the fullest development of all its powers, mental and moral, possible — the duty of society to provide the means of education for all, so that all may have within their reach the means of the best education that the age can confer.

Secondly. Politically, personal freedom for all — the abolition of bondage in all its forms and everywhere: and socially, the emancipation of women — the equality of all classes and both sexes, the abolition of all political and social privileges between men and women and between class and class.

Thirdly. Politically, the emancipation of the land — the right of the people to the soil, and the abolition of privileged political land castes: and socially, the emancipation of labour — and the advocacy of measures that shall make capital the servant of labour, and not labour the servant of capital.

Fourthly. Politically, the right of self-government — of national sovereignty by universal suffrage, the right of the nation, and the nation only, to rule, as the source of all power, and the destruction of class rule and dominance: and socially, the unity of humanity, of all mankind — the end of the dominance of race over race and nation over nation.

Fifthly, Politically, the protection of the rights of minorities by the principle of federalism and by decentralisation of power — so as to take away the temptation of the central government to trample on the rights of its opponents: and socially, the union of the nations to be a federal bond — so as to protect the rights of the weaker races and nations.

Thomas Smith, Secretary.

The Association meets every other Saturday Evening, at Eight o'clock, at the above Coffee House.

PREFACE

"What is a Republic?" is a question that has often been asked, and as yet has not been answered in a definite manner. In the following letters I have endeavoured to give, as well as the limited space would permit, a clear statement of the principles that are the essential bases of a democratic and of a social Republic.

That all phenomena are the results of laws eternal in their operation is a well established principle, and it is from the results of natural laws observed by man that we are enabled to first notice the sequence of their occurrence, and then to reason from that to the laws of which they are the results.

On this method I have acted. I have started no theory of my own, I have simply stated the principles that have successively developed themselves in the course of European progress; and as France is the country of all others whose people are the most logical in their methods of thought, so are they therefore the nation who have most logically developed the principles of human progress; and in whose history they stand forth as the most conspicuous landmarks. It is to the history of that country, therefore, that we naturally turn when we wish to discover the principles, and the order of their development, upon which the progress of human society depends.

If we look to Asia, the cradle of civilization, we everywhere see these principles almost wholly absent from the constitution of society, or but very imperfectly developed; and, as a consequence, progress has almost ceased. China is, of all Asiatic countries, the one where these principles have attained their best development; and is, consequently, the most prosperous, powerful, and progressive. If we turn to the history of Europe, we see nations prosperous, progressive, and free, in proportion as they have adopted these principles.

The course of European history may be divided into three parts — the history of Greece and Rome; the history of the time from the decline of Rome to the Reformation; and from the Reformation till now, or the era of the revolution.

The Republics of Greece and Rome seemed for a time as if they would solve the problem of liberty and self government, and their fall has been often cited against the success and stability of Republican Institutions; but we see when we examine them that they were deficient in one or more of the principles of modern society, and essential to real freedom, and that the result of this deficiency was to vitiate the action of the other principles, and ultimately to destroy them. The Republics of the Middle Ages were the same, and were destroyed from the same cause — the want of some of the real democratic principles, and consequently were not real Republics. In fact, all of them, both the ancient Republics and the Republics of the Middle Ages, may, from this cause and their limited extent, giving them small scope for action, be fairly regarded as preliminary experiments, preparatory to that great movement of all the peoples of Europe, who, advancing side by side, though by different methods, are marching to a real democracy, and which constitutes the modern or revolutionary era.

The period of European history, including the time from the decline of the Roman Empire to the Reformation, and appropriately called the Dark Ages was predominantly a time when the principles of democracy were almost unknown, and for generation after generation it seemed dounbtful whether any fresh principles of government would succeed in gaining ascendancy, or whether Europe would be practically a second edition of Asia.

But the advent of the Reformation announced that a new epoch had arrived in human history, and that instead of isolated efforts to solve the problem of liberty and self-government, the whole of Europe was to advance on one path, and that principle after principle was to develop itself, and, though persecuted and massacred, were to establish themselves as fundamental principles of government. This is the modern, or revolutionary era, through which we are now passing, and which has sufficiently advanced to enable us to see what are its course and principles, and the result to which it leads, namely, government of the people, by the people, and for the people.

In conclusion, as we approach the solution of the political problem, it is evident that there is a social problem next awaiting solution, and we may, by analogy of other general laws of nature, expect that its solution will also be affected on the same general principles as the political problem, modified by their application to the social instincts and necessities of human nature.

In the efforts made at different times, both theoretical and practical, to solve the social question, they have evidently failed from the same general cause, the want of a clear understanding of the fundamental principles at the base of the problem, and also from the failure to perceive the absolute necessity of the prior solution of the political question.

Firmly believing that it is only by observing the phenomenon of society in the past, not in its class aspects, but in its great movements, in which the whole mass of nations are stirred to their depths, that we can hope to throw light on the future, I have endeavoured, however imperfectly, to point out the light in which they present themselves to me, and if they in any way help to clear away the mists of the future, I shall be more than satisfied.

T. S.

LETTERS ON THE COMMUNE

To the Editors. — The present revolution in Paris has been described as a struggle between the capital and the provinces — between the artisans and the peasants; and, so far as the persons who are the chief actors, or forces, in the movement are concerned, truly enough. But it will be as well to endeavour to understand what are the Principles that are trying to gain acceptance through these masses. To talk as though the struggles of the people of Paris are merely wild outbursts of folly and passion, is simply ignorance.

I think it is an admitted principle that all phenomena, in both the moral and physical worlds, are governed by law, and that what we call chance are solely those things that we cannot refer back to their causes. It seems to me that the present movement in Paris is the natural growth and a compulsory stage of the revolution through which France has been passing the last eighty years, and may be described as a movement of decentralization for the preservation of the Republic.

Three times have the people of France proclaimed the Republic, and twice have they lost it through the same cause, namely, extreme centralization wielding great military power. Napoleon the First and the Third both stamped it out in blood in the streets of Paris by the aid of the army, and disarmed the people.

The third Republic yet lives, but the present reactionary Assembly are evidently prepared to destroy it by the same means — the disarmament of the people, the suppression of liberty of the press and speech, the maintenance of extreme centralization and the power of the army. Now all the demands of the present movement, warned by experience, are directed to the creation of local bodies who shall

246

act as a check on the central power. To accuse men who demand that the commune, or municipal councils, shall be elected by the people without the interference of the Government, of being ruffians and plunderers, is as absurd as to accuse the British Parliament that passed the Municipal Reform Act of 1837 of belonging to the same class.

If we look at the freest nations of the world, we find them all possessed of strong local self governments, and they regard them as the best guarantees of liberty, — as America, Switzerland, and England, and two of these have scarcely any standing army, and the other a small one compared to France. If these nations cherish local self government as necessary to liberty, how much more does France need them with her large army! We thus see that the present movement in Paris, Lyons, &c., is a natural growth of the Republician idea; having three times established the Republic, it now takes the form of demanding institutions that will preserve it. I would also point out to those self-styled friends of order who are so fond of abusing the artisans of France, that the best friends of order are those who wish to end the era of revolution by making it no longer necessary to progress, by establishing such local institutions as will command the attention of Goverment to popular wishes, and not compel them to descend into the streets, rifle to hand, before they can get their wishes listened to; and that to force France back under a system of centralization is simply to lengthen out the era of the revolution, as they cannot hope that the Republicans of France will ever give up the struggle till liberty is firmly established. At the same time it is plain that the same local institutions which are strong enough to hold reaction in check, and prevent liberty being drowned in blood, would also make revolution both unnecessary and impossible, as Paris would cease to be France, and progress could be made without these violent convulsions.

Hounds-gate, March 25th, 1871

THOS. SMITH

THE STRUGGLE IN PARIS

To the Editors, — The struggle in France between de-
centralization and centralization, between the Republic
and Monarchy, still, after eight weeks' fighting, shows but
little sign of ceasing.

When I, in a letter you published shortly after the
establishment of the Commune, pointed out that as the
real foundation of the struggle, it was not the generally
received opinion; but the progress of events and the logic
of facts have now shown to all who pay attention to
French affairs, that such are the real conditions of the
struggle. In endeavouring to estimate the Forces at work
on both sides, it will be as well to recur to the course of
political events since 1848. The middle class, who had
ruled under Louis Phillipe, thought they should be able to
make a middle class Republic, and use the peasantry and
the priests against the workmen of the large towns.
Accordingly, they commenced with the aid of the rural
delegates to suppress Radical papers, restrict the suffrage,
disarm the workmen of the towns and do other acts of
reaction. The Radical Republicans, seeing they should lose
all that had been gained, rose in June, 1848, and fought
for three days most heroically to save the Republic. The
middle classes in the National Guards fought along with
the army, and also many thousands of middle class
National Guards from other towns hurried to Paris to help
to put them down, and they were beaten, and reaction
held on its way. Soon it was seen who reaped the fruits.
The priests had felt their strength in the Assembly, and
soon after the election of Louis Bonaparte as president,
put the rurals into power. But it was necessary to teach the
middle class by a severe lesson who was master, and on
December 2nd, 1851, they got it. Bonaparte on that day,

with many thousand troops occupied the chief streets of the capital, and to strike terror, shot down all, right and left; and when they fled indoors the soldiers fired into the houses through doors and window at random. This was in the main streets, and not amongst the poorer quarters; and few, I think, will cry because the wealthy classes got a dish of the game meat they were so eager to serve to the workmen in June, 1848. It is true that the following night and day thousands of workmen came out and fought, hoping even at the last hour to save the Republic; but want of organisation and arms, of which they had been deprived by the middle class, made it useless, and the Republic was dead. The lesson then administered to the middle class has not been lost on them, and in spite of the proclamation and appeals of Thiers and the rurals, they decline to serve again as cats' paws for the priests and either join the Commune or stand aloof from both, their dream of a middle class Republic being dead and gone. We must also take into account the effect of nearly twenty years of political slavery, social degradation, heavy taxes, and still heavier conscription. The appeals of Thiers to the National Guard of other towns also meet with no response, eager as they were in 1848 to crush the Radicals, and from the same causes. Even the peasantry will not come. mainly from political apathy, and also because their share of the blessings of the reactionary style of order came to increased taxes, and heavier conscription. Thiers and the rurals are therefore compelled to rely on the remains of the army, and Bismarck returning them the prisoners from Germany, to conquer the Republicans, and any one may judge what stability there would be in a government on that foundation, without any moral support from the intelligent classes, and whose only hope of success would be in the ignorance of the peasantry, even if he succeed.

Now it is plain that if it had not been for the help of Bismarck returning him the French soldiers, the Government of Thiers would have been before now swept away, or obliged to grant large local powers; and the result of the elections for councillors in the towns shows that they sympathise with Paris, and if they will but act with energy, the rurals and Thiers will be compelled to give way. Their terror at their defeat is shown by their fear of the projected congress of delegates of the town councils, which they had hoped to have had in their own hands by terrifying the people with lies about the Communists; but the facts coming to be known, and Paris holding out, spoilt that game. The result now mainly lies in the action of the large towns — if they do their duty the rurals are beaten, but if they not having had the same lesson Paris had in '48 and 52, dally and wait, Paris, I do not doubt, will fight it out single handed; and even if beaten, every hour she holds out will be securing the future success of the principle of de-centralization, for we are sure that principle is now being discussed by every man in France. Switzerland, so close at hand, with its cantons, its Federal Government, light taxes, small army, and liberty, is being contrasted with the centralization of France, its absence of local powers, heavy taxes, conscription, and want of political liberty, and who can doubt that the Commune are gaining converts by thousands every hour? If the Assembly conquers Paris, all liberty of speech and press will be gone, and France will fall back to the old system of repression, based on an ignorant peasantry and the priesthood, until the outbreak of another revolution, and thus the struggle will go on till at last liberty, if we are to have any faith in progress, will triumph.

Hounds-gate, May 13th, 1871
THOS. SMITH

THE RECENT STRUGGLE IN PARIS

To the Editors, — The Martyr City of Liberty is once more stretched upon the rack — the wolves and vampires of repression, the army and the priests, are once more tearing her limbs and sucking her blood. Once more the enemies of liberty and justice, the foes of human progress, are showing to the world that, like the Bourbons, they have learned nothing and forgotten nothing — that their only arguments are blood and murder, the rifle and the bayonet — and that they still believe in the power of force to stay the progress of thought. Again and again they have tried to stifle in the blood of Paris new principles of progress which she has proclaimed for the acceptance of the nation, and which in despite of all the atrocities of its enemies the nation had adopted and firmly planted. In spite of failure after failure to prevent the adoption of fresh ideas, they still go on blindly endeavouring to stay the tide of progress by the same means which have so often proved futile, showing that in reality they have no other weapons on which they can rely.

Let us just consider as shortly as possible the occasions on which Paris has been subjected to the torture, what are the principles which it was hoped to annihilate by those terrible massacres, and what were the results that followed them; and from the total failure of the former efforts of the reactionists we may judge of the likelihood of the ultimate success of their present bloody doings. We should also keep in mind that in judging of the growth of the institutions of another nation we cannot justly measure them by our standard only; that because they do not travel on exactly the same road that we are going on we should not jump to the conclusion that they are therefore not progressing at all, but only going round in a circle. We

251

should keep as guides the great principles of liberty for all, of equal rights for all, as the goal to which all tend. Now as nations differ in their institutions, habits, and modes of thought, they naturally strike out different paths of progress, but all tending to the adoption in practice of those principles. Taking the above principles as guides in our investigation, let us go back to the history of Paris and see what have been the great principles she has upheld at those supreme crises of her history when her streets have run with blood — when she has fought and conquered; when she has been vanquished; and when she has been massacred — and see if the principles for which she suffered have not in every case ultimately triumphed. Without counting the continual persecutions, the imprisonments, the fines to which she has been subjected, let us turn to those supreme events which are epochs of history. Let us go back to the Massacre of St. Bartholomew, the struggle of 1789 and 1792, the revolution and battle of 1848, and massacre of 1852, and with these and their results before us, we may better judge of the events of 1870 and 1871. And in considering those mighty convulsions let us not be led away by the incidents attending them, which it is so much the object of certain classes to thrust into prominence, so as to shut out of view the great principles that lie at the root, for it is only principles of paramount importance to humanity that can be the cause of such mighty upheavals.

And first, the Massacre of St. Bartholomew, instigated by the priests, the object of which was to stamp out liberty of conscience. I need not ask, was the principle for which she then suffered just? Nor if the cause for which her best and noblest men died did not, in spite of that fearful deed, triumph? Coming to the great and double Revolution of 1789 and 1792-93, what were the principles she then proclaimed and called upon the nation to adopt? The liberation of the serfs; and the right of the people to the land.

For these she fought and won, and shed her blood like water. The nation accepted them, and need I ask if they were just, and that their triumph was the triumph of humanity and right? The kings and priests of all Europe fought for years to undo this glorious work, but without avail, and yet hate Paris with a deadly hatred for her glorious deeds, and for the reforms which her example compelled them to grant their own subjects. One thing they accomplished by compelling France to become a nation of soldiers, they raised up a military caste, the chief of which seized power, murdered the Republic, and again massacred the men of Paris who strove to defend it. But though Bonaparte destroyed the Republic and tried to found an aristocracy, he dared not attempt to undo either of the great works of the Revolution, the liberation of the serfs; and the right of the people to the land; neither dared the allied despots of Europe when France was under their feet.

Passing by the Revolution of 1830 in which Thiers, Guizot, and Co. were most prominent — mere office hunting politicians — and in which no great principle developed itself, and in which, therefore, Paris escaped fresh martyrdom, we come to the Revolution of 1848. What was the principle which pervaded this movement that was proclaimed and established? It was the right of the people to self-government, the sovereignty of the nation, universal suffrage.

Again was Paris doomed to suffer, again was her blood to be shed by privileged and priestly caste. The bourgeoisie who had ruled France since 1830 thought they could turn the Revolution of 1848 to the agrandisement of their own class, as they had that of 1830; but France had progressed since then, and was prepared for the adoption of the principle of national sovereignty.

The bourgeoisie, backed by the priests — for the priests are always on hand when the blood of the people is to be shed — blindly proceeded on a course of reaction, taxed the press, passed bills to restrict the suffrage, and tried to disarm the people. The terrible struggle of June followed, and the principle of the national sovereignty was sealed with the blood of Paris. But though Paris was beaten, the principle, baptised in blood, was too strongly planted to be uprooted. And, again, need I ask if that principle was right and just, and an enormous step in the path of progress? The bourgeoisie soon found that, standing alone, they were not powerful enough to keep power, and, having converted the workmen into enemies, were quickly supplanted by the priests. The murders of December 2nd, 1852, which fell mainly on the middle classes — though the workmen also suffered severely by taking up arms to defend the Republic — was the confirmation of power to the priests and the death knell of the dreams of the bourgeoisie of a middle class Republic, and fearfully have they paid for their blunder. This monstrous crime, and the years of terror and despotism that followed, had other results also, they had the effect of promoting a union of the middle class and the workmen, who are now struggling side by side in the present revolution of 1870 and 1871. Judging from the past we may be sure that when the blood of Paris is being spilt in torrents some great principle is asserting itself. What is that principle of the revolution of 1870 and 1871? It is the principle of the right of local self government, the rights of minorities, the principle of federalism — in short, the Commune. Having in 1848 established the rights of national self government in national affairs, she now proclaims the right of local self government in local affairs, and without it real liberty is hopeless. And does it need any argument to prove that that principle is right and just? That de-centralization would be the demand of the present revolution soon became evident; the establishment of communes at Lyons and Marseilles immediately following the revolution of September 4th, the springing up of newspapers in various parts of France devoted to the advocacy of that idea; the attempts to establish the Commune in Paris even during the Prussian siege, and the agreement on the 30th October of the Government of September 4th to the election of the Commune, and who then broke their word — all showed that this was to be no mere shuffling of the cards, no 1830 affair — the child of intrigue, but a demand for the adoption of a new principle, and that principle Paris having baptised with her blood, can we doubt, judging by the past, that it will triumph?

Paris, which is the Capital, the Leader of France, the Proclaimer of Principles, the Army of the People as the military is the army of repression, does not raise the standard of new principles — as 1830 and 1848 prove — till the national mind is prepared to adopt the new ideas. The priests, yes, always the priests, and royalist reactionaries may flatter themselves, in spite of past failures, that the murders and the massacres, the slaughter of men, women and children — yes, children — which they are now perpetrating, will rid them of the new ideas, but ideas are beyond the reach of arguments such as they alone trust to — the argument of force. In looking back on the events of the present revolution, it is to be regretted that the Government of September the 4th did not more fully comprehend the logic of the siutation, the forces that had raised them to power. If they had done so, and carried out the principle of de-centralization, proclaimed the abolition of the prefects and the election of Communes throughout France, it would have been at once accepted by the nation, strengthened the national defence, and could never have been destroyed any more than the principle of universal suffrage in 1848. The war in which they were engaged, though it may be pleaded in mitigation of their blunder, is no real justification for them; for men who consent to lead a revolution, ought to be imbued to their heart's core with the principle that causes it. It may be said that even if they had, the reactionists would never have acquiesced in the new order of things till, sooner or later, they had indulged in a saturnalia of blood; and, if we may judge by their past doings, it is a mournful truth. But the principle, once put into practical operation, would have been beyond their power to uproot, as past experience in former revolutions proves.

It has been said that to grant the claims of the Communists would destroy France by splitting her up into little Republics; but their most extreme demand, that the National Guards should be in the hands of the local authorities, is no more than the Cantons of Switzerland and the States of America enjoy; and France with her large army needs this counterpoise more than either of them. The logical character of French thought is universally admitted, and in considering the principles and causes of French progress in the past, nothing is more striking than the logical sequence of the principles enunciated and for which blood has been so freely shed.

First, the emancipation of the conscience; second, the emancipation of the person — the abolition of serfdom; third, the emancipation of the land — by putting it into the hands of the people: fourth, the principle of national sovereignty; and lastly, the principle of Federalism — the guarantee of the rights of minorities.

It will be seen at once that each of these principles is the natural sequence of the other, and should serve to modify the prejudice respecting French implusiveness of nations whose path of progress has been less logical, who have adopted their principles piecemeal, and put them into practice bit by bit, while France, when she adopts a principle, carries it at once to its logical results. In deploring the sufferings of France, we may remember that when another nation, America, in her late civil war, proclaimed and carried the principle of emancipation to its logical results, conferring all the rights of citizens on the slaves — and if she had not done that, all her efforts would not have saved the Union — what fearful sufferings and losses she had to endure, and which seem almost inevitable in these great epochs of progress; and this result of the struggle was not the result of logical conviction in the mind of the nation, but the logic of necessity.

We may also see at a glance that these principles could not be adopted and carried to their logical results in any other order than that in which they were adopted — the rights of the mind, the man, the land, the nation, and the minority. It also follows from the preceding facts, that the adoption of the principles of Federalism advocated by the Communists is the next natural logical step in its path of French progress; and as nations cannot stand still, but must either go on in the path of progress or retrograde, we may consider the result as certain as the result of any other natural law, for the most bigoted reactionist cannot hope to thrust a nation like France backwards. All through these long-continued struggles, it should be constantly borne in mind, the priests have always been as relentlessly opposed to every effort of France to advance, as Paris has been firm in the cause of progress, and to every argument and appeal of reason they have answered with one everlasting — No.

In the foregoing remarks I have referred but little to the individuals and the incidents which have been thrown into prominence by these mightly upheavals. The men of the great and double revolution, both civil and military — the Bonapartes, both great and small, even the allied kings of Europe, and the Lamartines, Alberts, Thiers, Bismarcks, Moltkes, &c, have but little influence on the ultimate results of these great movements of humanity. They must either go on with the great forces, be they reactionary or progressive, or be swept aside. The wars of the first Bonaparte were almost without effect on them, as they were too firmly established before he rose to power to be ever destroyed. And if it were so that the destinies of humanity could be largely influenced by the energies of one or a few individuals, how different would have been the history of the human race. Sometimes driven forward, sometimes backward, it would have sunk into the lethargy of despair; but no, it is the individual who is subordinate to the whole, not the whole to the individual.

Turning from the past, the immediate future of France looms dark and heavy. The present Assembly will doubtless proceed on the old course of repression to the end, as the same classes always have when they have regained power — reaction, so far as the great principles of former revolutions are concerned, they cannot indulge in. Compromise, which plays so important a part in the politics of other countries, seems adverse to the genius of French thought, and from the Girondins to the present Assembly, has always failed. Once it seemed during the present struggle that the Assembly were inclined to try a compromise, when it voted a clause in the Muncipalities Bill to allow the people to elect their own mayors and deputy mayors; but it at once backed out under the threat of Thiers to resign, and it was doubtful if it was more than a trap for the people of Paris. But, compromise or no compromise, it cannot be doubted that the principle of Federalism, the only guarantee of the rights of minorities, will in the end triumph over every obstacle. How that end will be attained, time only can tell; whether through renewed and fearful struggles — whether through the contagion of ideas in the army rendering it, as so often before, a broken reed for repression to lean on, and against which their panacea of force is powerless — whether by dissensions amongst the monarchical factions of the Assembly, who are already quarrelling amongst themselves, and whose only possible band of union is the cohesive power of the public plunder — or whether by the resistless march of the nation to the Standard Paris has raised, forcing a future Assembly to grant what the present Assembly has revelled in a saturnalia of murder to prevent — or whether by foreign war, or by any other means, when it comes it will be adopted in its entirety, and with all its logical consequences, never more to be stricken from the French constitution. The project of making some other town the capital of France, beside the danger of civil war, when Federalism would at once force its acceptance, would, if successful, only transfer the seat of conflict; for Paris is doubly the capital of France — it is the capital of the Government, where are concentrated the means of repression, and it is also the capital of the people, where are gathered together the growing forces of the nation, its thought, its earnestness, its intelligence, and its indomitable energy, and any other capital would soon gather up the same elements.

It is this which makes Paris feel and know when the time has come for the proclamation of new principles. The subtle threads of sympathy by which she is connected with all that is growing and progressive in the nation prevent her, as in 1830, from proclaiming them before the nation is sufficiently advanced to receive them. The elections which took place in the towns and communes during the present conflict, and in which Federalist Republicans so largely succeeded, in spite of Government opposition, show that Paris is again right in her estimate of the progress of French thought.

The repressive factions, having no principle to offer for the national acceptance, may, for lack thereof, with hideous hypocrisy continue to howl order, while they are themselves the real creators of disorder, by binding down the nation and for ever to its aspirations replying, "Be quiet, move not, Be torpid." But the nation is weary of the cuckoo cry, and gave no response to their appeals; and even the army long wavered — but left them to depend on the assistance of Bismarck to find them men, and Thiers now is little better than his viceroy. Paris, though beaten and tortured, is yet unbroken in spirit, and, recuperated by the living forces of the nation, will soon again face her foes; and if it is her fate to again shed her blood for humanity and progress, she will again undauntedly meet it, and the greater the repression the greater the explosion; and before long, however won, the crown of victory of principle will doubtless again, as so often before, rest on the brow of the martyr city. Come as it may, let us hope that when the time comes, the progress of France will be on a more peaceful path — that the baneful power of centralization broken, these terrible conflicts will cease — that power being more diffused, the conflicts of progress will also be spread over a larger area, instead of being concentrated in one volcano — and that we have seen the end of the long martyrdom of Paris.

Hounds-gate, Nottingham, June 7, 1871.

THOS. SMITH.

THE LAW OF THE REVOLUTION

To the Editors, — In a letter of mine which you were so kind as to publish on the 8th of June, I pointed out what appeared to me the five great principles of the political revolution, through which Europe has been passing for some generations — the five great objects to which all the efforts of reform have been devoted, though they have assumed in different countries such different phases — namely, the emancipation of the mind, the man, the land the nation, the minority.

Now these five great objective principles, which spring so naturally from the human mind, and are the reflex of its aspirations, feelings, hopes, and desires, have been struggled for and attained, in the most logical order in France of any country in the world; and when the present revolution, which has been thwarted in its course, shall have attained its object, namely, Federalism, the political revolution of France will be complete; and we may rest assured that France will never, having entered on the last stage of the revolution, be again in a settled condition, till the revolution has worked out its logical result, complete de-centralization.

As regards the progress of the political revolution in other countries, they have all adopted the policy of bit by bit reform more or less; and, therefore, while they have attained some of the above principle in full, they have only attained to the enjoyment of a part of others. As examples we may take England, where we have full liberty of conscience, both political and religious, and the total abolition of serfdom — as in fact, this last object has now by the abolition of serfdom in Russia been attained by all Europe; and we have also partly attained to the enjoyment of the rights of the minorities. The other two principles of the national sovereignty; and the right of the people to the land; we have yet to struggle for, though the first we have partly attained to. Or take Prussia, they have abolished serfdom, and they have got universal suffrage, the expression of the principle of national sovereignty, though by their imperfect political development in other respects it is crippled to the full development of its results, and they have also liberty of conscience, political and religious. But they have yet to liberate the the land, which is so largely held by a privileged aristocracy, as with us, though not to the same extent, and they have also to acquire, what we have partly got, the acknowledgement of the rights of minorities, now crippled by censorship of the press and denial of the rights of public meeting and speech. We thus see that the five great objective principles of the political revolution above stated, furnish us with a standard by which we may measure the relative progress of nations in the great movement of modern times. And France, by the logical development of her revolution, has put the world under an obligation, even though involuntary on her part, by showing by facts of history what are the principles, and the natural order of development of the modern era of thought. In watching the progress of the five great principles of the political revolution we must perceive that it progresses at an accelerated speed, that we make all over Europe more progress in one lifetime than they did in half a dozen in its earlier stages, say immediately following the Reformation — for though the causes were at work long before then, that was the first great national step in its progress; and we may therefore be sure that its full accomplishment will not be very many more years delayed in the principal nations of Europe. We may also perceive that other questions are being pushed into prominence along with these political principles, and that they are assuming more and more importance year by year, as the political revolution is drawing to its close; in fact they will soon excite an equal interest with the remaining reforms to be accomplished in the political revolution. They are the social questions that are growing larger and larger on the horizon, that are assuming shape and taking possession of the public mind; they are, in short, the social revolution, the necessary and inevitable complement of the political revolution.

I propose in the following remarks to endeavour to define the principles and objects of the social revolution. As that revolution is already demanding recognition of modern society, it will be better for all classes if its course and aims can be clearly defined, thus preventing that misrepresentation and exaggeration to which the political revolution has been exposed, and which spring from ignorance and fear; and I think the logical development of the political revolution in France gives us the key by which we may define the principles and objects of the social revolution, and its logical order of development. It is, I think, evident now that the political revolution would have been less violent in its course, less productive of bloodshed and suffering, than it has been if its principles and aims could have been clearly defined in its commencement; and with that object of preventing the evils which spring from exaggerated fears, and the mis-representations of ignorance and interest, and which have been the cause of so much misery in the course of the political revolution, I will, as shortly as possible, endeavour to state what are, in my opinion, the results the social revolution is destined to attain to. In pursuance of this purpose we must keep in mind that the social revolution springs from the same great humanity that the political revolution does — that it is an outgrowth of the same mental and moral organization — that the same feelings, aspirations, hopes, and desires are at the basis of both. Keeping these considerations in mind, we should naturally expect that the social is the climax, the complement of the political revolution, the carrying out in the social relations of society of the same great principles that the political revolution has forced, and is forcing, in its political relations, and I think we shall find that such is the case. With these considerations as guides, let us compare the principles of the two revolutions, one largely completed, the other rapidly approaching; and as France has shown us the logical order of development of one revolution, and as the social is the complement of it, we make it for certain that if it were developed logically, we should find its principles developed in the same order. Let us compare them.

The first principle of the political revolution was the emancipation of the conscience, the freedom of the mind; and in the social revolution the first necessity is universal education, its natural complement — not merely the mere rudiments but the facilities and opportunities of the most complete mental and moral cultivation of all, both male and female; and this first principle is already forcing itself into general acceptance even before, in most countries, the completion of the political revolution — though the political principle it springs from, the freedom of the conscience, of the mind, has been accepted at least in those countries where the education of the mass has received any attention.

The second principle of the political revolution was the emancipation of the man — the abolition of serfdom, the equality of all before the law.

The complementary principle in the social revolution is palpable at a glance; it is the emancipation of women, and this principle is also making rapid strides in our day, more especially in those countries where the corresponding political principle has made most progress. That the emancipation of women is one of the most important steps of the social movement, does not require much argument, her importance as a social force in human affairs is palpable to all, and the education of both sexes, which is now acknowledged to be necessary, carries with it the recognition of their equal rights. Being endowed with the same powers and capacities, though in different degrees — in some the man being superior, in some the woman, and in the social capacities the woman being better endowed than the man — the demand for the recognition of the equal rights of woman must be acceded to before the social movement can develop its full results. There is one fallacy of the opponents of equal rights — both those who oppose equal rights for all men, and also those who resist equal rights for women — which I should here point out, they assume that the claim for equal rights implies the claim of an equality of powers and duties, but it does nothing of the kind, the natural law being equality of rights, inequality of powers and duties, for if rights depended on the natural powers of individuals or sexes, there would have to be a scale of rights which in diversity and complexity would laugh the castes of India to scorn; for as there are no two individuals exactly alike in their capacities nor ever will be, there would have to be, if right depended on capacities, an endless scale of rights as varying as the powers of individuals and sexes.

The third principle of the political revolution as developed in France is the emancipation of the land, the right of the people to the soil. And the necessary complement of that in the social revolution is the emancipation of labour, now engrossing so much of the attention of the working classes. The emancipation of the land, which is yet so imperfectly accomplished in most countries, and least of all England, being in Europe the most advanced in Switzerland, France, and Belgium, has been resisted most strenuously of all the principles advocated by the revolution, and has caused, and yet threatens to cause, the most bitter animosities between the different classes of society; and the social complement of the emancipation of labour promises to be the most bitterly contested of all the principles of the social revolution. In Switzerland the land never was in the hands of a privileged class and used as a weapon of political warfare against the rest of the community, and Switzerland has been the first to complete her political development. In France the land was almost completely monopolised by her aristocracy and the church till the time of the double revolution of '89 and '93, when she secured the almost complete emancipation of it, and converted it into peasant freeholds; and provoked by the onslaught of the privileged classes of all Europe, on her newly acquired rights, massacred her nobility and priesthood, who were undoubtedly in league with her foreign foes. In consequence largely of this destruction of the land monopoly, France, lightened of the dead weight of a political caste with which most other countries of Europe are still cursed, promises to be the first of the great nations of Europe to complete her political revolution by her conversion into a Federal Republic, the principle at the root of the present revolution. Belgium, which largely owes her riddance of the curse of political land monopoly to France, is another instance of the beneficial effects of the emancipation of the land, and though torn from France, still clings to the laws she received from the French Republic, and when the principle of Federalism in France triumphs, she will very likely soon seek reannexation.

In considering the development of the corresponding social principle of the emancipation of labour, it is evident that it will take different phases in different countries, though all having the same end in view, the abolition of wages slavery. Now, before this can be fully accomplished, the first principle of the social revolution, universal education, must have made very considerable progress, as an ignorant people could never carry out a principle like this, and the acknowledgement of the rights of woman will very much strengthen the hands of its advocates and bring her as an active coadjutor into the movement, it seems to me that the main steps in the social elevation of labour, are an intelligent understanding and obedience to the laws of population, the forbidding of land being used as an instrument of wages slavery, the growth of individual self-reliance and the spirit of personal independence, and the development of the principle of co-operation. The first cannot be understood by an ignorant population, and, therefore, education is imperative. The second may be carried out in two ways; either by the land becoming national property and being let by the nation to actual cultivators only, either individually or co-operatively; or, secondly. by the nation taxing all lands let on rent, compelling their sale to actual cultivators.

To the objection that this would be an unjust interference with the rights of property, it may be answered that in land there is no absolute right of property, that no man ever made the land and cannot have an absolute title to it, that when men first enclosed land it was on the tacit understanding that they would make it produce more food, and if they ceased to cultivate it they surrendered all claim to it. Now if a man does not cultivate it, but lets it on rent, he is breaking the only title by which he has any claim to it. If it be urged that he may have by his labour improved it, and made it of more value to the one he lets it to, though that is not true of the great bulk of the land-letters, it still remains true that he is breaking his agreement, and would be more than compensated by allowing him to sell to actual cultivators. The growth of personal independence and co-operation will be other great means of doing away with wages slavery, and can be if needful, facilitated by loans to co-operative efforts, on the principle that loans are granted to the landlords of this country to drain their estates; and even as a last means, when the principle had made great progress, of taxing the employers of wages slaves to promote the destruction of a vicious system which tends to demoralize both sides, and thus injure society though in a less degree than chattel slavery.

The fourth principle of the political revolution is the national sovereignty, the destruction of all privileged castes, and of the dominance of class over class. The complement of this in the social revolution will be the sovereignty of the race, of all humanity, the equality of nations, and the end of the dominance of nation over nation. As it never was the interest of one nation to war upon another, but only of the privileged castes in nations, their abolition will speedily lead to the cessation of wars between nations, and the unity of mankind in one federation.

We shall thus get rid of the curse of war, and the scarce less curse of standing armies and warlike navies, with all their waste of wealth, and the keeping of millions of men in the prime of life in idleness, the prolific source of vice and demoralisation. The nations which have completed, or nearly so, their political development, and have thoroughly established the principle of national sovereignty, Switzerland and the United States, are the most advanced on this path of social improvement. When the other nations attain to the same stage of political development, it is plain from their example that the war curse will soon cease; and France, when this revolution has established Federalism, will speedily follow in their steps, and get rid of her standing army, and the odious conscription.

The principle of Federalism, of local self-government, the capstone of the political revolution, the guarantee of the rights of minorities, will be completed by the federation of the nations; a principle capable of indefinite extension, as centralization is not, by which the rights of the weaker races and peoples will be secured. As the guarantee of the rights of minorities, of the free expression of opinion, produces a spirit of tolerance between parties and sects in a country, so the federation of the nations will tend to destroy those senseless prejudices of race, of religion of nationality, of colour, which have been the cause of so much injustice and misery to mankind.

I have thus endeavoured to give a scientific form and order, to show the law of the development of that great movement of humanity, called The Revolution, with its two great branches of the political and social revolutions, each comprising five great objective principles. These two series of principles naturally sub-divide themselves into three divisions. The first two principles of each series, the emancipation of the mind and of the man is the first, and the education of the mind and the rights of woman is the second series, are the development of the rights of the individual, while the two last of each series relate to the rights of man as a member of corporate society; the middle one of each series, the emancipation of land, and of labour, being the connecting principle between man as an individual and society as a whole.

It is also certain that none of the principles of the second series can be acted on till the corresponding one of the political series has been adopted, and that none of the second or social series can be carried into full operation without very speedily compelling the full acceptance of the whole of the political series. In fact, only the first two of the social principles can be adopted at all till the full completion of the political revolution, and the adoption of even them will at once force its full acceptance.

It will be seen also that, contrary to the assertion of its enemies, the emancipation of labour does not aim at reducing men to one dead uniformity — a manifestly absurd idea in itself — but leaves free scope for all those diversities of individual powers and capacities so essential to the progress and improvement of the race; that it simply aims at the abolition of social or wages slavery, as that of chattle or political slavery has been. Neither does it necessarily abolish private property, but leaves each individual to his own choice as to whether he will live and work in a community of joint property and labour, or will live and work individually, or he may even combine the two; though it will undoubtedly throw great obstacles in the way of the accumulation of colossal fortunes, as the destruction of chattel slavery broke the political power of the barons.

In conclusion, I hope that it may tend to show that politics, or the science of government, is not a mere chaos and compromise of contending interests and passions, as is so often said and believed; but that it is based on great principles which may be defined and classified; and that as man progresses and adopts these principles, so is the prosperity and happiness of the race increased. As the principles which cause these revolutions are implanted in the very nature and constitution of man; we may be certain that their progress will be as resistless in the future as they have been in the past; that to prevent their triumph it would be necessary, not merely to stay the course of human progress, but to force mankind backwards, and as that is simply impossible, we may rest assured that their triumph is as sure as the stars in their courses. It may also show us how much human happiness depends on the influence of governments, and how large is the scope left for the influence of individual energies and virtues, and we shall find that the latter will always count largely in the scale. As liberty is the object of the political revolution, so is social equality the object of the social revolution, and the adoption of those two principles will inaugurate the fraternity of the human race.

THOMAS SMITH.

THE REVOLUTION IN FRANCE

To the Editors, — In some previous letters I have endeavoured to show what was, in my opinion, the principle that was the cause of the present revolution in France. I propose in the present one to give what appears to me to be the reason of its present failure to establish that principle; and also why I consider the present revolution to be the last of the series of physical force revolutions.

In considering the progress of the principle of the present revolution, we must go back to 1848. The revolution of that year established the principle of the National sovereignty, and the struggles and massacres of that revolution, combined with the establishment of the principle, naturally produced a state of political lassitude; for the nation was desirous of seeing what would be the fruits of that principle before it could take any further steps in advance; and time was also necessary to develop what was the next great national principle to be proclaimed, and, by the experience of suffering, to show the nation the true path of further progress. Yet, at the first election of the legislative Assembly after the massacre of December, 1851, there were indications of the direction in which French thought was tending. In that Assembly, consisting of about 290 members, were five opposition members only, and they were all pledged in opposition to the principle of "one man" government, the embodiment of centralization. That was their bond of unity, and they were all returned by Paris, the real Leader and centre of France. These indications of the direction of French political thought were borne out by the results of the election of the next Legislative Assembly, for in that body was an opposition numbering twenty-five pledged to opposition to personal

271

government, and they were returned by Paris and the large towns. These were pretty clear indications of the direction of political activity and thought, and culminated in the election to the legislative body a year last May of an opposition of ninety to one hundred, while there was also a body of about the same number holding a middle position, but which the current of events had a tendency to carry into opposition, leaving the official candidates in a minority. In counting up the votes cast at the election, also, it appeared that the number given to the official candidates, not-withstanding all the exertions of the officials, did but exceed those cast for the opposition by about 300,000. These results showed the Emperor that the country was slipping out of his hands, and the press, encouraged by them, assumed a liberty of discussion to which it had long been a stranger, and which the Emperor dared not attack. It was evident that a crisis was approaching and that France was preparing to take another step in advance. The Emperor, after a little hesitation, determined to try a plebiscite, to see if it would stem the torrent of approaching revolution: and as he could order the prefects to return what majority he chose, as there were no checks on the returns and no scrutiny, it was a safe game so far as getting his majority was concerned; but it was soon evident it had no effect on public opinion. He then, after some shuffling and pretending to surrender a part of his power and govern by a responsible Ministry, determined on a foreign war, as the best means of staving off a collapse, and if successful, of again seating himself firmly in power. We know the result, and that it precipitated the revolution, instead of letting it come to a natural head, as it would, though it might have taken several years. That, I have no doubt, is the reason of its present failure, the national mind not having time to be fully prepared for the new principle, as it would have been in another year or two; and then, as in 1848, the new principle would have been at once proclaimed on the outbreak of the revolution.

Nevertheless, if it has been once established, the most

THOMAS SMITH

active political thought of the nation had so far accepted it
that it could never have been reversed, and when established · it requires at once a great accession of strength.
There were, it appears to me, four times during the recent
events when it might have been successful — first, upon the
outbreak of the revolution, when the new Government, if
they had been honest and earnest, would have at once
proceeded to carry it into effect, instead of which, as Trou-
chu says in his speech, they were talking of capitulating from
the very day the seige commenced, and would have done
so if the people would have let them. Again, on the 30th
October, it might have been carried when Flourens,
Blanqui, and their compatriots seized the Hotel de Ville
and held the Government prisoner all day, if they, instead
of trusting to the worthless words of the men of the 4th
September, had been for an hour as merciless as the repressive always are, and shot them, or even kept them safe in
prison till the seige was over, and formed a fresh Government; then the principle of Federalism would have
triumphed, and how different would have been the current
of events. Again, when Gambetta assumed command at
Tours, if he, instead of using all his influence to induce
Lyons and Marseilles, which had elected Communes, to
defer the establishment of the new principle to the end of
the war, had followed their example up, and ordered the
election of Communes in all the great towns, it would have
taken firm root and held its ground. And again, if the
Communists, on the 18th March, had at once marched on
Versailles and compelled the Assembly to adopt the
principle of Federalism or else have dispersed it, and not
have allowed an Assembly elected to make peace to levy
war, in conjunction with the Prussians, on Paris again. But
all these failures doubtless arose from the same cause, the
revolution having been forced to a premature head by the
collapse of the army, and the national thought not being
sufficiently matured as in 1848.

The Government of Thiers and the Assembly, elected
only to make peace, and so evidently provisional in all

273

their arrangements, may be regarded simply as a makeshift — a continuance of the empire under another form, till the nation is more fully prepared for the new idea and the revolution comes to a natural denouement, and which recent events will tend to accelerate.

Whether this will be the last of the revolutions of force, is a question of great importance, and in a former letter I gave what seemed to me one great reason why it would be, viz, that it is the conclusion of the political revolution, the establishment of the sovereignty of the people, one and indivisible, no division of power, the people supreme. And as it cannot be the interest of any nation to go to war they would speedily rid themselves of a standing army, the tool of privileged classes, and if driven into war, raise an army from the people, as Switzerland and the United States; and without standing armies to overawe the people, the ballot box will decide all questions. I would also point out that both Switzerland and the United States keep a greater military organisation, from the force of external circumstances, than they would need for their internal order, or if other nations were as politically advanced. But there is another and as powerful a reason why nations which have completed their political development, or nearly so, should dispense with standing armies. It is, that the questions that then come up for solution, the social revolution, cannot be settled by force either yes or nay; they are not capable of that prompt settlement which may be adopted with political principles, either by revolutionary decrees or statutory enactment.

If we compare the principles of the political with the social revolution, this essential difference in their mode of solution will be at once apparent. The first political principle is the rights of the mind, the right to proclaim and inculcate the convictions of the individual. This was the right which was attempted to be stamped out by the massacre of St. Bartholomew the first great sign of the growing centralisation of France, and an indication that in future the struggle between progress and repression would be fought out in Paris. The complementary social principle is the right of education, and we can see at once this is a question that will require many years for its solution. While the first may be enacted and be at once fully enjoyed, the education of the people must be a growth of years, in fact it will be always growing and always being solved. Also, with the second principle, the emancipation of the man, the abolition of serfdom, it could be accomplished by revolutionary decree, but the social emancipation of women must be a work of years, her political rights might be enacted at once, but they are only secondary to, and helps to her social rights; her equal right to education, to property, to her earnings, to man in the marriage relations, to her children, in fact her social equality are questions not to be solved by force either, yea or nay.

It is the same if we take the other political principles and compare them with their social complements; the emancipation of the land from political caste ownership; the sovereignty of the people by universal suffrage; and the principle of Federalism, the guarantee of local rights, and the rights of minorities. None of the corresponding principles in the social revolution can be carried by force. The emancipation of labour is especially dependent on the increased intelligence of the people, a thing of growth, and not to be decreed, while the unity and federation of the nations must, by its very nature, be voluntary.

We have thus the two natural and logical reasons why nations, which have completed, or nearly so, their political organisation, no longer keep large armies; they are no longer wanted either for foreign aggression or domestic repression, and we may clearly see why, and approximately when we shall be done with the curse of war and war establishments.

Whether the present revolution will work itself out without further bloodshed seems doubtful. When we see how a logical Nemesis has avenged the former crimes of the repressives against the revolution, we may expect that it will still dog their footsteps. When we see how the villanies of the old aristrocracy and priesthood were avenged in '93 ;

275

how the assault of Europe upon France was avenged by the ravage of Europe for a generation; how the murder of the Republicans by the Bourgeoise in June '48, was avenged by such unlikely agents as the priests and Bonaparte, we may expect that the atrocities of Thiers and the rurals in '71 will not escape the same relentless deity.

Judging from the past it seems to me that the logic of events in the present points to the peasant as the arm of avenging destiny now. As the priests in '48 seemed the obedient servants of the bourgeoise, but so soon displaced them from power and avenged the workmen upon them, so the peasants now, who seemed the bond slaves of the priests, are already showing that they have ideas of their own, and dare to stand by them; that the power of the priests is a nothing when opposed to his feelings and interests, for the Legitimatists at the late elections, though backed by the priests who fondly hoped to again march on Rome, having only returned one candidate; yet the rurals who are the logical successors of the old aristocracy, in spite of the warning of 1793, and that the peasant, when driven into the field as an active revolutionist, is apt to say, like Thiers, "I shall be pitiless", and that he looks upon the remaining great landlords with no loving eye, but regards them as relics of the old system, who escaped the deluge of '93; and heedless of the warning of the elections of April 30th and July 2nd, 1871, and that he can strike the present possessors of power as surely and sharply as the army struck the bourgeoisie in '51: they seem possessed by the madness of crime and resolved to drive him to despair; they are already discussing bills to alter the inheritance of the land, that tender spot in the heart of the peasant; they talk of strengthening the rural gendarmes, their Swiss Guard — a significate sign that they feel the ground moving under their feet; they are going to extend the blood tax to every man, though so hateful even now, and they are now going to put fresh mountains of taxes on his already over-laden shoulders, while M. Thiers declares, amid the frantic shouts of the rurals, that he will die before he will put one

THOMAS SMITH

penny on the incomes of the rich. And all these things to uphold centralization, while federalism would not only spare him these fresh burdens but release him from the blood tax altogether by organising the country on the Swiss system, while the all but abolition of the army would do away with the necessity for fresh taxes. These things, to me, point to fresh catastrophes, and the growing infection of the army, as shown by the elections, should warn them how they drive the peasant to active revolution, or at the end of his long political drama with the peasant and the workman on the one side, and the priests and nobility on the other, he may again take a leading part and bring to a close this wonderful revolutionary epoch.

Hounds Gate, July 13, 1871.
THOMAS SMITH.

VIII

Occasional Voices 2

The International Herald. 18 January, 1873

EDITOR'S INTRODUCTION

In England, the Paris Commune stimulated class feeling
and the quest for socialist ideas while simultaneously
encouraging the revival of lost delusions and traditions. In
this respect the English response to the Commune may
have mirrored the elaborate complexities of the Commune
itself. At any rate, Jacobins and ultra-Democrats; champions of natural law and natural rights; land and currency
reformers, experienced a brief period of renewal: a false
Spring. Beside them were the advocates of the 'Social
Republic' and the few avowed 'socialists' and 'communists'
directly associated with the International. Hardly any of
the defenders of the Commune who sold Marx's *Civil War
in France* could themselves be properly described as
'Marxists'. They were eclectics who cheerfully combined
the old democratic and radical commonplaces with hard-
won socialist ideas. Their programmes fell apart. They
hardly survived the Commune itself. By 1873, as the
extract from the *International Herald* shows, "Our
Commune" had become no more than a return to the old
communitarian ideals of the first half of the century: what
Whigs, Marxists and other out-moded historians would
once have dared to call "an infantile regression" or a
relapse into an "archaic" form of social protest.

The Republican perished in February 1872 to be
replaced in the following month by the *International
Herald.* If the former failed thanks to its sectarian passions,
the latter came to grief as a result of "unscientific lump-
ing" to borrow a phrase from one of the most perceptive

and level-headed Labour journalists of the time, Lloyd Jones. The *International Herald* was edited by William Harrison Riley, an O'Brien-ite, land and currency reformer, advocate of producers' co-operation and, on the whole, of the position of Marx and Engels in relation to the split which occured within the International after the fall of the Commune.

On 20th July 1872 Riley published in the *International Herald* a set of 37 demands which he suggested should be adopted at the forthcoming Congress of the British Section of the International at Nottingham. They were:

1) Adult Suffrage.

2) Equalisation of Representation by means of Electoral Districts.

3) The payment by salary of all Members of Parliament and of all necessary election expenses . . .

4) Lawyers and Public Officers to be ineligible as members of Parliament . . . .

5) The abolition of Patent Fees . . .

6) The abolition of all money fines for breaches of law . . .

7) The abolition of all fees in courts of law or justice . . .

8) No feed lawyers to practice in public courts of law or justice.

9) All necessary household furniture, provisions, stores, and working tools to be exempt from seizure for debt.

10) The abolition of sinecure offices.

11) The discontinuance of State support to any Church.

12) Qualified Doctors, Chemists, Inventors, Architects, Surveyors, Mechanics.

13) The establishment of a National Bank of Issue in lieu of all other Banks . . . .

14)   The purchase and liquidation by the State of the so-called 'National Debt' . . . .

15)   The State, Districts, Counties, or Municipalities to purchase with National Money all the Railways, Tramways, Docks, Canals and Mines.

16)   The Nationalisation of the Land.

17)   The abolition of hereditary ranks and titles.

18)   The abolition of all taxes on imports.

19)   Substantial, convenient, and healthy houses to be built by the State or the Municipal Governments. All dwellings unfit for human habitation to be pulled down . . . . I speak of the State as of a co-operation of the People for mutual benefit not as an outside something managed by somebody somewhere . . . .

20)   The supply of water and gas in towns to be the business of the National or Municipal Governments.

21)   The Post Office to carry all parcels and packages at the lowest possible rates.

22)   All Fire and Life Insurance to be undertaken by the State.

23)   The State to supply coal to the people at the cost of procuring and transit.

24)   The National or Municipal Bakeries shall establish large steam bakeries and shall deliver clean and wholesome bread to the People at cost price.

25)   The present poor house system shall be abolished. The honest poor must not be punished . . . .

26)   Crank, treadmill and other similar penal labour must be discontinued . . .

27)   Eight hours shall constitute a day's labour for all persons employed by the State or Municipalities. This to apply to the labour of prisoners.

28)   Free Public Halls, gymnasiums, recreation grounds, and baths shall be provided in or near all towns.

29)   Saturday shall be recognised as a general holiday . . . .

30)   The sale of adulterated articles of food must be suppressed.

31)   Drunkeness must be treated as a crime.

32)   The sale of unadulterated wines and malt and spirituous liquors must be free from tax or licence.

33)   All citizens to have the right to arrest criminals . . .

34)   No person in the employ of the state or Municipalities to be allowed to vote at elections (sic!) or on any measure directly affecting the tenure, conditions, or remuneration of his office . . . . .

35)   The standing army to be reduced and gradually abolished . . . . .

36)   England, Ireland, Scotland, Wales the Colonies and Possesions each shall have a local House of Representatives in addition to being represented in the Federal Parliament . . . . .

37)   Our Federal Parliament shall invite all other States to unite in forming an International Congress . . . .

The final extract in this section, taken from the *International Herald* of 18 January, 1873 *Our Commune* shows how the exciting, if absurd eclecticism of the immediate post-Commune period was exchanged for a return to the old communitarian ideals of the Owenite period.

OUR COMMUNE

Responding to the invitation addressed to men and women willing to co-operate with others in the establishment of a village in which all shall help all, I have received a sufficient number of applications to warrant me in believing that ere many months one co-operative village may be established as a model for others, which, if the first answer my expectations, will, by the force of working example, cause the downfall of the heartless, cruel, and unscientific systems of political economy now practised in "civilised" and "christian" countries. As there are already several men co-operating with me in the preliminary proceedings, and for whom I write, I am justified in adopting the plural that I have ceased to use as editor.

We, like all other well disposed and thinking men, have wished improvement in the condition of all classes of people, and have thought that much improvement would result from the substitution of the co-operative for the competitive systems. We regard the competitive selling of the fruits of labour as being essentially injurious to the interests of the labourer, as stimulating the lowest instincts of human nature, and as being, in the greatest sense of the word, unprofitable. The "profit" of the seller is now the loss of the producer or buyer. In our Commune all material profit will be shared by all, as all material loss will be shared by all.

For our first Commune we purpose obtaining a few acres of land in the vicinity of London. On this land we shall build a village, in the centre of which will be the public buildings, comprising the Work Hall, a "Store", a steam laundry, a cookery and bakery, and a school-room (which shall be available for public meetings) a library and news-room, and a gymnasium and pleasure garden. Every

283

building will be as simply beautiful as our draughtsman, architect, and builders can make them. The Work Hall, inside and out, will be free from that ugliness that is born of sin, and shapen in iniquity. As our Commune will not be under the idler's and usurers' law of political economy, we shall make Industry more pleasant and profitable than voluntary idleness. Hitherto Industry has been punished, and Labour has been degraded. The prisoners in our goals are taught to hate Labour with undying hatred, by having it imposed upon them *as a punishment* by the State. Why not try to make then religious, by forcing them to repeat the Lord's Prayer a thousand times a day while in gaol?

Immediately surrounding the Halls will be a roadway or an area laid in asphalte, and outside that will be grass plots and "plantations" intersected with asphalte roadways to the cottages. Encircling the Halls the park will be artizans' houses, each with its garden. There will not be any church, chapel or salaried parson in the Commune, as every villager will be expected to do his duty every day in the week. Anyone will be at liberty to teach any who are willing to be taught, in such places and at such times as will not interfere with the rights of others. The means of education provided by the Commune will be as *good* on other days as on Sunday. We intend to recognise Sunday as a special day of rest, and Saturday as a special day of amusement. Co-operative amusements will be encouraged.

By scientific co-operative effort we hope to be able to secure a sufficiency of the material necessaries of life, by working eight hours a day during five days a week. We purpose obtaining the best machinery that we can get to aid us in manufacturing with the greatest economy. The machinery will be worked sixteen hours a day, for which purpose two sets of workmen will be employed.

There will not be any gold or silver money used in any dealing of the villagers with each other. Certificates, which will be issued in the first place by the trustees and treasurer, will suffice for proof of all transfer of value, debt, credit. or payment. For use with the "civilised" world (or the Philistines) pieces of their precious metals will be supplied, when necessary, to those who may require them. We shall be able to increase our wealth, even though we do not increase the number of pieces of precious metal. With abundance of good food, clothing, buildings and implements, we may manage to live, even though we don't see a "sovereign" or a "crown" once a year.

To aid the establishment of our first Commune, several large-hearted men will advance money to aid in obtaining the land and erecting the buildings. The co-operating artizans must supply the machinery and materials to be used in their business. The co-operators will purchase the village by means of weekly or monthly payments. No "rent" will be charged, excepting to those who may leave the village, and in such cases the amount charged will be estimated to pay for the "wear and tear" of the property.

The Commune will not permit those of its members who are disabled to be additionally punished by "stopping the supplies". The weekly income will not be forfeited by sick members. The Community will be so conducted as to provide for the ills common to all humanity. The dead will not be expected to bury the dead.

Some of the goods manufactured in the Commune will be exchanged for other goods manufactured by other co-operators, for coal at the co-operative mines, and food at the co-operative farms. We intend including co-operative farming in our work after getting established, and hope that in a few years other Industrial Communes will be in operation, with which we exchange labour for labour, to the common profit. Until our system has extended itself so as to include every branch of industry, it will be necessary for us to sell a portion of our goods for "sovereigns" and "crowns" with which to induce "civilised" traders to supply us with what the co-operators have neglected to occupy themselves in producing. If we were commencing business in central Africa, we should have to swap some of our goods for glass beads, with which to trade for raw materials. Our political economists assume to be sublimely superior to those who believe in glass beads, cowrie shells, or wampum, as the only natural and scientific meetings of exchange.

Scientific Co-operation will, if earnestly carried out, very soon abolish usury, "interest", rent and "profits". An opportunity is now offered to working-men to leave their wages slavery — their servitude — for industrial freedom. Let every man who reads and approves of this effort, and is willing to join, send in his address and occupation. He should not be content with that, but should talk with his fellow workmen, and form a local committee, which should correspond with the editor of the *Herald* until the central committee is fully organised.

No man will be allowed to make a "profit" out of this work, except such *real* profit as all will participate in. There will be no paid "promoters", or other speculators. Those who now form the nucleus of the Committee are men who would rather be robbed than be robbers, but who are firm enough to oppose any attempt to introduce orthodox commercial tricks into the preliminary operations. Let every well-disposed reader do something to help in this great work. This subject will be continued in next week's *Herald*.

W. H. R.

IX

William Morris

Pilgrims of Hope

EDITOR'S INTRODUCTION

MORRIS William (1834-1896) Designer, Poet, Socialist. Education at Marlborough — where he narrowly escaped being taught by Beesly — and Exeter College, Oxford. He was encouraged in his artistic work by Rossetti and in the year of the Commune the two of them bought Kelmscott Manor House where Morris subsequently established the Kelmscott Press. Morris appears to have made little response to the Commune at the time, but it became an important part of his understanding and immagination after he became a socialist. In 1884 he broke with H. M. Hyndman and helped to form the Socialist League. He edited the journal Commonwealth until 1890. In 1885 he published in its pages his *The Pilgrims of Hope*.

It was, perhaps, during the socialist revival which occured in England in the eighteen eighties, that the memory of the Commune came to be cherished with a peculiar intensity. Morris thought it was highly important that English workmen should know what happened in Paris between March and June, 1871. With Belfort Bax, whose turn towards Socialism began thanks to reading Beesly and Harrison, Morris wrote (1886) *A Short Account of the Commune of Paris*.

There may have been a few British citizens who went over to Paris to defend the Commune in something of the manner which Morris imagined in the *Pilgrims of Hope*. Adolphe Smith gave lectures in London on his experiences as an officer of the Commune. He subsequently served as a translator at many Congresses of the Second International.

J. Johnson, who was mocked in the press, as the 'Marat of Walworth Common,' declared himself ready to organise a British brigade to go to Paris, but nothing appears to have come of it.

MEETING THE WAR-MACHINE

So we dwelt in the war-girdled city as a very part of its
    life.
Looking back at it all from England, I an atom of the strife,
I can see that I might have seen what the end would be from
    the first,
The hope of man devoured in the day when the Gods are
    athirst.
But those days we lived, as I tell you, a life that was
    not our own;
And we saw but the hope of the world, and the seed that
    the ages had sown
Spring up now a fair-blossomed tree from the earth lying
    over the dead;
Earth quickened, earth kindled to spring-tide with the
    blood that her lovers have shed,
With the happy days cast off for the sake of her happy day,
With the love of women foregone, and the bright youth worn
    away,
With the gentleness stripped from the lives thrust into
    the jostle of war,
With the hope of the hardy heart forever dwindling afar.

O Earth, Earth, look on thy lovers, who knew all thy
    gifts and thy gain,
But cast them aside for thy sake, and caught up barren
    pain!
Indeed of some art thou mindful, and ne'er shalt forget
    their tale,
Till shrunk are the floods of thine ocean and thy sun is
    waxen pale.
But rather I bid thee remember e'en these of the latter
    days,

Who were fed by no fair promise and made drunken by no
praise.
For them no opening heaven reached out the martyr's
crown;
No folk delivered wept them, and no harvest of renown
They reaped with the scythe of battle; nor round their
dying bed
Did kindly friendly farewell the dew of blessing shed;
In the sordid streets of the city mid a folk that knew
them not,
In the living death of the prison didst thou deal them
out their lot,
Yet foundest them deeds to be doing; and no feeble folk
were they
To scowl on their own undoing and wail their lives
away
But oft were they blithe and merry and deft from the strife
to wring
Some joy that others gained not midst their peaceful
wayfaring.
So fared they, giftless ever, and no help of fortune
sought.
Their life was thy deliverance, O Earth, and for thee
they fought;
Mid the jeers of the happy and deedless, mid failing
friends they went
To their foredoomed fruitful ending on the love of thee
intent.
Yea and we were a part of it all, the beginning of the end,
That first fight of the uttermost battle whither all the
nations wend;
And yet could I tell you its story, you might think it
little and mean.
For few of you now will be thinking of the day that
might have been,
And fewer still meseemeth of the day that yet shall be,
That shall light up that first beginning and its tangled
misery.

For indeed a very machine is the war that now men wage;
Nor have we hold of its handle, we gulled of our heritage,
We workmen slaves of machines. Well, it ground us small
    enough
This machine of the beaten Bourgeois; though oft the work
    was rough
That it turned out for its money. Like other young soldiers
    at first
I scarcely knew the wherefore why our side had had the worst;
For man to man and in knots we faced the matter well;
And I thought, well to-morrow or next day a new tale will
    be to tell.
I was fierce and not afraid: yet O were the wood-sides fair,
And the crofts and the sunny gardens, though death they
    harboured there!
And few but fools are fain of leaving the world outright,
And the story over and done, and an end of the life and
    the light.
No hatred of life, thou knowest O Earth, mid the bullets
    I bore,
Though pain and grief oppressed me that I never may suffer
    more.
But in those days past over did life and death seem one;
Yea the life had we attained to which could never be undone.

You would have me tell of the fighting? Well, you know it
    was new to me
Yet it soon seemed as if it had been for ever, and
    ever would be.
The morn when we made that sally, some thought (and yet
    not I)
That a few days and all would be over: just a few had
    got to die,
And the rest would be happy thenceforward. But my stubborn
    country blood
Was bidding me hold my halloo till we were out of the
    wood.
And that was the reason perhaps why little disheartened I
    was,

As we stood all huddled together that night in a helpless
    mass,
As beaten men are wont: and I knew enough of war
To know midst its unskilled labour what slips full often
    are.

There was Arthur unhurt beside me, and my wife come back
    again,
And surely that eve between us there was love though
    no lack of pain
As we talked all the matter over, and our hearts spake
    more than our lips;
And we said, "We shall learn, we shall learn — yea, e'en
from disasters and slips."

Well, many a thing we learned, but we learned not how to
prevail
O'er the brutal war-machine, the ruthless grinder of bale;
By the bourgeois world it was made, for the bourgeois
    world; and we,
We were e'en as the village weaver 'gainst the power-loom,
    maybe.
It drew on nearer and nearer, and we 'gan to look to
    the end—
We three, at least — and our lives began with death to
    blend;
Though we were long a-dying — though I dwell on yet
    as a ghost
In the land where we once were happy, to look on the
loved and the lost.

DATE DUE

MAR 1 2 2003			